If the truth should trump all, then this book should persuade those it argues against. It is informed, heart-felt, and utterly reasonable. Christians can ignore the facts that Stark brings into the light of day only if they want to be wrong.

—Dale C. Allison, Jr.
Pittsburgh Theological Seminary, author of *Constructing Jesus*

The Human Faces of God is one of the most challenging and well-argued cases against the doctrine of biblical inerrancy I have ever read. The value of this bold and witty book goes well beyond posing challenges evangelicals like myself must face, however. All who hold the Bible in high regard will benefit from Stark's brutally honest, insightful, and well-researched investigations into the text, as well as from his own constructive proposal to interpret Scripture's "damnable texts" as "negative revelations." Rarely have I read a book with which I agreed *and disagreed* so much—which is precisely why I found this stimulating work to be deeply rewarding and believe it is a work that deserves to be seriously wrestled with by evangelicals and mainstream Christians alike.

—Greg Boyd
Senior Pastor, Woodland Hills Church, author of *The Myth of a Christian Nation*

Here is a book that answered a lot of questions that I had about what really transpires historically as it pertains to the revelation of God in Scripture. I learned so much from this book that I can strongly encourage anyone who is seeking to move from simplistic proof-texting to a comprehensive understanding of the Bible to read this book carefully.

—Tony Campolo
Eastern University, author of *Red Letter Christians*

The battle over the Bible is increasingly polarized between the absolutism of inerrantists who claim to speak for all Christians and the scorn of secularists who find easy targets for ridicule. With an engaging combination of honesty, goodwill, and wit, Thom Stark offers a vital third way. He explodes the "hermeneutics of convenience" of self-styled inerrantists, examines some of the most objectionable aspects of the Bible, and refuses throughout to sacrifice moral decency on the altar of inerrantist dogma—which is, after all, as much a human construction as the biblical criticism that inerrantists deride. This is must reading for Christians who have agonized over their own private doubts about Scripture—and for others who have given up hope that evangelical Christians can practice intelligent, moral interpretation of the Bible.

—Neil Elliott
United Theological Seminary, author of *Liberating Paul*

Thom Stark writes with intense passion and an almost brutal honesty. In doing so, he does thoughtful Christians a great service. In our chaotic, post-Christendom age, the teachings of the Bible are more relevant than ever—should we fight our way free from old patterns that make a doctrine about the Bible more important than the Bible's content. We need passion and honesty like Stark's to overcome the problems of an authoritarian theology of the Bible. And then, with the help of this book, we may discover that the Bible—when we read it in all its diversity and vulnerability—does bring healing words to those who keep listening.

—Ted Grimsrud
Eastern Mennonite University, author of *Embodying the Way of Jesus*

Thom Stark's book *The Human Faces of God* reflects an engagement with Scripture and a personal journey of faith that mirrors my own, and that of many others in our time who have found themselves grasped simultaneously by both a positive experience of and personal adherence to the Christian faith, and the conviction that the Bible does not fit the descriptions that conservatives and fundamentalists use to describe it, such as "inerrant." Stark's book offers a refreshingly honest engagement with Scripture as Scripture, acknowledging the bad as well as the good within the pages of the Bible, and explaining what the positive function of the Bible can be when read in this honest and critical fashion.

What the reader is offered on its pages is neither an attempt to defend the Bible from criticism for the sake of maintaining a worldview, nor an attack from without, but *criticism of the Bible from a Christian perspective*. Perhaps most importantly, *The Human Faces of God* highlights aspects of the Bible ignored or denied by the superficial reading of those who ironically proclaim themselves the Bible's defenders. Stark's book effectively demonstrates how the Bible, in practice, is the most dangerous enemy of fundamentalists, who regularly seek to defend their doctrine and idea of Scripture from the evidence found in the Bible itself.

I strongly recommend *The Human Faces of God*, and look forward to the conversations and growth towards maturity that I expect will be the experience of Christians who read it and engage with it as individuals and as communities.

—James F. McGrath
Butler University, author of *The Only True God*

For a few centuries now, conservative Protestants have been uncomfortable with the humanity of Jesus and the Bible. But momentum is building in new directions—a theological genre is appearing that is wholly comfortable with God's choice to redeem his fallen world through the finite and fallen horizon that stands in need of redemption. I welcome Thom Stark's contribution to the genre. May it advance us towards a healthier understanding of Scripture and of the Savior to which it points.

—Kenton L. Sparks
Eastern University, author of *God's Word in Human Words*

More than just the standard retelling of the horrors of the Bible, Stark's "confrontational" method of reading scripture exposes the deadly contradictions of biblical fundamentalism and gives thoughtful Christians a way forward by allowing them to "own" these troubling texts in a new way. Readers will breathe a deep sigh of relief at his suggestion that we can view the "dark side" of the Bible as scripture precisely through our condemnation of the way it too often portrays the character of God and the things that God calls human beings to do to one another. Perhaps most importantly, Stark provides a model for theology that is committed to hearing the voice of the victims of history, especially the victims of our own religious traditions. A powerful book.

—Michael J. Iafrate
PhD Candidate, Toronto School of Theology

Each chapter of *The Human Faces of God* is packed with information and draws one in deeper like a good crime novel. Unlike conservative Evangelical fare that confuses biblical scholarship with the practice of apologetics, Thom Stark has learned the difference. Apologetics relies on bits and pieces of biblical scholarship, any that can be used to support its preconceived notion that the Bible's unity is crystal clear and each book is unquestionably without error. But the questions are there, they've always been there, and with precision, wit, and passion, Stark guides the reader through some of the most challenging ones.

—Edward T. Babinski
Editor of *Leaving the Fold: Testimonies of Former Fundamentalists*

This book is for those who wish to understand the Bible and learn from it. It is not for those who seek handy Bible quotes, nor for those who have no urge to plumb the Bible's depths. Thom Stark shows how the scriptures confront us with the big questions such as suffering and identity. He provides a thorough and devastating critique of the "inerrancy of scripture." He offers persuasive rejoinders to those who try to get round some of the nasty bits of the Bible or dodge difficulties like the possibility that Jesus was wrong. If nothing in this challenging book causes you to think again, you have a very closed mind!

—John Henson
Author of *Other Prayers of Jesus*

The Human Faces of God will shatter any honest reader's preconceptions about the Bible and what it "says" and leave that reader with a stronger and better faith. This book is the most powerful antidote to fundamentalism that I've ever read. Literalism and fundamentalism have defamed God by defining God as someone or something as small-minded as God's interpreters. This book liberates God at last.

—Frank Schaeffer
Author of *Crazy for God*

Stark's book is a direct frontal assault against Evangelical Christianity, the exact likes of which I have not seen before in one volume. In it Stark exposes, in the words of Mark Noll, the "scandal of the Evangelical mind." While Noll was chiding Evangelicals for not producing the best and brightest thinkers capable of truly engaging and changing their society for Christ, the reality is that the real scandal is Evangelicalism itself. The best and brightest thinkers, like Stark, cannot remain Evangelicals once they truly become biblically informed. I can only hope his book will have a very wide readership within those same circles.

—John W. Loftus
Author of *Why I Became an Atheist*

The Human Faces of God reads like a guidebook to the Bible's most troubling passages, and Thom Stark our guide on this tour is not afraid to ask difficult questions of the texts. Though one may not agree with him at every turn, Stark's work is a bold and much-needed call to deeper reflection on the nature of Christian scripture and its place within the shared life of God's people.

—Christopher Smith
Editor, *The Englewood Review of Books*

The HUMAN
Faces of God

The HUMAN Faces of God

What Scripture Reveals When It Gets God Wrong
(and Why Inerrancy Tries To Hide It)

THOM STARK

WIPF & STOCK · Eugene, Oregon

THE HUMAN FACES OF GOD
What Scripture Reveals When It Gets God Wrong (and Why Inerrancy Tries To Hide It)

Ancient document quotations are the translation of the author unless otherwise noted.

Those marked NRSV are from the New Revised Standard Version Bible, copyright
1989 by the Division of Christian Education of the National Council of the Churches
of Christ in the USA. Used by permission.

Those marked NASB are from the New American Standard Bible, copyright 1960,
1962, 1963, 1968, 1971, 1972, 1973, 1975, 1977, 1995 by the Lockman Foundation. Used by permission.

Wipf & Stock
An Imprint of Wipf and Stock Publishers
199 W. 8th Ave., Suite 3
Eugene, OR 97401
www.wipfandstock.com

ISBN 13: 978-1-60899-323-9

Manufactured in the U.S.A.

FOR JIM

Thus may we gather honey from the weed,
And make a moral of the devil himself.

Share your thoughts about the book and see what others are saying

HUMANFACES*of*GOD.COM

(WITH ONLINE INDEXES)

CONTENTS

Foreword ~ xiii

Preface ~ xv

Acknowledgments ~ xix

1 **THE ARGUMENT**
   In the Beginning Was the Words ~ 1

2 **INERRANTISTS DO NOT EXIST**
   Dispelling a Myth of Biblical Proportions ~ 15

3 **INERRANCY STUNTS YOUR GROWTH**
   and Other Fundamentalist Health Hazards ~ 46

4 **YAHWEH'S ASCENDANCY**
   Whither Thou Goest, Polytheism? ~ 70

5 **MAKING YAHWEH HAPPY**
   Human Sacrifice in Ancient Israel ~ 87

6 **BLESSING THE NATIONS**
   Yahweh's Genocides and Their Justifications ~ 100

7 **THE SHEPHERD AND THE GIANT**
   Government Propaganda ~ 151

8 **JESUS WAS WRONG**
   or, It's the End of the World as We Know It and I Feel Fine ~ 160

9 **TEXTUAL INTERVENTIONS**
   On the Need for Direct Confrontations with Scripture ~ 208

10 **INTO THE LOOKING GLASS**
   What Scripture Reveals When It Gets God Wrong ~ 218

Bibliography ~ 243

FOREWORD

CONSERVATIVE CHRISTIANS OFTEN AFFIRM THAT THE BIBLE IS historically accurate, internally consistent, and morally edifying. Anyone who has had a good introductory course on the Bible at college level knows that it is not necessarily any of the above. Even people who profess to hold that the Bible is inerrant acknowledge in practice that this is not always the case. Nonetheless, biblical scholars, especially those of a more theological bent, have engaged incessantly in an enterprise of apologetics, to try to explain away apparent mistakes or to justify ethical attitudes that we now find unacceptable in the modern world.

Thom Stark's book, *The Human Faces of God*, is a refreshing exception. It presents many of the obviously problematic aspects of the Bible—polytheism, human sacrifice, genocide, mistaken eschatological expectations. It breaks no new ground in the historical critical understanding of these problems; Stark's objective is not to advance new hypotheses, but to focus on the significance of that which has already been established. He does this by brushing aside all apologetic evasion. Human sacrifice and genocide are atrocities, whether we find them in the Bible or not. Attempts to save Jesus from apocalyptic delusion are unpersuasive. Those who strive to evade that conclusion only become "enablers," who are complicit in the negative effects of these texts on modern communities. As Stark realizes, the most severe problems raised by modern criticism are not those that question the historicity of events but rather those that question biblical morality. If Christians struggle with these texts, it is not because they are inherently difficult, but because we find their viewpoints hard to stomach. But as Stark also realizes, it is only by confronting these problems honestly that we can find a firm basis for a constructive biblical theology.

Many critics will want to portray Stark's book as negative, as an attack on biblical values. Nothing could be further from the truth. As he states at the beginning of this book, the Bible does not have a single viewpoint, and one of its great strengths is its inbuilt tradition of self-criticism. No modern critic comes close to being as critical of the biblical tradition as were Amos and Ezekiel, or, for that matter, Jesus. If we are to appropriate the Bible as

xiii

Scripture, however, we cannot affirm the canon whole and in equal measure. Rather it behoves us to listen to the critical voices within the tradition and proceed in a similar spirit. This is not to say that we should excise anything from the canon, as Marcion did. Some texts teach by negative example, and function as scripture by exhibiting attitudes that we must now condemn. But our condemnations, too, are inspired by biblical values. There is much in the Bible to inspire us, so long as we do not lay on the ancient texts burdens of inerrancy and infallibility that no text can bear.

This is a courageous book, that challenges us to take the modern criticism of the Bible to its logical conclusion. It deserves a wide readership.

John J. Collins
Yale

PREFACE

IN 1978, EVANGELICAL HEAVYWEIGHTS NORMAN GEISLER, J. I. PACKER, and Francis Schaeffer, together with over three hundred leading Evangelicals from around the globe, gathered in Chicago, Illinois to draft a statement detailing the tenets of their doctrine of biblical inerrancy. Though many evangelicals today—in churches as well as in the academy—would take issue with several of the extensive number of claims made in the Chicago Statement on Biblical Inerrancy, the statement continues to be relevant as the standard-bearer for Evangelical orthodoxy. This is demonstrable in the fact that in 2006 the Evangelical Theological Society adopted the Chicago Statement as the official definition of inerrancy, a decision which caused an uproar within broader evangelical circles. Since its inception in 1947, the Society had required confession of the Bible's inerrancy as a condition of membership but had never provided an official definition of what precisely was meant by such a confession. This allowed many moderates to enjoy fellowship with the Society without compromising their informed convictions about the nature of scripture.

Inevitably this ambiguity led to difficulties. As watchdogs began to contest the "orthodoxy" of the views of some of the more moderate evangelicals within the Society, it became evident that a firm definition of inerrancy was necessary in order to legitimize disciplinary action taken against allegedly offending members. If the power to expel members whose doctrine was deemed by a two-thirds majority to be "heretical" was to be maintained, an official definition of "orthodoxy" seemed apropos. Thus, after more than fifty years without such a definition, the Society voted to adopt the 1978 Chicago Statement—a move, as already noted, decried by many moderates for having the effect of making the Society more exclusive and therefore less representative of broader evangelicalism.

The doctrine of biblical inerrancy dictates that the Bible, being inspired by God, is without error in everything that it affirms—historically, scientifically, and theologically. As one part of the Chicago Statement puts it, "Being wholly and verbally God-given, Scripture is without error or fault in all its teaching, no less in what it states about God's acts in creation, about the events of world history, and about its own literary origins under God, than in its witness to God's saving grace in individual lives."[1] This book is an argument against that doctrine, particularly as articulated by the Chicago Statement, and it is an argument in favor of a different, more ancient way of reading the books that comprise the Bible.

This book and books like it are, unfortunately I think, necessary for a number of reasons. The first pertains to my own faith heritage. I hail from the Stone-Campbell tradition, the so-called "Restoration Movement," and specifically the branch identified as the Independent Christian Churches (Non-Denominational). Although my tradition began as a protest against Evangelicalism, it has since become virtually indistinguishable from Evangelical Christianity. One of the defining slogans of the Stone-Campbell tradition historically has been, "No creed but Christ, no book but the Bible." However, after its gestational decades the Stone-Campbell tradition came to allow many of the creeds of mainstream Evangelical Christianity to infiltrate its religion and transform the nature of its commitments. For the sake of my own tradition, therefore, a critique of the tenets of the Evangelical creed of biblical inerrancy is necessary, if the Bible is again going to be allowed to speak for itself within our congregations.

Books like this one are also necessary because of widespread misconceptions within Evangelical spheres of influence and also outside Christian circles altogether. The problem is not just that honest, well-meaning Christians *believe* Evangelical authorities when the claim is made that this kind of fundamentalism is the only proper way to be Christian; non-Christians tend to believe them too. But the fact is that fundamentalism as it exists in the Western world today is a relatively new phenomenon and there are many ways to be Christian, some of them much more ancient and developed. Because of the volume at which leading Evangelicals tend to speak, however, this fact is well disguised from the view of many. I myself was once subject to the parochialism of Evangelical fundamentalism, but have since discovered, by the grace of God, a world that is much broader, more diverse, charitable, and vibrant than the "orthodoxy" that marked my youth.

That brings up another motivation for the writing of this book. The sad reality is that many Christians who are raised in sheltered fundamentalist homes and churches leave their nests for college or the outside world, unprepared, only to discover how untenable the tenets of fundamentalism in fact are. This frequently leads to disillusionment and despair, and to the subsequent abandonment of faith. It is my hope that a book like this one will help some to discover that there are better ways to be a Christian than to be a fundamental-

---

1. Henry, *God Who Speaks*, 212.

PREFACE xvii

ist, ways to be a Christian that do not preclude critical engagement with the numerous problematic aspects of the Christian scriptures and religion.

This book began as a series of blog posts and developed out of the conversations that ensued. Those conversations with friends, foes, and strangers helped shape this book. In fact, it was precisely those conversations that incited me to write this particular book in the first place; after completing the original blog series, a number of individuals contacted me and in various ways expressed relief at the prospect that there are ways to remain Christian without being intellectually dishonest. It is my hope that with this particular book, others will find *some* of the help they need in order to manage their transition without despair.

But this book is not only for struggling fundamentalists. I have also tried to engage postliberal and postmodern Christians, by offering some criticisms of common non-fundamentalist, non-critical appropriations of scripture. I have tried to engage them by displaying what I think are some of the problems with metaphorical, canonical, progressive, and subversive hermeneutical methodologies. At the same time, however, I have tried to show how such Christians who are committed to making scripture relevant to the church have nothing to fear from unabashedly critical readings of scripture. I hope, therefore, to contribute in some small way to the conversation between liberals and postliberals by displaying some ways in which critical scholarship may be used in service of the church as well.

I have tried to write a book that is relevant to Christians and to churches. In fact, very little of what I have said within the pages that follow will be particularly new to those who are trained in biblical studies. It is not my objective in this particular book to advance knowledge within academic circles. My intention rather has been to make biblical scholarship relevant to those who have had the good fortune not to have gotten caught up in academics. Nevertheless, I hope that this book will be relevant to a wide audience. Despite the fact that much of my material is a distillation of previous scholarship for the sake of the reading public, perhaps some trained in biblical scholarship will be able to glean some insights from my own appropriations of the data. Non-Christians or nominal Christians may find this book useful, or at least interesting, as an example of an *internal* critique of fundamentalist Christianity and of an alternative way of being Christian. As for died-in-the-wool fundamentalists and biblical apologists, I have no expectations that anything I have said within the pages that follow will convert them (although I hope it will); nevertheless, I have tried to pay them the deep respect of extensively engaging their arguments. I hope that they will at least find my book useful as a stone upon which to sharpen their own swords.

Most precisely, as I have pointed out, I am writing this book for Christians who have honestly struggled with some of the contents of the Bible and have not been able to find satisfactory answers from among the Bible's many apologists. I myself was once such a Christian—a fundamentalist who struggled with his faith but did not know of any alternative way of being Christian. Unfortunately, many of the books written to debunk biblical inerrancy have been written by non-Christians with no interest in articulating what a non-fundamentalist use of scripture might look like, or have been written by Christians who focus primarily on minutiae, such as historical and archaeological discrepancies, numerical contradictions, or scientific problems. Such books are fine but do not address many of the big problems—the kinds of things about which honest Christians are right to worry.[2] In this book I have tried to tackle the big problems and have tried (as much as possible) to leave the minutiae by the wayside, but I have also attempted to articulate an honest way forward for those who wish to continue to read the Bible as scripture. I have written about the kinds of things that were important to me in my own journey. I have tried to write the book that I wish someone had handed me years ago, a book that confronts problematic biblical texts head on, but one that also offers a way forward. My intention here is not just to tear down, but also to build up—not merely to show what kind of approach to scripture will *not* work, but also to suggest some approaches that might.

No doubt many Christians who read this book will find information or arguments that feel threatening to them. Some will conclude that I am motivated by unspoken hostility toward the gospel. This is not the case. This book developed out of my personal and honest struggle to come to terms with my own very sincere and active faith. It is the product, so far, of my quest for truth, and as threatening as the truth can often be, those who believe that all truth is God's truth should not feel threatened by the contents of this book. I do not claim to have a secure grip on truth, but the pages that follow reflect the truth as I understand it, and it is a truth that—while initially threatening to my identity—has now set me free.

My intention, therefore, is not to undermine the faith, but to pursue a mature faith, to faithfully integrate my religious convictions with my commitment to honesty, and thus to offer a *holistically faithful* account of scripture and its role within the church. I have tried to be honest in these pages, and all I ask in return is that the reader should come with an open mind and—like the Bereans—examine the scriptures everyday to see whether these things are so (Acts 17:11).

2. A good recent exception to the rule is Seibert, *Disturbing Divine Behavior.*

ACKNOWLEDGMENTS

THIS BOOK WOULD NOT HAVE BEEN POSSIBLE WERE IT NOT FOR THE help of a multitude of friends. I owe a deep debt to Ted Troxell, my copy editor and token *bel esprit*. Immense thanks are due to my editor Christian Amondson, also to James Stock, Jim Tedrick, Chris Spinks, and everyone at Wipf and Stock whose support has been overwhelming. My gratitude to Rollin Ramsaran for his encouragement, for the many formative discussions I've shared with him, and for permission to use the diagrams from his NT Intro course; thanks also to Derek Murphy for his help with their graphic design.

Special thanks are also due to John Collins for his generosity and to Christopher Rollston for his patient guidance and the time invested in the many discussions that helped shape pivotal sections throughout this book. Dr. Rollston's support for me has been tremendous and the extent of my indebtedness to him is incalculable. Those who know him will surely see his imprint on my thinking. Of course, his influence on my work does not indicate that he approves of every move I make, but even where we differ I believe his impact can be felt.

I am forever grateful to the many friends and strangers who invested their time reading drafts of this manuscript, and for the many useful suggestions, criticisms, and encouragements offered by them. For this thanks are due to Dale Allison, Hector Avalos, Ed Babinski, Joe Beal, Adam Bean, Greg Boyd, Jacob Paul Breeze, Landis Brown, Erica Calderon Stark, Tony Campolo, Michael DeFazio, Neil Elliott, Peter Enns, Aanna Greer, Ted Grimsrud, John Henson, Dustin Hite, Michael Iafrate, Golden Kennedy, John Loftus, Ra Lovingsworth, James McGrath, Stephen Paul, Frank Schaeffer, Chris Smith, Kenton Sparks, Jack Weinbender, Matthew Worsfold, and Jordan Wood.

This book has also been shaped through countless conversations I've had with friends and mentors, and would not look at all the same without the influence of Joey Azterbaum, James Bell, Lacey Bell, Jason Bembry, Paul Blowers, Solomon Burchfield, Erica Chu, Derrick Crowe, Kaitlyn Demien, Kip Elolia, Alex Giltner, Logan Greer, Ned Greene, Jason Hare, Frank House, Nathan Howells, Ira Jacobs, David Kiger, Stephen Lawson, Tom Lawson, Ryan

McCracken, Nick Parsons, Nathan Perry, Jared Poznich, Chad Ragsdale, John Sobert Sylvest, Tyler Stewart, and Michael Westmoreland-White. Most of what's right with this book no doubt originated from one of these people. As for what's wrong with the book, I share the blame evenly for that as well.

Finally, were it not for the spiritual, emotional, and financial support of certain people, this project would never have come to fruition. So I thank Julie and Tom Stark, Golden and Phil Kennedy, Debbie and Gil Calderon, Celia Sims, Jim Stark, Amanda Calderon, Darnelle and Tom Johns, Elizabeth and Zack Exley, Hiedi and Tarrell Morang, Mark Moore, and Mark Scott. And of course my deepest debt of gratitude is reserved for my wife Erica and my daughter Ela whose patience permitted me and whose love sustained me. After having written a book about the nature of the knowledge of God, I can safely say that the only thing I know for certain is that I love my ladies.

1 THE ARGUMENT
IN THE BEGINNING WAS THE WORDS

IN THE BEGINNING WAS THE ARGUMENT, AND THE ARGUMENT WAS WITH God, and the Argument was: God. God was the subject of the Argument, and the Argument was a good one. Who is God? What is God like? What does God require of us? What is God doing about injustice? What is God doing, if anything, to relieve the human condition? Is God benevolent, or malevolent, or simply indifferent? Is there any divinely-infused meaning to human existence, or is it all just senseless? Throughout history, worshipers of Yahweh have been engaged in this argument, and for every question posed, they have proposed a plurality of divergent answers. In the beginning, long before there was the Word of God, there were the words of God's people. That is to say, before there was a Bible—a "Word of God" as a singular entity— there was an argument about God, reflected in diverse texts and traditions; and it is in fact that argument that is today enshrined in the Judeo-Christian canons of scripture. As John Collins has it, the Bible is a "collection of writings that is marked by lively internal debate, and by a remarkable spirit of self-criticism."[1] To put it bluntly: the Bible is an argument—with itself.

Biblical Bickering

Nationalism vs. Universalism

One dispute takes place between xenophobic nationalists such as Ezra on the one hand, and those (like the prophet Amos or the author of the book of Jonah) who tend to have a more universalistic, inclusive mindset on the other. The nationalistic and ethnocentric perspective is represented very openly in the book of Ezra, which is set after the exiled Jews had begun to migrate from Babylon back to Judea and to rebuild the temple in Jerusalem. According to Ezra chapter 4, when the inhabitants of the land of Israel, which is north of Judea, heard that the Judeans had returned and were building a temple to Yahweh, they came to

1. Collins, *Introduction to the Hebrew Bible*, 604.

1

the Judeans and offered to help in the building of the temple. Like the Judeans, the northerners also worshiped Yahweh, and had been sacrificing to him for centuries. In response, the leaders of the Judeans, Joshua and Zerubbabel, said, "We will not allow you to participate with us in the building of a house for our God. We alone will build to Yahweh, the God of Israel, as King Cyrus of Persia commanded us" (Ezra 4:3). The Judeans, who were taking their marching orders from the Persian emperor, refused the help of fellow Yahweh worshipers. Why? Because the northerners were "race-traitors."

About 135 years before the southern kingdom of Judah fell to the Babylonians, the northern kingdom of Israel, whose capital was Samaria, was taken by the Assyrian empire. One Assyrian method for keeping conquered territories compliant was to integrate them with people from other regions. So the Assyrians relocated some of the population of Israel, and in turn relocated other groups to Israelite territory, in order to integrate them with the locals. Those who were sent to Israel married Israelite men and women, and adopted the worship of the local deity, Yahweh. Nevertheless, despite the fact that Samaritan religion was fiercely Yahwistic, the Judean religious elites could not abide them. Because they were not purebred Israelites, the northerners were anathema. When the Judean elites refused to worship Yahweh with the people of the north, they instigated a religious rivalry that would never be resolved.

Some years later, a priest named Ezra was commissioned by another Persian emperor to return to Jerusalem and finish restoring the temple. Ezra would come home to discover that Judeans had begun to intermarry with "the people of the land," i.e., non-Jewish inhabitants of the region. These people were supposedly anathema to Yahweh, and were therefore *verboten* to his people. Thus, despite the fact that many of these marriages had already produced numerous children, Ezra decreed that every Jewish man married to a non-Jewish woman was to divorce her and, moreover, that every non-Jewish wife and her offspring were to be expelled from the land, abandoned to fend for themselves (Ezra 10:2–11). The book of Ezra presents Ezra's decree in a pious light, an act done out of fear of Yahweh. Indeed, fearful of Yahweh's wrath, and fearful of having their personal property confiscated by Ezra's government (10:8), the people complied with Ezra's demand and sent their wives and children away, never to return.

Yet there is no hint in the narrative that the intermarriages posed any threat to genuine Yahwism. In point of fact, intermarriage with people of other religions had long been permissible. Moses took an Ethiopian woman as a second wife. The Canaanite prostitute Rahab and her family were allowed to integrate with Israel on account of Rahab's fear of Yahweh. King David's great-grandmother Ruth was a Moabite woman, even though the Moabites were stanch enemies of Israel. Moreover, in Deut 20:14, Yahweh expressly permits the Israelites to intermarry with women from other regions and religions. Again, in Numbers 31, Yahweh *orders* that 32,000 Midianite virgins should be integrated with the tribes of Israel, virgins who had been raised, according to the text, to worship Baal of Peor. We are left to wonder how Ezra must have scolded Yahweh for permitting such pervasive perversions. The irony is that in their xenophobic and nationalistic quest to keep Judea pure from foreign influence, Ezra, Joshua, and Zerubbabel were (perhaps unwittingly) serving the interests of the Persian empire. These self-proclaimed vassals of Yahweh were in reality vassals of Persia, having received their authority from the Persian kings, kings who had shrewdly tasked them with unifying and consolidating religious and political power in Judea in order to keep the region pacified.

This fact did not escape the notice of other prominent Jews at that time. Ezra's policies were opposed by others. Some factions did not consider it either wise or faithful to submit to Persian hegemony; but Ezra's faction enjoyed the backing of the empire, and thus it is from Ezra's perspective that the history was recorded. Ezra's policy of racial segregation and the forced expulsion of women and children was also opposed, namely by Jonathan ben Asahel and Jahzeiah ben Tikvah (Ezra 10:15). Probably in light of the fact of Judea's own recent experience of exile, these men did not agree that breaking up families and forcing women and children into exile reflected the will of Yahweh.

Ideologically, the self-assured nationalism so widespread among Judeans, which was represented so profoundly in Ezra, would have been roundly opposed by the prophet Amos, who condemned Israel for putting more stock in their genes than in their justice. Amos warned them that without institutional justice, Israel is no different in Yahweh's eyes than any other nation. Moreover, all nations are equally under Yahweh's providential care. In Amos 9:7, Yahweh taunts them: "Are you not just like the Ethiopians in my eyes, O people of Israel? Did I not deliver Israel from the land of Egypt, and the Philistines from Caphtor, and the Arameans from Kir?" According to Amos, what Yahweh did for Israel was nothing special. Yahweh does not distinguish by nationality or ethnicity, but by conduct, and Israel's conduct had condemned them to utter destruction. It should come as no surprise that Amos was not a very popular prophet among the religious and political elites. Another prophet, also not very popular among the elites, would later offer a sharp critique of the ideology reflected in the book of Ezra, particularly with reference to his parable of the "Good Samaritan," in which, controversially, he challenged the widespread assumption that Jews were inherently superior to those "race-traitors" up north.

A similar critique of Judean nationalism and xenophobia is offered in the book of Jonah. Although it is set in the eighth century BCE during the ministry of the historical Jonah, a prophet mentioned virtually in passing in 2 Kgs 14:25, its vocabulary and theological concerns reflect a post-exilic date of composition (sometime between the sixth and fourth centuries BCE).[2] It may reflect an older tradition about the actual Jonah, but in all likelihood Jonah's name was selected by the author precisely because so little was known about him. Aspects of the story such as Jonah's being swallowed by a large fish, then spat out in one piece onto dry land several days later, are big clues that what we are dealing with is a fictional short story with a theological message.

> Digression: The fictional short story was an established genre among Jewish sacred writings, another prominent example being that of Tobit. Their purpose was to tell stories that encouraged God's people to be faithful and that challenged them to be self-critical. To say that it is fictional is not to discredit it or to deny its status as inspired scripture. It is simply a matter of recognizing its proper genre, and treating it as such. We do not accuse Jesus of lying when he told fictional parables splashed with historical details; neither should we accuse the author of Jonah of attempting to pull the wool over our eyes by doing the same thing. Inerrantists will insist on its historicity on the grounds that Jesus referred to Jonah's experience in the belly of the fish as a sign of his burial in a tomb (Matt 12:39–40). But this hardly amounts to a claim on Jesus' part that Jonah should be taken to be historical. Jesus regularly used parables to make theological points that pertained to the real world, and he was not duplicitous in doing so. The genre of the fictional short story was very common in Jewish literature of the second temple period, and Jesus no doubt would have been astute enough to recognize it when he saw it. Bluntly put, when I tell my wife that I love her as Westley loved Buttercup, I do not thereby imply that I think *The Princess Bride* is a historical narrative. Digression concluded.[3]

And the theological message of the book of Jonah is clear. Jonah is a profound and brilliant piece of satire. In it, the prophet Jonah represents those ardent nationalists and xenophobes who want to keep Yahweh's blessing all to Israel's self. The events that transpire in the book are designed to ridicule the reluctant prophet, to expose his narrow-mindedness for what it is. It is a piece of comedy, and Jonah is the butt of the joke. Its aim is to expose the absurdity of the perspective of people like Ezra, and to encourage

2. *Eerdmans Dictionary of the Bible*, 730.

3. For a fundamentalist attempt to deny the genre of Jonah, see Alexander, "Jonah and Genre."

God's people to change their minds. One of the key messages of the book is that Gentiles can worship Yahweh too. This point is made throughout the narrative in startling ways. The Gentiles in the story are portrayed as better worshipers of Yahweh than Jonah himself. While Jonah is stubbornly resisting Yahweh's will, the Gentiles keep recognizing Yahweh's authority. Yahweh tells Jonah to go to Nineveh, the capital city of Assyria, to prophesy doom upon its inhabitants as recompense for their utter depravity. But Jonah does not want to preach to the Assyrians, because Jonah does not want to afford those "philistines" the opportunity to repent. So instead, he attempts to flee to Spain. On the voyage there, a storm threatens to destroy the vessel. All the Gentiles aboard the ship pray to their respective gods in an attempt to assuage the deity's anger, calm the storm, and save their skins. When it is ascertained that Jonah's disobedience is the instigator of the divine tantrum, Jonah elects to be thrown overboard. After praying to *Yahweh*, the Gentiles cast Jonah into the sea, and the storm ceases. Then, when they had seen his power, "the men feared Yahweh even more, and they offered a sacrifice to Yahweh and took vows before him" (Jonah 1:16). The irony is not lost on the audience. Jonah's very attempt to dodge his responsibility to preach to the Gentiles results in gentile conversions.

After being swallowed by a big fish and spewed out onto shore, Jonah reluctantly proceeds to Nineveh and begins to announce impending doom. "In forty days time, Nineveh will be laid waste!" What do the Ninevites do? Do they ignore him? Do they mock Jonah, spit on him, and kick him out of the city, as one would expect? No. They immediately heed his message and repent. "The people of Nineveh believed God. They declared a period of fasting. Everyone, from the greatest to the least, put on sackcloth" (3:5). As soon as the news made its way to the king, he too immediately repented, stripped off his clothes, put on sackcloth, and sat in ashes. He issued a citywide decree, ordering every human being and animal to fast and to mourn, crying out to Jonah's God for mercy. Even the *dogs* of the "gentile dogs" repented! The hyperbolic depiction of the Ninevites' unprecedented conversion to Yahwism is again designed to make Jonah look like an insufferable oaf. Meanwhile, Jonah went off and sulked. He may not have been able to escape his destiny, but God couldn't make him embrace it. The narrative invites the audience to laugh at Jonah's obstinate closed-mindedness. In achieving this reaction, the satirist has successfully undermined the ideology driving ethnocentric policies such as those of Ezra and his brand of Yahwism. The *raison d'être* of Jewish existence is to be a light to the Gentiles, but people like Ezra, Joshua and Zerubbabel—represented by Jonah—just want to hide that light under a bushel.

A similar clash of ideologies can be detected between Jonah's satirist and the architects of the Canaanite conquest narratives. In Deut 20:16–19, one faction's version of Yahweh is giving instructions to Israel about how they are to treat the Canaanites when they invade the land:

> But as for the cities that Yahweh your God is giving you for your inheritance, you must not let anything that breathes remain alive. You shall devote them to utter destruction . . . just as Yahweh your God has commanded. You must kill them all, or else they may teach you to do all the abhorrent things that they do for their gods, causing you to sin against Yahweh your God. If you besiege a city for a long time, attacking it in order to take it, *you are not permitted to destroy its trees with an ax. You may take fruit from them, but you must not cut them down. Are the trees human beings that they should be destroyed by you?*

To Yahweh, according to this perspective, trees apparently have more intrinsic value than humans. Contrast this with the humorous and revealing conclusion to the book of Jonah. As the story goes, after Nineveh had repented, Jonah was feeling sorry for himself outside the city under the hot Assyrian sun. Even as Jonah was sulking, God provided a bush to shade him. The next day, however, God caused the bush to wither, and Jonah was exposed to the elements. Suffering from the heat of the day, Jonah begged God to kill him. "I would rather die than live," he said. God asked him if he was right to be angry about the loss of the bush, and Jonah retorted that he was angry enough to die. The book concludes when Yahweh chastises Jonah for being so concerned over the life of a bush and yet so indifferent to the lives of the more than 120,000 human beings and the countless animals in the great city of Nineveh.

The contrast between the two perspectives is sharp and obvious. According to the Yahweh worshiped by the architects of the Canaanite conquest narrative, Yahweh cares more about trees than he does about human beings. According to the Yahweh worshiped by the author of the book of Jonah, Yahweh cares more about human beings than he does about trees. It's an interesting argument. Perhaps some extreme environmentalists would side with Deuteronomy's Yahweh. Which Yahweh's side would *you* take in this debate?

Just Deserts or Just Desserts?

Perhaps the most significant argument in the Bible has to do with suffering. Traditional Hebrew wisdom looked at suffering and attributed it to sin. The wicked suffer on account of their wickedness, while the righteous prosper on account of their righteousness. "Life is the wage paid to the righteous, sin the reward of the wicked. . . . The nightmares of the wicked will become their reality, while the wishes of the righteous will come true. When the storm rolls over, the wicked will be taken; but the righteous are established forever. . . . The fear of Yahweh leads to long life, but the wicked's years will be cut short. The hope of the righteous comes to fruition, but the aspirations of the wicked come to naught. The way of Yahweh upholds the upright, and destroys the downright evildoers. The righteous will never be taken away, but the wicked will be removed from the land" (Prov 10:16, 24–25, 27–29). According to the traditional wisdom, everybody got what they deserved *in this life*. Those who prospered did so because they were blessed by Yahweh, rewarded for their righteousness. Those who suffered and whose lives came to ruin must have been culpable for some sin. Reward and punishment occurred in this life, and they took the form of prosperity or poverty, long life or suffering and death.

This is the perspective exhibited in John 9 by Jesus' disciples when, faced with a man who had been born blind, they asked their rabbi, "Who sinned, this man or his parents, that he should be born blind?" This was the perspective of the Hebrew prophets who interpreted Israel's suffering at the hands of foreign nations as Yahweh's punishment for their collective sins. This is the perspective that has been revived again by the modern "health and wealth gospel," the mammoth popularity of which should tell us that despite the patent absurdity of this simplistic worldview, it is still attractive to many people. The reasons for this should be obvious. For one thing, it gives people a sense of control over their lives. Their misfortunes are their own fault, and can be overcome with just the right amount of willpower, or faith, or piety, or financial investment. From another angle, this perspective is very popular among religious elites. The promise of tangible blessing is the carrot on the end of the stick held out by those who are in a position to determine what faith looks like, what righteousness is, and how much money it costs to acquire.

But this perspective is sharply opposed in the Bible by the authors of Job and Ecclesiastes, representatives of a non-traditional, more subversive wisdom. In Ecclesiastes, the Teacher decries the traditional propaganda, just as the character of Job clashes with the traditional wisdom, represented in the story by the characters of Eliphaz, Bildad, Zophar, and Elihu—Job's less than helpful companions. Job accuses the traditional Hebrew wisdom of lying for God, covering over Yahweh's misdeeds with platitudes and misdirection, calling its proponents "worthless physicians" (Job 13:4). Conversely, unseemly as the facts are, Job and the Teacher are not afraid to face them. The facts are that the righteous are *not* always rewarded, and the wicked are *not* always punished. Too often, the wicked prosper while the righteous suffer. Thus, says the Teacher,

> In my vain life I have seen it all; there are righteous people who die in their righteousness, and there are wicked people whose evil deeds serve to prolong their lives. . . . There is a vanity that takes place in this world—that the righteous are treated as though they were wicked, and that the wicked are treated as though they were righteous. I saw this and concluded that this too is vanity. Therefore, I recommend pleasure. There is nothing better under the sun than for people to eat, drink, and be merry. This at least is something they can carry with them as they slog through the days of their existence under the sun, which God has [so graciously] granted them. (Eccl 7:15; 8:14–15)

If the Teacher's critique of Yahweh's tolerance of injustice is subtle, Job's is less so: "If I summoned him and he saw fit to respond, I still do not think that he would really hear my complaint. . . . When disaster results in sudden death, he makes fun of the innocent in their calamity. . . . If he would put down his club, and stop bullying me, then I would not be afraid and I would speak my mind without holding back, for I know that I am not what people say I am" (Job 9:16, 23, 34–35). Later in 10:3–7, Job hurls these charges directly at Yahweh: "Do you take pleasure in oppression? Do you so loathe what your hands have made that you would support the plans of the wicked? Are your eyes made of flesh? Do you see as humans see? Are your days numbered like those of mortals, your years like human years, that you spend your time spying on me, trying to catch me in some sin? You know full well that I am not guilty. Do you do this simply because you know you can, because there is no one strong enough to pry me loose from your grip?" Ultimately, the book of Job never acquits Yahweh of the charges brought against him by Job. In fact, the narrative does not shrink back from impugning Yahweh, vindicating Job's accusations that Yahweh does what he will simply because he can. Yahweh's only response to Job is to remind him how thoroughly Job's significance pales in comparison to Yahweh's. Job is never told why he had to suffer, and today's pious readers tend to see an air of mystery and profundity in that fact. But they miss what would have been obvious to the ancient audience. Although Job does not know why he suffers, *the audience is privy*. Job is suffering because the gods in the heavens had made a wager.

While in the end Job is rewarded with a new family, the satire is not lost on the astute audience. "Yahweh gives and Yahweh takes away; blessed be the name of Yahweh." This is not a statement of happy confidence in a benevolent deity, but a sigh of resignation—resignation to the fact that justice may be too much to hope for in this life. Job does not say "blessed be the name of Yahweh" because what Yahweh does is right, but because there is nothing that can be done to make Yahweh do otherwise than what he will. The Teacher in Ecclesiastes would look on Job's life before, during and after his calamities, and his conclusion would be the same in each case: "Vanity of vanities; all is vanity."

Why is it all vanity? Why such resignation? Because neither Job nor the Teacher expect any recompense or restitution beyond this life. In fact, both deny the possibility. Job contrasts the fate of humans with that of trees. Unlike humans, "there is hope for a tree, if it is cut down, that it will grow up again, and that its roots will not die" (Job 14:7). Water can bring a tree back to life, says Job, but when mortal humans die, there is no coming back. "As waters evaporate from the lakebed, as a river wastes away and dries up, so mortals lie down, never to rise again" (14:11–12). Although such a view of mortality may sound like a council of despair for us, for Job, in light of his afflictions, death is the only thing he has to look forward to. Job despairs not in the thought of eternal sleep, but only in the thought of another day among the living. His life is simply biding his time "until my release should come" (14:14). When death comes knocking at Job's door, he will gladly answer, for only in death will calamity find him no longer (14:15–17). Indeed, Job sees in death an escape from the tormenting hand of Yahweh. "As the cloud fades and ebbs away, so those who go down to the grave do not come up. They will never return to their homes, nor will they be seen again from whence they came" (7:9–10). This fact emboldens Job to accuse Yahweh: "Therefore I will not hold my tongue; I will speak up out of the torment of my spirit; I will protest out of the bitterness of my existence" (7:11). Without restraint, Job indicts Yahweh for unjustly afflicting him. He can do this because he knows that death is near, and that then he will be beyond Yahweh's reach: "For I shall lie down in the dust of the earth; you will seek me, but I will not be there to be found" (7:21).

Similarly, the Teacher resigns himself to the fact that everything that comes to the righteous in this life—whether love or hate—is vanity. Why is it vanity? "Because the same fate comes to everyone—the righteous and the wicked, the good and the evil, the clean and the unclean, the religious and the nonreligious. As are the pious, so are the impious. Those who keep oaths are in the same boat as those who break them. This is what's wrong with everything that happens under the sun—that the same fate comes to everyone" (Eccl 9:2–3). The same fate that comes to everyone is death. Good, bad, rich, poor—everybody ends up in the ground. If the Teacher believed in an afterlife in which rewards and punishments were handed out like exam results, then everything would not be vanity. Everything would have a purpose, and that purpose would be to pass the exam. But everything is vanity for the Teacher precisely because he does not believe in such an afterlife. Just as with Job, the Teacher's perspective is shaped by the finality of death. "The hearts of everyone are full of evil. Insanity possesses their hearts while they are alive, and then they're dead. But those who are still alive have some hope; after all, a living dog is better off than a dead lion. The living at least know that they're going to die, but the dead know nothing. The dead have no more reward. Eventually, even their memory will disappear among the living. Their love, their hate, their jealousies—all of that dies with them. Never again will they take part in anything that happens under the sun" (9:3–6). In light of this, the Teacher concludes that the only thing to be done is to live one's life to the fullest measure. In the absence of just deserts, there's just dessert. "Go ahead and eat your bread with satisfaction, and drink your wine with a happy heart. . . . Enjoy life with the wife whom you love, every last day of your vain life under the sun. That's all that has been allotted to you. That's your whole task" (9:7, 9). The Teacher concludes that if one is to find any meaning in existence, it will be in what one does on this side of the grave; there will be no meaning on the other side (9:10).

Sometime later, however, a third voice would join the argument. This third voice conceded Job and the Teacher's critique of the traditional wisdom literature. It conceded that reward and punishment are frequently not meted out in this life according to the dictates of justice. In fact, this third voice knew that fact all too well, for this was the voice of the martyrs. The traditional wisdom and the promises of the prophets had failed them. Their suffering was not tied to their disobedience. Their suffering only seemed to increase to the degree their obedience became more fervent. It was almost as if they were being punished *because* of their obedience to Yahweh. And this is in fact what they concluded. They *were* being punished for their obedience to Yahweh; only they were not being punished by Yahweh, but by forces hostile to Yahweh. They were being punished by the Devil and his demonic delinquents—the spiritual puppet masters pulling the strings on foreign tyrants.

Nevertheless, unlike Job and Ecclesiastes, these faithful Jews refused to believe that death would have the last word—that their suffering was meaningless. Unlike Job, the martyrs did not see death as a sweet release from Yahweh's unjust afflictions; they saw death as a grave injustice that Yahweh, in his justice, could not let pass. Unlike the Teacher, the martyrs did not believe that life was vanity in light of the finality of death; they believed that life was meaningful in light of the impermanence of death. Their experience was too painful to accept the Teacher's counsel of despair. They took Ezekiel's valley of the dry bones, a metaphor for the restoration of the nation of Israel after exile,[4] and read it literally, giving rise to belief in a resurrection, a life after death in which all wrongs would be righted and in which they would once again have a share in all that happens under the sun. Thus the author of the book of Daniel tells those who are suffering of an imminent deliverance: "At that time Michael, the great prince and guardian of your people, shall stand up. Then there will be a period of suffering more intense than any other since the nations first came into existence. But when that happens, your people will be delivered, everyone whose name is found inscribed in the book. At that time, many of those who sleep beneath the dust of the earth will wake up, some of them to everlasting life, and some of them to shame and to everlasting condemnation" (Dan 12:1–2). Another pseudonymous book, the Wisdom of Solomon, speaks similarly of the significance of the deaths of God's faithful:

> For God created us for incorruption,
> and made us in the image of his own eternity [or nature],
> but through the devil's envy death entered the world,
> and those who belong to his company experience it.
> But the souls of the righteous are in the hand of God,
> and no torment will ever touch them.
> In the eyes of the foolish they seemed to have died,
> and their departure was thought to be a disaster,
> and their going from us to be their destruction;
> but they are at peace.
> For though in the sight of others they were punished,
> their hope is full of immortality.
> Having been disciplined a little, they will receive great good,
> because God tested them and found them worthy of himself;
> like gold in the furnace he tried them,
> and like a sacrificial burnt offering he accepted them.
> In the time of their visitation they will shine forth,
> and will run like sparks through the stubble.
> They will govern nations and rule over peoples,
> and the Lord will reign over them forever.
> (Wis 2:23—3:8, NRSV)

These three voices would be carried on in various ways until the destruction of the temple in 70 CE. The apocalyptic voice of the martyrs, which originally took shape during the reign of Syrian king Antiochus IV Epiphanes in the 160s BCE, would continue to be heard in some quarters of the Qumran community, in the Zealots, in the Pharisees, and in the Galilean

---

4. On the interpretation of Ezekiel 37, see Wright, *Resurrection of the Son of God,* 119–21.

Jesus movement. The message of the wisdom tradition, which ascribed suffering to wrongdoing, would continue to be propagated by the ruling elites—the Sadducean regime that governed the temple and did the bidding of Rome. Yet it seems that despite what the temple regime preached, the elites themselves adopted something closer to the perspective of the Teacher, albeit with a more nefarious bent: life is short; acquire much.

Of these three voices, the most subversive is clearly that of Job and Ecclesiastes. After the eventual triumph of the perspective of the martyrs over the others, it is remarkable that Job and Ecclesiastes were kept within the sacred curriculum. Job was likely kept because its satire could easily be read flatly—the narrative which impugns Yahweh by exposing him as a self-indulgent tyrant came to be read by the pious as a reverent testament to Yahweh's incalculable power. The status of Ecclesiastes was disputed among the rabbis. To them it was questionable because of its hedonistic and skeptical message, but it was ultimately salvaged with the help of some earlier editorial emendations, and by virtue of a tradition (wrongly) attributing the book to King Solomon. A redactor had added an introduction (Eccl 1:1) and conclusion (Eccl 12:9–14) to the body of the Teacher's book. The editorial conclusion essentially gives the audience permission to ignore the contents of the book, undermining its message by adding a reference to a final judgment in which all that is wrong will be made right—a possibility the Teacher himself had repeatedly denied.

Manufacturing Conformity

Before there was a canon, there was a curriculum—a collection of literature that for a variety of reasons was important to Yahwists. As we have seen, within this curriculum there was a broad spectrum of ideas about God, justice, the role of Israel, and the meaning of human existence. Most of this literature made no claim to divine inspiration, but these texts were nonetheless important to the Jewish people because they were points of reference in an ongoing argument that they saw as vital to the faith. As Collins explains, claims to divine inspiration were originally only made about the laws of Moses and the prophetic oracles. Certain parts of the Torah were supposedly dictated directly to Moses by Yahweh, and the prophets were believed to have spoken under divine inspiration. But the historical books made no claim to divine inspiration, and writings such as Ecclesiastes and Job were very humanistic in their perspective; far from claiming to be inspired by Yahweh, they were critical of him. Nevertheless, Collins writes, "the claim of inspiration was gradually extended to the whole corpus, by analogy with the laws and the prophets."[5]

This process was slow, but probably inevitable. After the loss of the monarchy, the vassal rulers of Judea— under the authority of the Persians, then the Greeks, and then the Romans—struggled to find ways to maintain political control over the people. The obvious resources at their disposal were the institutions of sacrifice and the corpus of literature that had been acquired over the centuries. Maintaining the geographical centralization of the rites of sacrifice ensured that people would continue to depend on the temple in Jerusalem for the favor of their deity. This also guaranteed a steady stream of income for the ruling elites in the capital, and marginalized the significance of rival religious factions. Moreover, bringing the broad corpus of literature under the domain of the establishment helped to ensure that it could not be used to inspire dissenting ideas. The genius of appropriating dissenting texts in service of establishment orthodoxy lies in that fact. Thus editors were put to work revising the texts, reframing the perspectives to give them a pro-establishment spin. We saw this already with the conclusion that was added to Ecclesiastes. The collection of oracles from the radical prophet Amos was also amended to include a happy ending for the Davidic pedigree, and so on down the line. Because of widespread illiteracy, the vast majority of the general population was none the wiser.

This is not a phenomenon unique to second temple Judaism by any means. It has always been standard practice for ruling elites to attempt to re-cast revolutionary figures and anti-establishment gadflies as national heroes of the first order. We see this in the United States, for instance, with Martin Luther King Jr., who after his death would come to be celebrated as an icon of the American spirit; in reality he was while alive increasingly considered by the government to be a dangerous radical. By making King over into a brand name, elites were able to minimize the impact of his crusade against the Vietnam War and his growing opposition to free market capitalism. In the same way, the broad corpus of Hebrew and Jewish writings was gradually incorporated into the canon of official Jewish religion, where its interpretation and transmission could be controlled to a significant degree.

It was during this period also that names of authoritative figures from Israel's past were attached to these otherwise anonymous documents. Moses became the author of the Pentateuch; Joshua was written by Joshua; Samuel became the author of Judges and 1 and 2 Samuel; Jeremiah was said to have written the books of Kings; the books of Chronicles were ascribed to Ezra; many of the Psalms were attributed to David; and Proverbs and Ecclesiastes

5. Collins, *Introduction to the Hebrew Bible*, 600.

were both said to have been written by Solomon. In this way, a sense of unity and authority was brought to a diverse set of texts. Although the Pentateuch is clearly composite in nature and was obviously composed in pieces over the course of centuries, the tradition that the entirety was composed by Moses brought legitimacy to any and all late additions to the narratives.[6] By attributing both Proverbs *and* Ecclesiastes to the same man (King Solomon), the elites were able to disguise the fact that the latter book constituted a fairly incisive critique of the former. As one would expect, with the progression of time, traditions about the composition of the Bible became ever more incredible. For instance, in the second century BCE, two separate books (Baruch and Ben Sira) would both identify the Torah as the earthly instantiation of preexistent personified Wisdom. In other words, the books of Moses had already been written before the foundation of the world![7] This idea would later become commonplace among the rabbis.

To summarize, the process by which these disparate books were collected together into a single curriculum was undertaken in large part in order to contribute to the consolidation of political power—as a way to safeguard religious identity and group cohesion. This does not necessarily imply any unsavory motives, but at the very least it is clear that this was a process overseen by the political elites at every turn. Absent more effective institutions of political control, the texts were brought together to form a sort of divinely-commissioned legislature. It should be clear, therefore, that it was only *after* the texts had been brought together for these purposes that it even began to make sense to think about them as a singular "Word" from God. It was the process of canonization itself that created the so-called "problem" of errancy and with it the need to harmonize these originally argumentative texts historically, morally, and theologically. The roots of the doctrine of inerrancy can thus be found in rabbinic interpretation, which became an exercise in manufacturing conformity—the conformity of one biblical voice to another, and the conformity of Yahweh's people to the dictates of Yahweh's Persian-appointed and self-appointed representatives.[8] The *man*ufactured Word had eclipsed its ancestor, the Argument.

---

6. An example of such additions can be found in Deuteronomy 17, which gives detailed regulations restricting the powers of the monarch. If we are to take seriously the claim to Mosaic authorship, these instructions were given more than two hundred years before Israel had a monarchy!

7. See Bar 3:35—4:4; Sir 24:1–23.

8. For a concise and very accessible introduction to this whole process, see Coote and Coote, *Power, Politics, and the Making of the Bible.* For a comprehensive yet still very user-friendly treatment, see Collins, *Introduction to the Hebrew Bible.*

2 Inerrantists Do Not Exist
Dispelling a Myth of Biblical Proportions

PERHAPS I SHOULD BE MORE CIRCUMSPECT WITH MY LANGUAGE. It is not my intention to demonize inerrantists. In the last chapter I portrayed incipient inerrancy as a concoction of powerbrokers for power-brokering ends. I argued that the canonization process gave rise to the doctrine of inerrancy, which is an ideological construct projected onto a set of otherwise morally and theologically disparate texts that functions to eradicate dissenting views and to help preserve the status quo. It all sounds frightfully Orwellian.

One may find consolation, however, in reality: *there are no such things as inerrantists*. Certainly, there are those who *claim* to be inerrantists. There are those who *think* that they are inerrantists. But in truth, nobody is *really* an inerrantist. Inerrantists do not and cannot exist. It's a logical impossibility. An inerrantist, simply put, is someone who believes that everything the Bible affirms is true, and good, and that it comes from the mind of a kind, loving, merciful, and just God. Now admittedly, anybody who knows anything about the horrible kinds of things the Bible tends to say would be well within their right mind to be afraid of an *actual* inerrantist. But inerrantists are mythical creatures, no more real than the bogeyman, or the monsters in my daughter's closet; no professing inerrantist has ever scored 100 percent on the acid test of scripture.

It would be difficult to find an inerrantist who believed that Ashur, Asherah, Marduk, and Kemosh were real gods in the ancient Near East; equally difficult to find an inerrantist who believed that when Yahweh was a young deity he received the land of Israel as an inheritance from his father, the mountain god El Elyon. Yet that's what the Bible says.[1] Try finding an inerrantist who does not have a problem with the fact that, according to the Bible, Yahweh not only desired, but commanded and expected Israelites to sacrifice their children to him as an act of gratitude for delivering them from slavery.[2] Speaking of slavery, no inerrantist nowadays would agree that it is

1. See chapter 4.
2. See chapter 5.

15

morally acceptable even to own a slave, let alone to beat that slave. Yet the Bible says that not only is it morally acceptable to own a slave and to beat a slave, it is also morally acceptable to beat a slave *to death*.[3]

If you were to ask an inerrantist if she agrees with Ezek 18:20, she would certainly answer in the affirmative. *Of course* she concurs that children should not be made to suffer for the sins of their parents! But ask her if she agrees with Isa 13:16, where Yahweh's idea of justice is to punish parents by dashing their infants' heads against large rocks. Ask her if she concurs with Lev 26:29, or Ezek 5:9, or Jer 19:9, where Yahweh chooses to punish misbehaving parents by force-feeding them their own children for lunch. Is the inerrantist still an inerrantist? Is the Bible still God's perfect word?

Furthermore, good luck finding an inerrantist who believes the final judgment and general resurrection of the dead occurred in the first century CE, because that's when Jesus said it would happen.[4] Ask an inerrantist if he agrees with 1 Tim 2:12–14 that women should not be teachers of doctrine, on the grounds that all women are inherently more susceptible to deception than men, as evinced in the fact that Eve ate the fruit before Adam did. Ask him if he agrees that Genesis 3 constitutes an accurate depiction of the credulity of all women everywhere, because that's what the author of 1 Timothy claimed. Is the inerrantist still an inerrantist? (Admittedly, *some* find this perspective amenable to their tastes.[5]) If so, ask him again, this time in front of his wife. She will probably not hesitate to remind her inerrantist husband of the fact that the vast majority of cults and superstitions throughout history have been propagated and mostly populated by males. Any male is just as capable of

---

3. See Exod 21:20–21.

4. Although I suppose conceding that Jesus was not inerrant is not quite the same as conceding that the Bible, which accurately reported his words, is not inerrant. At any rate, see chapter 8.

5. Such as Mars Hill pastor Mark Driscoll: "Without blushing, Paul is simply stating that when it comes to leading in the church, women are unfit because they are more gullible and easier to deceive than men. While many irate women have disagreed with his assessment through the years, it does appear from this that such women who fail to trust his instruction and follow his teaching are much like their mother Eve and are well-intended but ill-informed. . . . Before you get all emotional like a woman in hearing this, please consider the content of the women's magazines at your local grocery store that encourages liberated women in our day to watch porno with their boyfriends, master oral sex for men who have no intention of marrying them, pay for their own dates in the name of equality, spend an average of three-fourths of their childbearing years having sex but trying not to get pregnant, and abort 1/3 of all babies—and ask yourself if it doesn't look like the Serpent is still trolling the garden and that the daughters of Eve aren't gullible in pronouncing progress, liberation, and equality." Driscoll, *Church Leadership*, 43. I see no need for further comment.

being deceived as any female. The reality is that the author of 1 Timothy was simply the product of a patriarchal society, and was thus blinded to the irony that he himself had been deceived by the misogynist myth of male intellectual superiority. The joke was on him.[6]

There are countless thousands of test questions to put to the professing inerrantist, and the thing about being an inerrantist is that, in order to qualify, one has to score a perfect 100 percent on the acid test. All it takes is one miniscule disagreement with the Bible for the whole house of cards to come tumbling down. And eventually, if they allow themselves to be pressed, it will happen to every honest would-be inerrantist. There is no such thing as an inerrantist. Inerrantists just haven't realized it yet.

That is not to say, however, that professing inerrantists have not, like the Wizard of Oz, devised strategies for maintaining the illusion of their existence. One such strategy predominates among them, and that is the attempt to define inerrancy in such a way that it cannot be disconfirmed. They do this by employing what I call a "hermeneutic of convenience," disguised as a historical-grammatical hermeneutic. The principles of the hermeneutic of convenience are constructed specially for the purpose of "resolving" what by historical-grammatical criteria would be patent contradictions and discrepancies. In this way, professing inerrantists are enabled to *change the meaning of the text*, so that the illusion of their agreement with it—and thus of their status as inerrantists—can go on unabated.

Article sixteen of the Chicago Statement on Biblical Inerrancy (CSBI) affirms that "the doctrine of inerrancy has been integral to the Church's faith throughout its history," denying that the doctrine is of recent origin.[7] The exposition of this article further states that inerrancy is a doctrine affirmed (1) by Jesus of Nazareth, (2) by his apostles, (3) by "the whole Bible," (4) by "the mainstream of church history from the first days until very recently," and (5) by the Chicago inerrantists themselves.[8] If this were true, this would ostensibly put the Chicago inerrantists in reasonably good company. We might even be able to let this claim pass if it were not for a second claim they make. Article eighteen of the CSBI stipulates that "the text of Scripture is to be interpreted by grammatico-historical exegesis, taking account of its literary forms and devices."[9] Article fifteen of the Chicago Statement on Biblical Hermeneutics

6. See below, p. 41.

7. Reproduced in Henry, *God Who Speaks*, 214. The Chicago Statement on Biblical Inerrancy is also easily accessible online.

8. Ibid., 219.

9. Ibid., 214.

(CSBH) reiterates this point, referring to the historical-grammatical sense also as the "normal" or "literal" sense of the text.[10]

They do not literally mean "literal," however. For them, the "literal sense" is whatever sense the author intended to convey. If the author was using metaphorical speech, then the "literal sense" is the metaphorical sense. The important thing for our purposes is to make it clear that the Chicago inerrantists insist on the historical-grammatical interpretation of scripture. They "deny the legitimacy of any approach to Scripture that attributes to it meaning which the literal sense does not support. . . . The correct interpretation is the one which discovers the meaning of the text in its grammatical forms and in the historical, cultural context in which the text is expressed."[11] In other words, for the Chicago inerrantists, the text of scripture is not merely inspired in some allegorical or metaphorical sense; it is without error in its strict historical-grammatical sense. Records of errors are accepted, but not errant records; thus, the Bible can recount a character's lies or mistakes, but the Bible itself cannot lie or make a mistake. According to the Chicago inerrantists, essential to the doctrine of inerrancy—correctly construed—is the historical-grammatical hermeneutic.

It is exactly in their insistence on this point that the inerrantists shoot themselves in the foot. The reality is that, contrary to their claims, neither the Old Testament writers, nor the New Testament writers, nor "the mainstream of church history," nor the Chicago inerrantists themselves utilize a historical-grammatical hermeneutic. The biblical writers and many of the Church Fathers did not do so for the simple reason that they were not generally *interested* in the historical-grammatical meaning of the text. The Chicago inerrantists do not do so because their commitment to inerrancy frequently prevents them from accepting the historical-grammatical meaning of the text. In all cases, it is much easier to be an "inerrantist" when the intended meaning of the original author can be disregarded.

Ancient Jewish Hermeneutics

Before we discuss how ancient Jewish hermeneutics generally worked, we need to establish precisely what the Chicago inerrantists are claiming. To begin with, articles seven and eight of the CSBH establish the principle that "the meaning expressed in each biblical text is single, definite and fixed." The Chicago inerrantists deny the existence of any "double" or "deeper" meaning of the text, and insist upon "the unity and fixity of meaning as opposed

10. The CSBH is reproduced in Radmacher and Preus, *Hermeneutics*, 889–904.
11. Ibid., 898.

to those who find multiple and pliable meanings."[12] Secondly, they disallow the possibility "that later writers of Scripture misinterpreted earlier passages of Scripture when quoting from or referring to them,"[13] and insist that "the Bible's own interpretation of itself is always correct, never deviating from, but rather elucidating, the single meaning of the inspired text."[14] As they elaborate on this point, the Chicago inerrantists expose their fundamental lack of understanding of ancient Jewish hermeneutics: "The Bible never misinterprets itself. It always correctly understands the meaning of the passage it comments on. . . . For example, that Paul misinterprets Moses is to say that Paul erred. This view is emphatically rejected in favor of the inerrancy of all Scripture."[15]

It is precisely here that the flaw is betrayed. They present themselves with a false dichotomy: either Paul interprets Moses correctly or incorrectly. If incorrectly, then Paul is wrong and the Bible is not inerrant. The problem is that interpreters like Paul were not concerned with interpreting Moses "correctly," if by "correctly" one means, "historically-grammatically." Like most other Jewish interpreters of his day, Paul was interested in the text not for what it said in the past, but for what it was saying to Paul's own generation. When the Chicago inerrantists insist that a given passage can have only one fixed meaning, they are—unwittingly or not—rejecting a principle of interpretation that was axiomatic for Paul: the text had both a historical meaning and an eschatological meaning.

Paul shared this assumption with virtually all apocalyptic Jews of his day. To such thinkers, the text had *at least* two meanings, if not more, none of which were necessarily tied by any fixed principle to any of the other meanings. Moreover, the meaning that was important to them was not the historical one, but the one they were able to derive from the text for their own edification or for the elucidation of contemporary events. This was in fact true of Jewish interpretation generally, not just apocalyptic or eschatological varieties. As James Kugel explains, "The past was not approached in the spirit of antiquarianism but for what message it might yield, and this is necessarily predicated on an interpretive stance, indeed, a willingness to deviate from the texts' plain sense. The words of prophets, the accounts of ancient historians, were to be 'translated' into present-day significance, referred to (and sometimes distorted) in order to support a particular view of the present, or a program for the future."[16] Thus, there is no question of "misinterpretation."

12. Ibid., 893.
13. Ibid., 885.
14. Ibid.
15. Ibid., 900.
16. Kugel and Greer, *Early Biblical Interpretation*, 38.

Interpretation was not a careful process of historical-grammatical exegesis, but an inspired identification of a "hidden meaning" in the text with a present-day reality or concern.

Milking the Prophecy

This approach may be discerned in the author of Daniel's appropriation of Jeremiah's "seventy years" prophecy. The author took a prophecy that had already been fulfilled in the sixth century and retooled it to make it relevant to the concerns of his audience in the second century BCE. This requires an excursus on the dating of Daniel:

> Although the book of Daniel is set in the sixth century BCE, critical scholars are virtually unanimous that it was not completed in its final form until the mid-second century BCE. The evidence for this date is readily apparent. Daniel chapter 11 is presented as a prophecy of future political events, beginning with the rise of Alexander the Great, who overthrows the Persian empire, before his life is cut short and his kingdom is divided in four directions (Dan 11:2–4). The prophecy then proceeds through a detailed description of the rise and fall of the various kings of the Ptolemaic (Egyptian) and Seleucid (Syrian) empires, the two of which battled one another for control of Palestine. This account of the succession of kings culminates with the Syrian king, Antiochus IV Epiphanes (175–163 BCE). Antiochus IV was a fierce persecutor of the Jewish people, who desecrated the Jerusalem temple by converting it into a temple for Zeus. This incident, which took place in 167 BCE, is referred to as the "abomination that causes desolation" in Dan 11:31. The prophecy continues to describe the events of Antiochus's career, culminating with a prediction of his death. The relevant factor here is that the author predicts that Antiochus would be killed in the land of Israel, "between the sea and the beautiful holy mountain." There he would "come to his end, with no one around to help him" (11:45). The problem is that Antiochus IV did *not* die in Israel. In fact, he did not die anywhere *near* Israel. He died in Persia, after an unsuccessful attempt to loot the temple of Artemis-Nanaia in Elam.
>
> What does this tell us? The predictive prophecy in Daniel 11 is stunningly accurate, right up until about 164 BCE. Then, suddenly, a glaring failed prediction: Antiochus did not die where the author said he would die.[17] Furthermore, the author goes on to assert

17. Even revered inerrancy apologist Gleason Archer acknowledged that the prediction in Dan 11:45 does not correspond to the actual demise of Antiochus IV. Archer, however, attempted to ignore the obvious conclusion—that the author's prediction of

that following the death of Antiochus IV Epiphanes, the archangel Michael would arise and deliver Israel from its foreign oppressors, whereupon the faithful departed would be resurrected to life (12:1–3). It should not be necessary to point out that this did not happen either. What this tells us is that these portions of Daniel were written sometime after 167 and before 163. The author was engaging in what is called "prophecy *post eventum*," or "prophecy after the fact." Because they had already occurred, he was able to predict with amazing precision all the details of the battles and the successions of kings from Alexander the Great to Antiochus IV. The one *actual* prediction the author made—namely, that Antiochus IV would die in Israel and that Israel would then be delivered from bondage to the nations with the help of Michael—did not come to pass.

It is easy to understand why the author would have predicted what he did. The author had hopes that the Maccabean revolutionaries—Jewish freedom fighters who rose up in response to Antiochus IV's desecration of the Jerusalem temple—would kill Antiochus in battle on their own territory and that that victory would lead to Israel's immediate independence from and sovereignty over the nations. Thus, by disguising his description of past events as "predictive prophecy," the author's intent was to inspire hope that what had not yet taken place would happen just as surely as had all the rest. In order to explain why the "prophecy" given to Daniel had not been in circulation until the time of Antiochus IV, the author has the angel Gabriel instruct Daniel to "keep these words a secret and keep the book sealed until the time of the end" (12:4). With that, the author solved the problem. The Jewish people were not aware of Daniel's prophecy because it had been "kept a secret" and "sealed until the time of the end," which the author believed was his own time—the period of the Maccabean revolution.

This type of prophecy *post eventum*, or prophecy after the fact, was in fact a very common literary genre in the ancient world. Its

---

Antiochus IV's death was mistaken. Archer's hermeneutical gymnastics are mildly humorous. He referred to "the startling way in which the figure of the Greek emperor Antiochus suddenly blends into the figure of the latter day Antichrist in Dan. 11, beginning with verse 40. (Note that the Little Horn is said in 11:45 to meet his death in Palestine, whereas Antiochus IV actually died in Tabae, Persia.)" Archer, *Old Testament Introduction*, 439. Indeed, it would be "startling" if the author suddenly, and without any warning or indication, changed subjects from a Seleucid king in the 160s BCE, to an otherwise unmentioned figure at some indeterminate point in the distant future. What Archer did was to abandon the historical-grammatical hermeneutic when it did not suit him, projecting onto the text his own ideas, which are entirely foreign to Daniel, in order to salvage a failed predictive prophecy. If, on the other hand, this failed prediction had been found in a book outside Archer's accepted biblical canon, he would have been the first in line to denounce it as such.

intent was not so much to deceive—although a little deception was necessary—but to exhort and to inspire. The prophecies in Daniel were written to encourage the Jewish people in a time of intense crisis, to assure them that by remaining faithful, they would live to see the deliverance of Israel from the hands of the enemy.

Inerrantists frequently make the claim that "liberal" scholars argue for a "late date" for Daniel because of an alleged anti-super-naturalist bias. It is alleged that so-called liberals simply *cannot* accept that such accurate prophecy is possible—their "worldview" doesn't have room for it. There are two things to say in response to this. First, inerrantists are guilty of precisely that same bias when claims to the supernatural are made in texts outside of the biblical canon. When miracles occur in other sacred or quasi-historical texts, and are attributed to powers other than Yahweh, inerrantists do not hesitate to come up with natural explanations for the alleged phenomena. Second, such an anti-supernaturalist bias exists only in the minds of inerrantists. Critical scholars use the same methodology across the board, and the aim is not to disprove any and all supernatural claims, but to follow the evidence where it leads. In this particular case, the evidence in the text itself leads directly to the conclusion that the prediction of the location of Antiochus's death was mistaken. This factor in combination with late linguistic features in the book of Daniel, and not any anti-supernaturalist bias, is what leads critical scholars to date the final form of the book, quite correctly, in the mid-160s BCE. End of excursus.

As I was saying, biblical interpretation was not a careful process of historical-grammatical exegesis, but an inspired identification of a "hidden meaning" in the text with a present-day reality or concern. This is what we see in the author of Daniel's appropriation of Jeremiah's "seventy years" prophecy. The author took a prophecy that had already been fulfilled in the sixth century and retooled it to make it relevant to the concerns of his audience in the second century BCE. Jeremiah had prophesied that Babylon would make Jerusalem into a desolate wasteland, and that Babylon would rule over the nations for seventy years. However, after the seventy years had passed, Yahweh would send other nations against Babylon and make it a desolate wasteland in turn (Jer 25:9–12). After the seventy years had been fulfilled, Yahweh would restore his people to their homeland, bringing them back to Judea (Jer 29:10). This prophecy was fulfilled in 538 BCE, after the Persian King Cyrus had defeated Babylon and issued an edict releasing all Babylonian prisoners to return to their own lands. The "seventy years" should not be pressed for exactitude. It is a round number and symbolic of the "perfect" amount of time. In reality, the Jews had only been in exile for about forty-eight years. Regardless, the point is that Jeremiah's prophecy had already been fulfilled.

The author of Daniel, however, writing about 400 years later, was living during a time in which Jerusalem was once again being made desolate, this time not by the Babylonians but by Antiochus IV Epiphanes, a Syrian king. There was a sense among the Jewish people that Jeremiah's promise—that the land would be restored to Israel—was as yet unfulfilled, because while they had been *returned* to the land, control of the land had never been returned to them. Now the dire ramifications of that fact were being brought to the surface in the intense persecutions of Antiochus IV. Thus, the author of Daniel revisits Jeremiah's prophecy. At the outset of Daniel chapter 9, the character of Daniel ponders the prophecy, making explicit reference to Jeremiah and to the prophesied seventy years. At the time in which the narrative of Daniel is set, the "seventy years" of Babylon's reign would have been just about up. Daniel therefore begins to make supplication, pleading with Yahweh to deliver them from Babylon, now that the time is up. What happens next is telling. The angel appears to Daniel and gives him a vision of seventy *weeks* of years. In other words, each day of the week for seventy weeks represents one year. This totals up at 490 years. Again, these are round and symbolic numbers— seventy times seven (cf. Matt 18:22)—and should not be pressed for accuracy. The angel revealed to Daniel that the "real" meaning of Jeremiah's prophecy was not seventy years, but seventy weeks of years. Using Jeremiah in this way lends the authority of the prophet to the author's own agenda.[18] In other words, according to the author of Daniel, Jeremiah was not prophesying about Daniel's time at all, but about the period of the Maccabean revolt! *That* is when Israel would experience its true deliverance and restoration.

Now, if the Chicago inerrantists conceded this to be the case, they would no doubt characterize Daniel 9's use of Jeremiah 29:10 as a *misinterpretation*. But it is clear that "misinterpretation" is not an accurate description of what is going on. The author of Daniel 9 is not *misinterpreting* Jeremiah—he is reconfiguring Jeremiah. He is not misunderstanding the historical sense of the text; rather, he is "discovering" the hidden, eschatological sense of the text. According to Collins, this marks "a hermeneutical shift in the history of ancient Jewish exegesis. It is the first case where a prophetic oracle is explicitly interpreted allegorically, or understood to mean something other than what it literally says."[19] As we have noted, this assumption that the scriptures contained hidden, eschatological meanings was axiomatic for apocalyptic Jews

18. Collins, "Prophecy and Fulfillment," 272, writes that the prediction in Daniel 9 "is not really derived from the prophecy but that the prophecy is invoked to lend authority to a prediction that is made for other reasons."

19. Ibid., 270.

who believed they were living in the end times. This kind of interpretation of the scriptures, prefigured here in Daniel 9, would become pervasive in the Qumran sect, as reflected in the Dead Sea Scrolls.

Inspired Revisionist Readings

The Qumran sect, an ascetic Jewish community, seems to have come into existence sometime around the mid-second century BCE and survived until 68 CE when they were wiped out in battle by the Romans. Not much is known about the history of this sect. Most of what is known is derived from their biblical commentaries, in which their history is encoded within idiosyncratic interpretations of the prophets.[20] Scholars have attempted to reconstruct their history from these encrypted commentaries—called the *pesharim*—but many details remain ambiguous. It is clear that they were led by a charismatic prophet who is referred to as the Teacher of Righteousness, and that this prophet was opposed by a "Wicked Priest."[21] They were a millenarian sect who believed they possessed a special covenant relationship with Yahweh and that their community would serve as the primary agent of eschatological renewal.[22] These beliefs in fact underwrote the hermeneutics of the *pesharim*.

The word *pesher* is a Semitic word meaning, simply, *interpretation*. In the Hebrew Bible, the word occurs only once in Hebrew (Eccl 8:1), but 31 times in the Aramaic portion of Daniel, in which it refers primarily to the interpretation of dreams.[23] In the Qumran commentaries, a biblical (prophetic) text is cited one section at a time, each section followed by an interpretation, which is introduced by a stock phrase—"the interpretation (*pesher*) of which is" such and such. This methodology tended to produce atomistic interpretations "with scant regard for the original literary context, much less the original historical context." In fact, "disregard for the historical context is integral to the method."[24] This is so because the Qumran community believed that the biblical prophecies were written *not* for the contemporaries of the prophet but for their own community. The prophecies—so they believed—were encrypted descriptions of Qumran's contemporary experience and eschatologi-

---

20. Cohen, *Maccabees to the Mishnah*, 153. For a good example of this see Ehrman, *New Testament*, 49.

21. For a basic reconstruction of Qumran history, see Vermes, *Complete Dead Sea Scrolls*, 49–66; also Collins, *Apocalyptic Imagination*, 148–50.

22. On the covenantal theology of the Qumran sect, see Sanders, *Paul and Palestinian Judaism*, 239–328.

23. Bruce, "Pesher," para. 1.

24. Collins, *Apocalyptic Imagination*, 268.

cal destiny. These reinterpretations of prophecy are achieved in a number of ways, most commonly by exploiting ambiguities in the language of a passage, by rearranging the letters of a word or dividing a word into two or more parts, and sometimes by allegory. This process served the primary function of the commentaries which was not to exegete scripture but to address the community's concerns and reinforce its identity.[25]

The basic technique of interpreting sacred texts atomistically is not entirely unique to ancient Judaism. The method is attested in Egyptian literature, going back to the *Book of the Dead*, in which there are some surprising parallels to Jewish messianism. There is, however, no evidence that the Qumran sect was influenced by the Egyptian literature.[26] Another source of Qumran's technique can be found in Daniel in the interpretation of dreams. In Daniel, the dreams of Nebuchadnezzar are considered *razim* (mysteries) that require a *peshar* (interpretation) which is given to the prophet by direct divine revelation.[27] These two words (*raz* and *peshar*) occur frequently in the Qumran literature. In the commentaries, the *razim* are the "mysteries" of the biblical prophets (hidden from the prophets themselves) that are able to be unlocked only by the Teacher of Righteousness, who is specially inspired by God to give the interpretation.

What this indicates is that for the Qumran sect, "the distinction between biblical and nonbiblical was not hard and fast."[28] Although they revered scripture[29] and were committed to it as special revelation from God, they were just as committed to the belief that as God's eschatological community, their interpretation was equally divinely inspired.[30] More than that, they believed that encrypted in the prophets was a unique divine revelation from God pertaining to the end time, a revelation that *could not be unlocked* without the interpretation of the Teacher.[31] "It is the gift of the 'spirit of knowledge' from God, or the 'spirit of holiness,' . . . that allows the Qumran interpreter to penetrate the 'secrets,' 'mysteries,' or 'hidden things' in ancient Scripture and read aright their message for himself

---

25. Collins, "Prophecy and Fulfillment," 273.

26. Ibid., 269–70.

27. Bruce, "Pesher."

28. Lim, "Qumran Scrolls," 57.

29. Lim indicates that at this stage, when the textual traditions are marked by diversity and canonicity is still a fluid concept, it is more appropriate to talk about "authoritative writings" than scripture, *per se*. Ibid.

30. Ibid., 72. So too Ferguson, *Backgrounds of Early Christianity*, 525.

31. Collins, *Apocalyptic Imagination*, 152.

and his contemporaries."[32]An understanding of the prophetic message in its original historical context was entirely irrelevant to the community. What this "inspired interpretation" entails, then, from a "modern critical viewpoint," is the "manipulation of the prophetic text to meet the needs of the community."[33] Of course, to the members of the Qumran sect, the methodology was perfectly legitimate, especially given their eschatological assumptions and convictions about their collective identity; nevertheless, Collins concludes that "the claim of revelation appears here to be a rhetorical device, however sincerely employed, that masks the actual process of Biblical interpretation."[34]

Competing Inspired Revisionist Readings

There are numerous parallels between the assumptions and the techniques of Qumran interpretation and that of the New Testament writers.[35] Both groups used the same set of authoritative texts to "unlock a mystery" with eschatological and messianic significance. Both groups were trained by a charismatic personality (the Teacher of Righteousness; Jesus) how to find the mysteries hidden within the prophets.[36] Both groups seem to have had no qualms about changing the meaning of a text in order to give a sense of antiquity to their present experience. Both groups considered themselves to be living in the end times, and this is reflected in their hermeneutic.[37] Moreover, as both groups' expectations of the timing of the end were disappointed, each turned to the prophets in order to make sense of the "delay." The Qumran commentary on Habakkuk (1QpHab 7:6–13) turns to Hab 2:3 just as 2 Pet 3:8 turns to Ps 90:4.[38]

Some see a notable distinction between them in that New Testament "*pesher*" is retrospective (seeing the past events of the death and resurrection of Jesus in the texts) while that of Qumran is forward looking.[39] But this is certainly overblown. Qumran *pesher* also referred to past events, and

---

32. James Kugel in Kugel and Greer, *Early Biblical Interpretation*, 61.

33. Collins, "Prophecy and Fulfillment," 276.

34. Ibid.

35. There are even greater parallels between the two communities in general, some of which are spelled out in Vermes, *Dead Sea Scrolls*, 22–23.

36. Collins, *Apocalyptic Imagination*, 151. Compare the role of the Teacher of Righteousness in "unlocking" the scriptures for his disciples with that of Jesus as depicted in Luke 24:25–27.

37. Lim, "Qumran Scrolls," 72.

38. See chapter 8, pp. 204–05.

39. DNTB, 782.

Christian "*pesher*" likewise spoke to events yet unfulfilled. Nevertheless, their methods are not identical. As Collins shows, there is no actual example of *pesher proper* in the New Testament.[40] Lim has adopted the more cautious terminology of "pesheresque" to refer to the broad exegetical similarities in the New Testament. Such caution is perfectly appropriate. Nevertheless, the parallels are unmistakable.

Conceiving Prophecy

For instance, in its account of the virgin birth of Jesus, the Gospel of Matthew quotes a brief excerpt from the prophet Isaiah. According to Matthew, after Mary had conceived, Joseph was visited by an angel who assured him that Mary had been chaste. The angel announced to Joseph that Mary had conceived by the power of the Holy Spirit and that the child was to be named Jesus, and that he would grow up to be a savior of Israel. Matthew then comments, "All this took place to fulfill what the Lord spoke through the prophet: 'Look, the virgin will conceive and bear a son, and they will call him Emmanuel,' meaning, 'God with us'" (Matt 1:22–23). In other words, according to Matthew, the miraculous virgin birth of Jesus was the fulfillment of Isaiah's prophecy. Let's take a look at this prophecy in its original context.

The prophecy takes place in Isaiah chapter 7. The story is set during the reign of King Ahaz of Judah. The northern kingdom of Israel has made an alliance with the kingdom of Aram in order to siege the southern kingdom of Judah and lay waste the city of Jerusalem. The kings of Israel and Aram led their armies against Jerusalem, but initially failed. At this point, King Ahaz of Judah becomes mortified—his kingdom is no match for the combined strength of Israel and Aram; it is only a matter of time before they are successful and his kingdom is overthrown. Ahaz begins to contemplate making an alliance with a stronger nation, but Yahweh sends the prophet Isaiah to encourage Ahaz. Isaiah tells the king that the alliance between Aram and Israel will come to naught. Before long, Israel will fall. Isaiah encourages Ahaz to trust in Yahweh and not to be afraid of Aram and Israel, whose destruction is imminent. Isaiah tells Ahaz to ask Yahweh for a sign as evidence that the northern alliance will fail. Ahaz refuses to ask Yahweh for a sign, apparently out of a feigned sense of piety disguising his fear. But Isaiah insists:

> Yahweh himself will give you a sign. Look, the young woman is with child and will bear a son, and he will be called Emmanuel. He will eat cheese and honey by the time he knows how to refuse what is

40. Collins, "Prophecy and Fulfillment," 277.

evil and choose what is good. Indeed, before the child knows how to distinguish wrong from right, the land of the two kings—whom you dread—will be deserted. Yahweh will bring upon you and upon your people and upon your ancestor's dynasty such days as have not been seen since the day that Ephraim split from Judah. That is to say, the king of Assyria will descend upon you. (Isa 7:14–17)

Much ink has been spilled in vain in the debate over the meaning of the word for "young woman," in verse 14. The Hebrew word used is *almah*, which means "maiden" or "young woman." It is simply the female form of *alem*, "young man." It does not mean "virgin," except indirectly in the sense that most young women would be virgins. The Hebrew word for "virgin" is *betulah*. The cognate word *almah* in both Aramaic and Ugaritic is sometimes used to refer to a young woman who is not a virgin. Thus, *almah* does not relate to sexual experience but simply to age. An *almah* could be a young un-married woman, or a young married woman. It is used in both ways. If Isaiah had intended to specify a young unmarried woman who was yet a virgin, the simplest recourse would have been to use the word *betulah*. The trouble began when the Jewish translators of the Greek Septuagint (LXX) translated *almah* using the Greek word *parthenos*, which by Matthew's time *did* mean "virgin." Since Matthew used the Greek Bible, he would have understood the meaning to have been "virgin," thus his reapplication of the prophecy to sup-port the tradition of the virgin birth of Jesus.

Having said all that, the point is moot. Even if Isaiah *did* mean "virgin," he was not predicting a miraculous birth. If the woman had been a virgin at the time Isaiah uttered the prophecy, she would not have been by the time she had conceived the child. However, the verb here, "to conceive" (*harah*), is in the perfect tense, which means it is a completed action. The best translation of the verse would reflect that the young woman was *already* pregnant, that Isaiah was predicting the child's *gender*, and directing her how to name him: "Look, this young pregnant woman is going to have a son, and she shall name him Emmanuel."[41] That said, even if it *were* written in the imperfect (future) tense, it could not be the distant future to which Isaiah is referring. According to his prophecy, by the time the child has matured, Assyria will have invaded the land of Israel and the child will have felt the effects of it. The reference to the child's eating "cheese and honey" refers to the fact that the land has recently been ravaged by the Assyrians; the people are consequently forced to eat uncultivated food—cheese and honey as opposed to bread and wine.

The child is to be called "Emmanuel." As Matthew points out, this means, "God with us." But the name does not imply that the *child himself*

41. For a discussion of the syntax here, see Bratcher, "Isaiah 7:14."

is God. Ancient names frequently included reference to some god or divine activity. Joshua's name means, "Yahweh saves," and Azariah means "Yahweh helps," but neither Joshua nor Azariah were therefore understood to be Yahweh in the flesh. The significance of naming the child "God with us" is that the child was a sign to King Ahaz that Yahweh was going to protect the kingdom of Judah from the hostile alliance presently threatening it. *The child's significance was purely as a measurement of time, a way of expressing the fact that, before long, the northern kingdom of Israel is going to be laid waste by Assyria.* The prophecy was completely fulfilled within a few short years after it was given. The child was born, and not too long thereafter, Assyria had indeed defeated the kingdom of Israel in battle. That is the "single, fixed meaning" of Isaiah's prophecy.

It is apparent, then, that what Matthew is doing is emphatically *not* historical-grammatical exegesis. The Chicago inerrantists would only see this as an "error" on Matthew's part, a "misinterpretation." Because they recognize the difficulty involved in the fact that Isaiah 7 was fulfilled within one generation's time, they attempt to argue not that there is a second meaning to the text, but that there is a "fuller meaning," which was in God's mind, although "the prophet may not have been conscious of the full implications of this meaning when he wrote it."[42] But this is pure equivocation. By appealing to a "divine intention" in the text that is not in anywise discernible from the text itself, the Chicago inerrantists have abandoned the historical-grammatical hermeneutic they insist must be operative at all times.[43] Moreover, this is nothing more than special pleading. Matthew is not "misinterpreting" Isaiah, nor is Matthew revealing the "fuller meaning" of the prophecy. The prophecy was that Assyria would destroy Israel within a short span of time after the reign of King Ahaz—there is nothing further to fulfill. What Matthew is doing is essentially what the Qumran interpreters did with the prophets. He is "discovering" the second, eschatological meaning of the text by means of "inspired interpretation." Like the Qumran community, the Matthean community is not interested in the text for its historical meaning; they are only interested in using the text to elucidate their own present-day experiences and to reinforce their sense of identity.

The Chicago inerrantists may think this constitutes a deception or an error, but that is only because they do not think like apocalyptic Jews in the second temple period. Rowan Greer clears this up, explaining that as good

42. Radmacher and Preus, *Hermeneutics*, 900.

43. This is to say nothing of whether God could have, would have, or did intend something more than the prophet in this or any other instance; it is rather to call attention CSBH's inconsistency on the level of method.

moderns "we tend to think of an original sense, understood historically, and to regard theological interpretation as a departure from the true meaning of the text. Nothing could be farther from the point of view of religious writers in late antiquity. Pagan, Jew, and Christian were united in assuming the general correlation of sacred texts with the beliefs and practices of religious communities. Scripture represented the authority for those beliefs and practices, but at the same time the religious convictions of the community unveiled the true meaning of Scripture."[44] Thus, as an ancient interpreter, Matthew's intent is not to derive a message from the prophetic texts and to adjust himself and his community to it, but rather to mine the prophetic texts for language that may be used in support of religious experiences and structures that were already in place for him. Matthew's "pesheresque" use of Isaiah 7 is just one example of hundreds from the New Testament. Early Christian interpretation of the scriptures was thoroughly a product of its milieu.

God's Indifference toward Oxen

This goes especially for Paul. Morna Hooker affirms that "Paul's methods of exegesis are those of his own day. They may well make preachers in the twenty-first century uneasy, for he tears passages out of context, uses allegory or typology to give new meanings to old stories, abandons the 'original' meanings of texts, and turns them on their heads."[45] After an extensive investigation of Paul's intertextual use of the Hebrew scriptures, Richard Hays concurs, concluding that "for Paul, original intention is not a primary hermeneutical concern. . . . The scriptural text as metaphor speaks through the author; whether such speaking occurs with or without the author's knowledge is a matter of little consequence, for Paul's readings of Scripture are not constrained by a historical scrupulousness about the original meaning of the text. Eschatological meaning subsumes original sense."[46] As Hays explains, Paul "believes himself, along with his churches, to stand in a privileged moment in which the random clutter of past texts and experiences assumes a configuration of eschatological significance."[47]

Paul's axiomatic conviction that the text of scripture contains eschatological meanings unrelated to its historical-grammatical sense is so strong that it applies even to the most obscure texts. For instance, in 1 Corinthians 9, Paul is arguing that "those who proclaim the gospel ought to get their living

44. Kugel and Greer, *Early Biblical Interpretation*, 126.
45. Hooker, "Authority of the Bible," 46–47.
46. Hays, *Echoes of Scripture*, 156.
47. Ibid., 165.

by the gospel" (9:14), even though Paul himself is choosing not to exercise that right. In order to "prove" that this is the right of apostles, Paul quotes Deut 25:4: "Do not muzzle an ox while it is treading out the grain." Paul then asks, "Does God really care about oxen, or is he speaking exclusively to us?" Paul concludes that "it was indeed written for our sake" (9:10). Paul's claim here is astounding: God does not care about oxen; the historical-grammatical meaning of the text is of no concern to God or to us—that is not its usefulness as scripture. The *real* reason that passage is in the text is that it was intended for the last days, a message to the Pauline churches. "Paul reads the text as bearing direct reference to his own circumstances and reads this commandment of the Law of Moses as a word addressed directly to Gentile Christians."[48] Hays remarks in conclusion, "Even the most mundane apodictic pronouncements in Scripture gain unforeseen spiritual gravity when read with the ruling conviction that Scripture must speak to us and must speak of weighty spiritual matters."[49]

Conclusion

To claim, as many inerrantists do, that Paul and the other writers of scripture are permitted such "artistic license" in their interpretations because they were specially inspired by God to find *real hidden meanings* in the text is just another case of apologetic special pleading. The reality is that they shared basic hermeneutical assumptions with other apocalyptic sects much like their own, all of which made similar claims about "inspired interpretation." Such claims are just part and parcel of the hermeneutic itself. Regardless of the question of which group or groups may have been legitimately inspired to interpret the scriptures in ways that defy the historical-grammatical sense of the text, the important points for our purposes are these: (1) the Chicago inerrantists claim that the biblical authors always accurately represent the historical-grammatical sense of any scriptural text they quote or to which they allude; (2) it is clear that the biblical authors do not share the Chicago inerrantist's concern for the historical-grammatical meaning of the text; and (3) this does not mean that the scriptures were not authoritative for such interpreters, only that their account of scriptural authority is very different from that of the Chicago inerrantists. We might only add that—granting for the purposes of discussion that the New Testament writers all unanimously assumed that the scriptures (being inspired by God) were without error—it is clear that their lack of commitment to the historical-grammatical sense of the text makes it

48. Ibid., 166.
49. Ibid., 165.

much easier for them to deal with problematic passages should they arise. The eschatological hermeneutic turns out to be a very convenient hermeneutic to espouse if one is a professing inerrantist.

Patristic Hermeneutics

We recall article sixteen of the CSBI, which claims that "the doctrine of inerrancy has been integral to the Church's faith throughout its history."[50] In the exposition, the Chicago inerrantists go on to claim that the doctrine of inerrancy was upheld by "the mainstream of church history from the first days until very recently."[51] Article eighteen of the CSBI further stipulates that "the text of Scripture is to be interpreted by grammatico-historical exegesis, taking account of its literary forms and devices."[52] To reiterate, the Chicago inerrantists have made two claims: (1) that the doctrine of inerrancy has been held by "the mainstream of church history" from its inception onward, and (2) that the doctrine of inerrancy entails a commitment to the historical-grammatical interpretation of the text. As we will see, these two claims cannot at all go together. Inerrantists will regularly cite proof-texts from the Church Fathers which indicate that the scriptures were taken to be authoritative, but as we have seen, in the ancient world, taking a text to be authoritative does not mean one is committed to the historical-grammatical sense of the text. And there is the rub. It is much easier to be an "inerrantist" when the intended meaning of the original author can be disregarded, and in the Patristic world, problematic texts were often "managed" in precisely this way—through the use of allegorical interpretations which have the effect of ascribing some meaning to a text other than the meaning intended by the author.

Allegorical Apologies

The use of allegory for apologetic purposes in fact has a long tradition, going back to the Greek intellectuals in Alexandria who employed the allegorical method in order to gloss over the shameful conduct of the gods in the Homeric epics.[53] Later, this methodology would be adopted by Jewish thinkers in their apologies for the Torah. Most notable among them was Philo of Alexandria, who employed the allegorical method to explain away the more unsavory as-

50. Henry, *God Who Speaks*, 214.

51. Ibid., 219.

52. Ibid., 214.

53. For a good survey of allegorical readings of Homer, see Dawson, *Allegorical Readers*, 38–52.

pects of the Hebrew scriptures in order to make them palatable to Hellenistic sensibilities. The canonical status of the book of Song of Songs was threatened because of its explicit sexual nature. It is essentially erotic poetry. It was salvaged as scripture, however, by the imposition of an allegorical sense upon the text; Rabbi Akiva pronounced a curse upon anyone who did not read Song of Songs allegorically. In his letter to the Galatians, the apostle Paul used allegorical interpretation as an apologetic for his scandalous departure from mainstream Judaism—a departure that was even more radical than other factions of Christian Jews. The early second century Epistle of Barnabas used allegory to rehabilitate the dietary codes in the laws of Moses. The author contended that the laws were not meant to be taken literally, but were metaphors for spiritual principles. For instance, the prohibition of the consumption of pork was *really* meant to dissuade God's people from assorting with "swinish" people—those who only pray to God when they want something for themselves. The author contended that the metaphors were mistakenly read literally by the Jews because the Jews were carnal and dull-witted.

Marcion of Chicago

Most troublesome for the early Christians were the plague and conquest narratives in Exodus, Deuteronomy, and Joshua. Their problematic nature was especially intensified as a result of the teachings of one person in particular. The first notable Christian to reject the legitimacy of allegorical interpretation was Marcion. Like the Chicago inerrantists, Marcion *insisted* that the Bible must be read literally, according to the historical sense of the text. Because of this axiom, Marcion felt it necessary to reject the Old Testament. Because of his commitment to a literal reading of the text, Marcion believed the God of the Old Testament was a morally atrocious deity, a God of violence and vengeance, far removed from the New Testament's God of love. Thus Marcion and his followers cut the Old Testament out of their canon and were branded by other Christian factions as "heretics."

In this case, the relevant point for us is that Marcion was not considered heretical because of his reading of the violent Old Testament texts. He was branded a heretic in part because he *abandoned* those texts.[54] In fact, many "orthodox" Christians tended to *agree* with Marcion that, on a literal reading, the conquest narratives were morally repugnant and unacceptable. Contrary to the tendentious picture of church history painted by the Chicago inerrantists, the reality is that the Old Testament scriptures were *saved* precisely because of the predominance in this period of allegorical interpretation.

54. His Gnosticism may also have had something to do with it.

Saving Scripture

For example, Origen, an orthodox theologian in Alexandria, insisted that the allegorical reading is *necessitated* by the problematic content of the conquest narratives, in which Yahweh commands Israel to engage in the wholesale slaughter of the inhabitants of the land of Canaan: "As for the command given to the Jews to slay their enemies, it may be answered that anyone who looks carefully into the meaning of the passage will find that it is impossible to interpret it literally" (*Cels.* 7.19). In his *Homily on Joshua*, Origen reiterates this position. Referring to the genocidal narratives in the book of Joshua, he stipulates that "unless those carnal wars were a symbol of spiritual wars, I do not think that the Jewish historical books would ever have been passed down by the apostles to be read by Christ's followers in their churches" (*Hom. Ios.* 15.1).[55] In other words, Origen asserted that the only alternative to allegorizing the texts is to go the way of Marcion; they could *not* be maintained as scripture if they are to be read historically-grammatically. Origen's alternative was to read them as allegories of Christ's conquest of the individual Christian's soul; the inhabitants of Canaan are symbols of our own vices, against which we are commanded to wage war.

The Upside of Genocide

Another orthodox theologian, John Cassian, would adopt precisely the same strategy. Cassian referred to the apostle Paul's axiom in 1 Cor 9:10, which we noted above, that the ancient text "was written for our sake." The *real* meaning of the text is not the historical meaning, but its reconfiguration in the Christian dispensation. When Cassian addresses the genocides committed by the Israelites, he writes, "We must accept the fact that, according to the Apostle, everything that happened to them was figurative and was written for our instruction." He then quotes Deut 7:1–2, in which Yahweh commands the Israelites to devote to utter destruction the seven nations inhabiting the "promised land." He then offers his interpretation—the *real* meaning of the text: "The reason that [these seven nations] are said to be more numerous is that there are more vices than there are virtues" (*Conf.* 5.16).

Ezekiel versus Exodus

In similar fashion, the Cappadocian Father Gregory of Nyssa—one of the chief architects of the orthodox doctrine of the Trinity—used the allegorical

---

55. Quoted in Swift, "Early Christian Views," 286.

method as an apologetic for the tenth plague (the indiscriminate slaughter of Egypt's firstborn children). In his *Life of Moses*, Gregory issues an incisive critique of the immorality of the tenth plague. Despite the Chicago inerrantists' emphatic denial that a later revelation can ever correct or contradict an earlier revelation (CSBI, art. 5), Gregory quotes Ezek 18:20 *against* the book of Exodus in order to show that it is contrary to God's nature to punish a son for the sins of his father. Gregory launches into an impassioned appeal to our moral reason, using emotive language to describe the innocence of a child, in order to demonstrate that a literal reading of the tenth plague would be nothing short of monstrous (*Mos.* 2.91). Gregory concludes that the only legitimate recourse is an allegorical reading. The solution must be that the murderous events on the night of the first Passover took place "typologically," as a lesson for believers. According to Gregory, the lesson is this: "When through virtue one comes to grips with any evil, he must completely destroy the first beginnings of evil" (*Mos.* 2.92).[56] Once again, the historical sense of a text about divine or divinely-sanctioned murder is salvaged by turning it into an allegory pertaining to the pious destruction of one's own vices.[57]

Literally, All You Need Is Love

Of course, there were other Church Fathers who were opposed to the allegorical hermeneutics. They (rightly) contended that there was no way to ground such interpretations to orthodox doctrine in a consistent way. When faced with problematic texts such as the conquest narratives, however, the historical-grammatical school was not as well equipped to engage in apologetics. For instance, when confronted with the question of the morality of such texts, Irenaeus simply answered that it is not appropriate to question God. It was perhaps Augustine's late conversion from the allegorical school to the literalist school that helped eventually to make literal interpretation the predominant hermeneutic in the Western church. Perhaps this is what the Chicago inerrantists mean when they cite the "mainstream" of church history. The "mainstream" would refer to the stream preferred by them and their Reformation forebears. As evidence for their contention that this mainstream of church history has always held to the doctrine of inerrancy, modern inerrantists will often cite Augustine's letter to Jerome, in which Augustine confesses his belief that the canonical books of scripture are "wholly free from error" (*Ep.* 82.3), whereas he reads non-canonical books by default

56. This is the translation of Mahlerbe and Ferguson, *Life of Moses*.

57. For a fuller treatment of Origen and Gregory's allegorical apologies for the genocide texts, see chapter 6, pp. 138–40.

with a hermeneutic of suspicion. It is statements like this that incite many modern inerrantists to parade Augustine as a stalwart champion of inerrancy and historical-grammatical exegesis. The only problem for this thesis is that Augustine was *not* a proponent of historical-grammatical exegesis. Augustine was committed to what he called the "literal" meaning of the text, but for Augustine the literal meaning of the text was not always to be equated with the historical-grammatical meaning.

The attempt to find the literal sense was not an attempt to find the author's intended meaning. First, Augustine did not believe that it was possible to really know the intended meaning of a deceased ancient author.[58] Second, and more importantly, the author's intended meaning is irrelevant to Augustine because, as Thomas Williams explains, "what guarantees the veracity of the author, and thus the text, is the divine truth; and that same divine truth is available to us even apart from our interpretation of the text."[59] Augustine believed that the Holy Spirit was an "inner teacher" from whom we learn what is true. According to Augustine, we are able to recognize the truth of scripture not because scripture teaches us what is true, but because the inner teacher has already told us what is true, making it possible for us to identify truth when we find it in scripture. When the meaning of a text is disputed, Augustine—contrary to the Chicago inerrantists—insists that there can be more than one "literal" meaning of the text: "So when one person says 'He meant what I say,' and another says 'No, he meant what I say,' I think it would be more pious to say, 'Why not both, if both are true?' And if someone should see in his words a third truth, or a fourth, or indeed any other truth, why not believe that Moses saw all these truths" (*Conf.* 12.31.42)? Augustine could even suggest that there are truths in the text unknown to the original human authors to which later readers are privy on account of the presence of the inner teacher (*Conf.* 12.32.43). Finally, Augustine believed that the principal truth to which scripture pointed was love, or *caritas*, and that this conviction must be known prior to the reading of scripture and must function as a controlling presupposition throughout the hermeneutical process (*Doctr. chr.* 1.40–44). Augustine maintained that by reading the text of scripture with the expectation of finding *caritas*, the reader will find *caritas*.

For Augustine, this *caritas* reading is in fact the true meaning of the text. The "literal" meaning is not the historical-grammatical meaning, but the spiritual-theological one (although the two may often overlap). This definition of the "literal" meaning of the text was in fact axiomatic not only for Augustine, but for the majority of theologians and pastors until the Enlightenment. Thus,

58. See Williams, "Biblical Interpretation," 62–66.
59. Ibid., 65.

when modern inerrantists cite Luther's commitment to the "literal" sense of the text in support of their own views, they fail to recognize the important distinction between Luther's "literal" meaning, which is the theological sense of the text, and their own professed espousal of a strict historical-grammatical hermeneutic. The trouble with the Augustinian definition of the literal sense of the text, of course, is that it is not derived from the text. It is a predisposition that is brought to the text, sometimes a dogmatic reading of the text. It is not primarily concerned with ascertaining what the author meant; rather, it is a confessional reading of the text with the expectation that the text is fundamentally about love. Obviously one is going to find love in the text when one approaches the text with that expectation. In the same way, one would find violence in the text when one approached it expecting to find violence; one would find Arminianism when one sought Arminianism, and Calvinism when one sought Calvinism. In the end, we must acknowledge that, as morally fruitful an exercise as it may be to read the scriptures with the expectation that they are essentially about *caritas*, such a hermeneutic is sharply at odds with a commitment to historical-grammatical exegesis. One can choose to employ one or the other, but not both in the same breath.

Conclusion

The reality is that the insistence on the exclusive use of the historical-grammatical hermeneutic was something that developed in reaction to the findings of critical scholarship which emerged as a byproduct of the Renaissance and Enlightenment. Prior to that point, theological and allegorical hermeneutics prevailed. For our purposes, however, it is only relevant to point out that the Alexandrian allegorical method, the Augustinian hermeneutic of *caritas*, and other varieties of theological hermeneutics which come to scripture expecting to find some central theme (e.g., "justification by faith"), a central theme that is known to the reader *prior* to his or her engagement with the text—these are all hermeneutics of convenience. When it comes to problematic texts such as the conquest narratives, it is very convenient to be able to transform dead Canaanite children into conquered vices such as lust and greed; it is very convenient to come to a text which depicts the indiscriminate slaughter of Egyptian children with the knowledge that the text is *really*, in truth, all about love. Inerrancy is an easy doctrine to maintain when any text that threatens to overthrow it can be, in the case of Luther, declared non-canonical by fiat (as he wished to do with Esther, Hebrews, James, Jude, and Revelation), or somehow rendered innocuous by reference to an undisclosed inner truth known only to the Spirit-filled interpreter.

Fundamentalist Hermeneutics

The Chicago inerrantists claim that the doctrine of inerrancy is affirmed by "the whole bible," by "the mainstream of church history," and by themselves. They also claim that integral to the doctrine of inerrancy is a commitment to the historical-grammatical hermeneutic; they believe that in order for the text of scripture to be "true" and "without error," it must be true and without error historically-grammatically, not merely in some ephemeral spiritual or allegorical sense that cannot be isolated consistently by a coherent methodology. Thus far, however, we have seen that neither "the whole bible" nor "the mainstream of church history" live up to the standards set by the Chicago inerrantists. Frankly, the historical-grammatical hermeneutic was of little interest to ancient interpreters. Our agenda now is to show that neither is the historical-grammatical hermeneutic of much interest to the modern fundamentalists. Despite pretensions to the contrary, the inerrantists do not abide by the very methodology upon which they insist. Moreover, it is not merely that individual inerrantists fail on occasion to live up to the ideal methodology; the reality is that the historical-grammatical hermeneutic is undermined and eviscerated by confessional formulas and presuppositions long before the process of interpretation even begins. What the fundamentalists *actually* employ is a conspicuous hermeneutic of convenience.

Shakespeare via Stoppard

Earlier we looked at article eighteen of the CSBI, which affirms "that the text of Scripture is to be interpreted by grammatico-historical exegesis, taking account of its literary forms and devices." But we did not see the affirmation in its entirety. The affirmation continues: ". . . *and that Scripture is to interpret Scripture.*"[60] Underlying this axiom is the dogmatic assumption that "all Scripture is the product of a single divine mind."[61] The logic goes that, since all scripture was written by a single author, namely God, it is legitimate to interpret an obscure passage in, say, Genesis, in light of a more straightforward statement made in, say, 1 John; the fact that the two texts were written over a thousand years apart and by human authors with very different perspectives and agendas is irrelevant, because the texts were *really* written by the same author—God. The trouble is, the moment this methodology has been employed, the historical-grammatical hermeneutic has been abandoned.

60. Henry, *God Who Speaks,* 214.
61. Ibid., 218.

To wit, when a Renaissance historian wants to understand the background to Shakespeare's composition of *Hamlet*, he does not typically consult Tom Stoppard's *Rosencrantz and Guildenstern Are Dead*. When a historian of classical Greece attempts to interpret a particular saying of Plato, she does not turn to the twenty-first century theologian John Milbank to clarify Plato's meaning. Milbank has his own agenda (and he is harder to read than Plato at any rate). The historian turns to the antecedent and contemporaneous sources of the historical subject (Plato) in order to ascertain what was meant *in that context*. A classical historian cannot rule out by fiat the possibility that Milbank might get Plato wrong. In fact, a historian cannot rule out by fiat the possibility that Xenocrates, one of Plato's own students, got Plato wrong. A historian may look to Xenocrates to see if he brings some sort of elucidation; she may even look to Milbank. But she cannot determine in advance that either or both of these men *must* bring elucidation. That is not the way historical investigation works. Thus, when the Chicago inerrantists stipulate that "the text of Scripture is to be interpreted by grammatico-historical exegesis, taking account of its literary forms and devices, *and that Scripture is to interpret Scripture*," what they are essentially saying is this: "we utilize the historical-grammatical hermeneutic until the historical-grammatical hermeneutic reveals a discrepancy between two texts, or between one text and a particular fact that we cannot bring ourselves to deny, at which point we revert to dogmatic interpretation." Historical-grammatical exegesis is employed only to the extent that it suits fundamentalists. When it works in their favor, it is touted proudly; when it works against them, it is quietly swept under the rug. Some examples:

A Flat Reading

Article twenty of the CSBH provides a splendid illustration of the fundamentalists' dogmatic suspension of historical methodology. They begin with an admission: "Although only the Bible is the normative and infallible rule for doctrine and practice, nevertheless what one learns from sources outside Scripture can occasion a reexamination and reinterpretation of Scripture."[62] In other words, if what we thought was the plain sense of a biblical text is proved wrong by an undeniable fact, then our understanding of that text must be mistaken. "For example, some have taught the world to be square because the Bible refers to 'the four corners of the earth' (Isa 11:12). But scientific knowledge of the spherical nature of the globe leads to a correction of this

---

62. Radmacher and Preus, *Hermeneutics*, 901.

faulty interpretation."[63] Thus, by virtue of the controlling presupposition that "canonical Scripture should always be interpreted on the basis that it is infallible and inerrant,"[64] the Chicago inerrantists are forced to conclude that it is the *interpretation* that is wrong, and not the text itself.

But what would a historian conclude? The observation that the earth must be spherical was first made by Pythagoras in the sixth century BCE, two centuries after the time of Isaiah. Prior to Pythagoras, it seems to have been ubiquitously believed that the earth was flat. The ancient Near Eastern view was that the earth was a flat surface covered by a solid dome ceiling ("the heavens"), with water above and below. This is attested in Enuma Elish, and in numerous places throughout the Bible (e.g., Ps 104:5; Job 38:13; Jer 16:19; Dan 4:11; Mark 13:27; Matt 4:8; Rev 7:1), in addition to the passage cited in the CSBH (Isa 11:12). A flat earth cosmology is further attested in the Epic of Gilgamesh, and in other sources from Egypt and Mesopotamia. All of the historical and grammatical evidence points to the conclusion that when Isaiah refers to the "four corners of the earth," he is assuming a flat earth cosmology, in which the earth literally has four corners. To critical scholars, this is a small thing. No one, except the fundamentalist, is of the opinion that Isaiah's assumption of a flat earth discredits everything else he ever says. But the fundamentalist believes that one miniscule error in the text renders the entire Bible unreliable.[65] Consequently, and against the historical-grammatical evidence, the inerrantists claim that Isaiah is simply using a *metaphor* when he refers to the "four corners of the earth." By their own rules they have backed themselves into a corner, and the historical-grammatical hermeneutic must be abandoned in the name of inerrancy.

It is important, therefore, that we not confuse inerrantists with "literalists." Professing inerrantists actually rarely read the text literally; that is how they are able to remain professing inerrantists. As James Barr puts the matter, on the one hand, the fundamentalist "ties himself not to the 'literal' meaning, which would be methodologically controllable, but rather to the 'plain' meaning, the meaning which is clearly the right one. But since the principle of inerrancy is the overriding one in all interpretation, no meanings turn out to be 'plain' if they disagree with the inerrancy of the Bible."[66]

---

63. Ibid.

64. Henry, *God Who Speaks*, 217.

65. So Warfield, *Inspiration and Authority*, 220.

66. Barr, *Fundamentalism*, 52.

Only *Some* Women Are Inherently Stupid

Another example is the inerrantist treatment of texts such as 1 Tim 2:12–14. The author writes, "I allow no woman to teach or to have authority over any man. She is to remain silent. After all, Adam was made first, then Eve; and it was not Adam who was deceived, but the woman who was deceived, and who became a sinner." Some inerrantists accept this basic picture, and comply with the author's imperative, refusing to place women in teaching roles in the church. Yet, Mark Driscoll notwithstanding, one would be hard pressed to find many professing inerrantists who are willing to verbally consent to the author's expressed *justification* for this policy. To do so, they would have to acquiesce to the notion that women are inherently intellectually inferior to men. That is what the author is claiming—because Eve was deceived, and *not* Adam, therefore women cannot be trusted in positions of authority. It is rare to find an inerrantist nowadays who will give verbal assent to this.

The most common strategy to explain away this blatant misogyny is to impose a distinction between the "cultural" and the "universal," or between the "particular" and the "universal," upon the text. Some will say that this was a "cultural" truth (whatever *that* would mean), but does not apply in our own culture. Others will posit imaginative scenarios, such as that, in this particular church, some women were falling prey to heretical doctrines. Therefore, the author's words apply to *those* women, but not to all women everywhere. The problem is, that is not at all what the author says. The author does not make a distinction between the cultural or the particular on the one hand, and the universal on the other. The author is making what is called an "argument from the order of creation." He is claiming that women are secondary, and men are primary, *because that is how God chose to order the cosmos.* Moreover, the author's misogynistic perspective fits right in with the broader Jewish and Greco-Roman worlds. But most professing inerrantists today do *not* believe that women are inherently intellectually inferior to men. Most recognize, furthermore, that if women ever *were* intellectually inferior to men, it was because men did not afford women the same educational benefits they afforded themselves. Thus, once again, in order to reconcile a problematic text with an undeniable fact, inerrantists abandon the historical-grammatical reading of the text and replace it with their own imaginative and anachronistic interpretations.

Angels Don't Go There

In some cases, they abandon other of their principles as well. We have noted already how the professed commitment to historical-grammatical exegesis is undermined by the principle that "scripture is to interpret scripture." The striking thing is that, in defense of inerrancy, this principle too is abandoned when necessary. For instance, a narrative in Genesis 6 tells us that as the population of the world grew, and more and more beautiful women began to develop, the "sons of God" looked upon them and decided to have relations with them. The narrative then tells us that the daughters of men conceived children by the sons of God, and that these children were the "Nephilim," the heroes of old—renowned warriors. Num 13:33 tells us that the Nephilim were giants. Now, all the biblical and historical evidence tells us who these "sons of God" were. The comparative historical evidence tells us unequivocally that "sons of God" was a term used for celestial beings—not humans.[67]

More importantly for our purposes, *the Bible itself* identifies the "sons of God," unambiguously, as celestial beings. The "sons of God" are said to have convened in Yahweh's council, with Satan among them, in Job 1:6 and 2:1. Job 38:7 says that when the stars were first created, the "sons of God" shouted for joy. In Psalm 82:1–7, the "sons of God" convene in the divine council where they are judged by God and are cast down and made to be subject to mortality. In every case, the term "sons of God" refers to celestial beings. If we were to follow the principle touted by the inerrantists, allowing "scripture to interpret scripture," then it should be clear: Genesis 6 narrates that celestial beings descended upon the earth, took human women as wives, and caused them to conceive, giving birth to a race of giants. In this case, the historical evidence and the broader scriptural usage converge to make the meaning of Genesis 6 unambiguous. But this creates a problem. The historical and scriptural evidences *threaten* the doctrine of inerrancy. How?

As inerrantist scholar Walter Kaiser points out, Jesus said in Mark 12:25 that the "angels in heaven . . . neither marry nor are given in marriage." In other words, according to Jesus, angels are non-sexual beings. If this is true, then either the tradition in Genesis 6 is wrong or—God forbid—Jesus is wrong. But this is unacceptable to Kaiser, because the assumption of the inerrancy of scripture is the overriding principle—the controlling presupposition—that trumps all other principles of interpretation. Thus, the commitment to historical-grammatical exegesis *and* the principle that "scripture should interpret scripture" are both discarded in service of the meta-commitment—inerrancy.

---

67. We will have more to say about what *kind* of celestial beings these were in chapter 4.

The "sons of God" in Genesis 6 are therefore not celestial beings; they must be humans.[68] To an inerrantist, the "best" interpretation is ultimately not the historical-grammatical interpretation but the one that does not threaten the doctrine of inerrancy. Nevertheless, as Barr explains, "the fundamentalist interpreter is not at all insincere in his oscillation back and forward between literal and non-literal interpretations. Given his principle of inerrancy, fed in as the architectonic control in his approach to the Bible, it is obvious that the meanings he discovers are to him indeed the 'plain' meanings."[69] Barr's summary of the *actual* methodology of inerrantist hermeneutics warrants quotation at length. Barr points out that the principle of inerrancy

> is fed into the interpretative process at its very beginning. That is to say, one does not first interpret the passage on the basis of linguistic and literary structure, and then raise the question whether this is true as a matter of correspondence to external reality or to historical events. On the contrary, though linguistic and literary structure are respected as guides, and indeed conservative literature contains a good deal of boasting about the command of these disciplines by conservative interpreters, the principle of the inerrancy of scripture has an overriding function. It dominates the interpretative process entirely. . . . The question is, therefore, which of the various interpretations is supported by the linguistic and literary evidence, under the overriding assumption that the passage is inerrant as a description of external events and realities? The passage is inerrant: the only question is, which is the correct path to the necessarily inerrant meaning?[70]

In other words, if the best available historical-grammatical interpretation of one text happens to contradict the best available historical-grammatical interpretation of another text, then any other less plausible yet *non-contradictory* interpretation is proffered as the "best" of the available options.

Constructive Criticism

Inerrantists attempt to maintain a façade of critical methodological credibility by concocting a distinction between what they call "lower criticism" and "higher criticism." So says article sixteen of the CSBH:

> We affirm that legitimate critical techniques should be used in determining the canonical text and its meaning. We deny the legiti-

68. Kaiser et al., *Hard Sayings*, 106–108.

69. Barr, *Fundamentalism*, 52.

70. Ibid., 51.

macy of allowing any method of biblical criticism to question the
truth or integrity of the writer's expressed meaning, or of any other
scriptural teaching. . . . Implied here is an approval of legitimate
techniques of "lower criticism" or "textual criticism." It is proper to
use critical techniques in order to discover the true text of Scripture,
that is, the one which represents the original one given by the biblical authors. Whereas critical methodology can be used to establish
which of the texts are copies of the inspired original, it is illegitimate
to use critical methods to call into question whether something in
the original text is true. In other words, proper "lower criticism"
is valid but negative "higher criticism" which rejects truths of
Scripture is invalid.[71]

Only three things need be said in response to this. First, they attempt
to paint ordinary critical scholarship as "negative," as if biblical critics were
motivated by a need to prove the Bible wrong. This is pure fantasy. The historical critic (in any field) is not motivated to prove the historical sources
wrong *or* right; the only objective is to achieve perspicuity on what the texts
are saying and how that relates to the other historical evidence, so that valid
conclusions may be drawn and invalid assumptions revised. Conceptions of
the "hostile liberal" who is out to "attack scripture" and "rebel against the
God of the Bible" are purely the imaginings of conspiracy theorists. These are
what psychologists call self-reinforcing mechanisms. Second, the inerrantists
claim that (what they call) "higher criticism" *rejects* the truths of scripture.
Such a claim certainly strains credulity. Not once have I encountered this
infamous critic who "rejects the *truths* of scripture." In my experience it is the
untruths that are wont to be rejected. Biblical scholars tend to have no trouble
acknowledging the truths. Finally, the terms "higher criticism" and "lower
criticism" are the inventions of fundamentalists. It is merely an attempt to
disguise the fact that the inerrantist methodology is not itself a thoroughgoing criticism; it is critical when it serves the fundamentalist agenda, and
uncritical when ordinary criticism would threaten that agenda. The distinction is not, in reality, between "higher" and "lower" criticism, but between
historical description and dogmatic apologetics.

Conclusion

If an inerrantist is someone who assents to everything the Bible affirms, in
its *historical-grammatical* sense, then inerrantists, I have argued, do not exist.
Those who claim to be inerrantists have defended their identity by defining

71. Radmacher and Preus, *Hermeneutics*, 885; 898–99.

inerrancy beyond the possibility of disconfirmation; they espouse a herme-neutic of convenience that allows them to dispense with any problematic text by *appeal to the possible*. A problematic text may be rendered unproblematic if, in the words of B. B. Warfield, "any conceivable hypothesis of its meaning"[72] can be proffered to resolve a discrepancy. Although they ballyhoo allegiance to the historical-grammatical process, in the end, the best candidate for a text's meaning is not the most probable by historical-grammatical standards, but the "best" of the *possible* choices that do not threaten inerrancy—no mat-ter how improbable that "possible" choice may be. In this manner, professing inerrantists are able to disguise the fact (more from themselves than from others) that they do not agree with the Bible on every point. The myth of the inerrantist is thus preserved, and the Wizard of Oz can continue to proclaim that he has all the answers.

72. Warfield, *Inspiration and Authority*, 220.

3 Inerrancy Stunts Your Growth
and Other Fundamentalist Health Hazards

In the last chapter I argued that in reality inerrantists do not exist. We looked at various strategies would-be inerrantists have utilized in order to maintain the illusion of their commitment to the text, and saw how those strategies undermine fundamentalists' professed commitment to a historical-grammatical hermeneutic. In this chapter we are going to take a further look at some serious problems with inerrancy. I will argue that the doctrine of inerrancy undermines some basic tenets of fundamentalist theology, and that it threatens the very moral fabric of the church. We will begin, however, by evaluating some apologetic defenses of inerrancy, showing that in every case, double standards are employed.

For the Bible Tells Me So

The Sentient Bible

Perhaps the most basic claim made in defense of modern-day inerrancy is that it is derived directly from the teachings of the Bible about itself. Article fifteen of the CSBI states that "the doctrine of inerrancy is grounded in the teaching of the Bible about inspiration."[1] There are two things to be said in response to this claim. First, it is simply not the case that "the Bible" ever makes claims about "itself." It is true that some of the Psalms make statements about the goodness and the perfection of the laws of Moses. The author of 2 Timothy makes a claim about the usefulness of the scriptures and their status as "God-breathed," but he does not make any such claims about New Testament texts, nor does he provide a list of the books he considers to enjoy canonical status.

The author of 2 Peter implicitly ascribes scriptural status to Paul's letters, but which of those letters is not specified. The author tells us nothing about his view of other books that are now in our New Testament. Marcion

1. Henry, *God Who Speaks*, 214.

accepted Paul's letters, but not other New Testament books. As late as the sixteenth century, Martin Luther approved of Paul's letters, but not James, Jude, or Revelation. Moreover, 2 Peter makes no claims about its own status as scripture, which perhaps would have been useful since 2 Peter is itself one of the most disputed texts in the New Testament canon. Finally, the author of 2 Peter tells us nothing about whether he considers scripture to be inerrant. He considered them to be inspired (2 Pet 1:19); we may assume he considered them to be authoritative, but what "authoritative" would have meant for him is open to debate; any idea put forward could be nothing more than conjecture. Thus, it is clear that "the Bible" does not make claims about "itself." The inerrantists talk about the Bible as if it were some self-aware being, like an artificial intelligence that, once assembled, achieves a sort of quasi-consciousness. As James Barr elucidates, "It is only if one begins by looking at the Bible unhistorically, as if it was a variegated but in principle unitary system of thoughts and facts, all of which alike had come straight from God, that any talk about its 'claims' or its 'view of itself' could even appear to have any standing."[2]

Inspired Does Not Equal Inerrant

The second problem with the claim made in the CSBI is that the case *has not been made*—nor could it be made—that "authority" or "inspiration" necessarily entails "inerrancy." Again, we turn to Barr to put things into perspective for us: "The link between authority or inspiration on the one side and inerrancy on the other rests on one basis only: supposition. Here conservative evangelicals go over to a purely philosophical and non-biblical argument: if it was inspired by God, then how could there be error of any kind in it? This is in fact that core of their argument. But, since this link has no rootage in the Bible and belongs to purely philosophical assumption, the entire attempt of conservative evangelicals to derive their position from 'the Bible's view of itself' is a waste of time."[3] For instance, 2 Tim 3:16–17 describes scripture as "God-breathed," and therefore as useful for instruction and rebuke, but the author does not provide any indication of what he means by "God-breathed." Could it be that God breathed *out* the words of scripture? Or is it that God breathes *into* the text of scripture, in the sense that the Spirit of God brings life into the dead letter? Either is plausible, but the latter seems to be much more consistent with the hermeneutics of the period, and with Paul's use of scripture, as we saw in the last chapter. To say that scripture is "God-breathed"

2. Barr, *Fundamentalism*, 78.
3. Ibid., 84–85.

could very well mean that God breathes *new life* and *new meaning* into even obscure texts that are outdated, irrelevant, and perhaps even wrong. Recall Paul's reconfiguration of the law of Moses regarding oxen in 1 Corinthians 9, in which he asserted that the text was written not for the sake of oxen but for the sake of Paul's own generation. On the other hand, even if 2 Tim 3:16 *does* mean that scripture is breathed *out* by God, in the sense that it is divinely uttered, that does not necessarily entail that it is without error. Perhaps God lied. (We shall have more to say about this possibility below.)

The Dominical Trump Card

A related strategy of the Chicago inerrantists is to attribute the doctrine of inerrancy to the teaching of Jesus of Nazareth. For instance, in his exposition of article one of the CSBH, Norman Geisler avers that the "divine authority of Old Testament Scripture was confirmed by Christ Himself on numerous occasions (cf. Matt 5:17–18; Luke 24:44; John 10:34–35). And what our Lord confirmed as to the divine authority of the Old Testament, He promised also for the New Testament (John 14:16; 16:13)."[4] The exposition of the CSBI states that "the authority of Christ and that of Scripture are one. As our Prophet, Christ testified that Scripture cannot be broken."[5] In Geisler's mind, "one cannot reject the divine authority of Scripture without thereby impugning the authority of Christ, who attested Scripture's divine authority. Thus it is wrong to claim one can accept the full authority of Christ without acknowledging the complete authority of Scripture."[6]

There are two things to say in response to these latter claims, before we evaluate their use of the passages cited above. First, the inerrantists are again conflating the concept of authority with that of inerrancy. It is not self-evident that scripture must be inerrant in order to be authoritative. In fact, such a requirement is logically unwarranted.[7] Thus, to reject inerrancy is *not* to impugn the authority of Christ or of the Bible. Those are logically separate issues, even if there is some *prima facie* relation between them. Second, what the inerrantists are essentially doing with this claim is manipulating the believer into accepting their doctrine of inerrancy by appealing to their devotion to Christ. James Barr, again, is helpful here: "This endlessly repeated argument seeks to use the personal loyalty of Christians towards Jesus as a lever to force them into fundamentalist positions on historical and literary matters. There is no

4. Radmacher and Preus, *Hermeneutics,* 889.

5. Henry, *God Who Speaks,* 216.

6. Radmacher and Preus, *Hermeneutics,* 889.

7. I will have more to say about this in chapter 10.

part of the fundamentalist world view that should inspire so much distaste in the mind of other Christians. Its distortion of the proper proportions of the Christian faith is extreme."[8] Having said that, let's turn to evaluate the texts cited by Geisler in support of the thesis that Jesus taught inerrancy.

A Legal Controversy

First, Matt 5:17–18: "Do not imagine that I have come to do away with the law or the prophets. I have come not to do away with them, but to fulfill them. I mean it when I say that, until heaven and earth disappear, not one letter, not even a stroke of a letter, will disappear from the law, until everything is accomplished." There are three things to say in response to the fundamentalists' use of this text.

First, the reasoning behind their use of this text is viciously circular. The only reason they are able to claim that these verses represent "Jesus' teaching" on scripture's inerrancy is because *they already presuppose* that the Gospel of Matthew is giving an inerrant record of Jesus' words. In other words, inerrancy is supported by the assumption of inerrancy. But the reality is that there is *good reason* to suspect that some of these words may have been *attributed to Jesus* by Matthew, in support of Matthew's own theological agenda. By the time Matthew's gospel was written, there had already been mass conversions of Gentiles to Christian Judaism. The policy of Paul and others was that the laws of Moses did not apply to the Gentiles, and this policy was highly controversial. Many Jewish Christians dissented from Paul's position, arguing that the laws of Moses were still in effect. Matthew's gospel seems to take that stance of opposition to the policy of Paul and other gentile churches. In Matthew, Jesus says that "until heaven and earth disappear, not one letter, not even a stroke of a letter, will disappear from the law." This phrase, "until heaven and earth disappear," is an idiom in Hebrew which basically means, "until forever." In other words, in Matthew, Jesus says that the laws of Moses will *never* become irrelevant. There will *never* be a time when they should not be obeyed.

On the other hand, the Gospel of Luke quotes this same saying of Jesus, with a minor but significant variation in the wording: "But it is easier for heaven and earth to disappear than for a single stroke of a letter in the law to be cut out" (Luke 16:17). Note, however, that in Luke, this saying is preceded by a rather different claim: "Until John came, the law and the prophets were in effect; since that time, the good news of the kingdom of God is proclaimed, and everyone is rushing madly to get into it" (16:16). In Luke's gospel, the same saying of Jesus is given *the opposite meaning* to that of Matthew. In

8. Barr, *Fundamentalism*, 74.

Luke, although it is difficult for the law to pass away, it has! It was only valid until the ministry of John the Baptist, after which point it was set aside in order to allow the Gentiles to come into the kingdom. This also happens to be Luke's theological agenda—being a Gentile himself. Thus, the Gospel of Luke takes Paul's side in the controversy, and the Gospel of Matthew takes the side of the Jewish Christians who are highly polemicized in Paul's letters as "Judaizers." Both Luke and Matthew use the same saying of Jesus to articulate polar opposite positions.

The second thing to say in response to the inerrantists' use of this passage in Matthew is therefore precisely that the inerrantists themselves do not agree with it. Matthew says that the laws of Moses will be in force forever,[9] yet the Chicago inerrantists tend to believe that the laws of Moses were abolished after Christ's death on the cross—an explanation given nowhere in these texts. Luke himself says that the laws of Moses passed away at the time of the ministry of John the Baptist. Thus, Matthew, Luke, and the Chicago inerrantists all disagree with one another.

Finally, the fact remains that even if this saying *is* original to Jesus, and conceding that by it he meant that the law and the prophets were *inerrant* (a claim he does not make, but which the Chicago inerrantists believe is inferred), Jesus still makes no statement about the Writings—the books of Hebrew scripture that fall outside both the categories of the Law and the Prophets.

It's All About Me?

Of course, inerrantists will then point to Luke 24:44, which includes the other writings in Jesus' canon: "These are the words which I spoke to you while I was still together with you—that everything that was written about me in the law of Moses, in the prophets, and in the psalms must be fulfilled." Here "the psalms" is just shorthand for the third section of the Hebrew Bible ordinarily called "the Writings." Jesus refers to it as "the psalms" because the book of Psalms is the first book in that section of the Bible. The Writings include Psalms, Proverbs, Job, Song of Songs, Ruth, Lamentations, Ecclesiastes, Esther, Daniel, Ezra-Nehemiah, and Chronicles. According to the Chicago inerrantists, Jesus' reference to "everything that was written about me . . . in the psalms" *must mean* that Jesus believed that every detail of every book in the Writings must be inerrant. But this claim is certainly overstated. At most, all Jesus claims is that any messianic prophecies in these texts must be fulfilled. That says nothing about the *vast majority* of these texts, which say nothing about the Messiah.

9. The qualifying clause, "until everything is accomplished," refers to the consummation of God's kingdom.

Moreover, as we saw in the last chapter, the assumption that these texts actually make claims about an end-times messianic figure is an assumption Jesus shared with other apocalyptic sects of his day. It is not a belief rooted in a historical-grammatical reading of those texts, but one that is rooted in an eschatological hermeneutic which presupposes that those texts *must be talking about the present generation,* a presupposition that is based on the belief that the present generation was the last generation before the end of the world.[10] In short, this passage can hardly be used as "evidence" that Jesus affirmed the inerrancy of the scriptures. At most it is a statement of the infallibility of any perceived messianic prophecies in those texts, but it says nothing about, for instance, Job and Ecclesiastes' denial of the possibility of the afterlife. There is no doubt that Jesus disagreed with them on *that* point.

For the Purposes of Discussion

A favorite text of modern inerrantists, which they use as a proof-text for Jesus' belief in the doctrine of inerrancy, is John 10:34–36: "Isn't it written in your own law, 'I said, you are gods'? If those to whom the word of God came were identified as 'gods'—and the scripture cannot be annulled—how is it that you're able to say that the one whom the Father has sanctified and commissioned to go into the world is blaspheming, just because I said, 'I am God's Son'?" Here the inerrantists capitalize on Jesus' statement that "the scripture cannot be annulled," and assert that this constitutes Jesus' "teaching" on the doctrine of inerrancy.

Hardly! Let's take a look at what Jesus is really doing. His opponents at the temple are accusing him of usurping God's place of authority, charging him with setting himself up as God's agent. They do not like the fact that Jesus refers to himself as "the son of God." So Jesus appeals to the scriptures. He points them to Psalm 82. The standard interpretation of that passage in Jesus' day was that the ones who are called "gods" are the Israelites at Sinai. Jesus assumes this interpretation when he says, "those to whom the word of God came." In other words, when Israel was given the law at Sinai, according to this interpretation of the psalm, they were called "gods." This meant either that they were God's representatives on earth, or that they were rendered immortal at that time, until they later sinned again (as some Rabbis concluded). Regardless, in order to defend his application of the term "son of God" to himself, Jesus appeals to the fact that Israelites are all called "gods" at Sinai. What Jesus is doing is using his opponents' own scriptures against them. Note that Jesus begins his question with the word "if." "*If* those to whom

10. We have much more to say about this in chapter 8.

the word of God came were identified as 'gods'—and the scripture cannot be annulled . . ." In other words, this is a conditional clause (a hypothetical), and Jesus' statement about the impossibility of the scripture's annulment is a subordinate conditional clause. Jesus is not "teaching" that scripture cannot be annulled; he is merely arguing that *if* the scripture cannot be annulled, then it must follow that his opponents are wrong. At most, one could look at this passage and conclude that Jesus is assuming his opponents' perspective for the purposes of the debate. This is standard practice in debate.

In fact, in chapter 8 of this book, I myself *assume* that the gospel accounts of the Olivet Discourse are accurate in order to make my case that Jesus wrongly predicted when the final judgment would occur. I do not *necessarily* believe that the gospel accounts are accurate (they couldn't be, in fact, because they differ in some significant ways at points), but all I need to show is that if they *are* accurate, then Jesus was inaccurate. In the same way, all John 10:34–36 tells us is that Jesus was using his own opponents' assumptions about the infallibility of scripture against them. Jesus even makes this clear when he uses the plural second person possessive pronoun to modify "the law." Jesus identifies it as "*your* law," referring to his opponents. Now, I do not mean to imply that Jesus did not consider the Psalms to be his own as well. Of course he did, but the fact that he identifies them as *your* law is a clear indication that Jesus is intentionally using his opponents' own assumptions against them. As for Jesus' *own* views—they are not stated. Jesus may believe that the Psalms and other of the Writings could not meet with his approval 100 percent of the time. But all he needs to do for the purposes of this particular debate is to accept the assumptions of his opponents. Without denying that Jesus took the Psalms to be authoritative, this is still a very slender reed upon which to hang the claim that Jesus "taught" the inerrancy of the scriptures.

A Spirit-Filled Proof-Text

Finally, in order to support their belief in the inerrancy of the New Testament, the Chicago inerrantists point to Jesus' words in Luke 14:16 and 16:13: "I will ask the Father, and he will give you another Advocate, to be with you forever. . . . When the Spirit of truth comes, he will guide you into all the truth. He will not speak of his own accord; he will only tell you what he hears [from the Father], and he will announce to you the things that are yet to come." Once again, the proof-text fails to make the claim the inerrantists wish it to make. Jesus says nothing here of the writing of scripture. He is speaking to the apostles about the role of the Holy Spirit in their ministries. Much of the New

Testament was not written by these apostles. Even if it were, the claim that the Holy Spirit would guide them in truth and instruct them about future events (future events which, as we will see in chapter 8, did not in fact transpire) does *not* constitute any sort of claim that everything they write down is going to be 100 percent accurate. Nor is it a claim that they would be prevented from writing down their own ideas and conflating them with divine revelation if they so chose.

Literary Allusions

Inerrantists also make regular mention of the fact that Jesus sometimes referred to biblical stories, such as the one where David ate the showbread, or the one where Jonah was in the belly of the fish, or the one where Daniel "predicted" the desecration of the temple. To fundamentalists, these allusions to biblical stories somehow constitute evidence that Jesus "taught" the inerrancy of these texts. Barr exposes the faulty assumption underlying this sort of claim:

> The high status that the Old Testament holds in the minds of Jesus and the early Christians will be granted by the most critical as a matter of historical fact, and therefore the fundamentalist efforts to prove this are of no importance. On the other hand, the fundamentalist attempts to argue that these sayings of Jesus and the New Testament writers about Jonah, Daniel, Moses and other persons and events prove the historical accuracy of the Old Testament are futile, because they make no attempt to show that Jesus or the early Christians were interested in such questions as the authorship of books, the presence of sources, or the historical accuracy of data and figures.[11]

Or as John Huxtable put the matter, "Jesus Christ came into the world to be its Saviour, not an authority on biblical criticism."[12] Jesus never *taught* that David wrote Psalm 110, or that Daniel wrote the book of Daniel, or that the book of Jonah is historically accurate. At the very most, he *assumed* these things. But not even this is guaranteed. It is quite possible that by alluding to these traditions, Jesus was simply conceding to standard assumptions. He may have known better, he may not have. As I showed in chapter 1, perhaps Jesus was aware that Jonah was an example of a fictional short story. By alluding to the story, he does not commit himself to its historicity, any more

---

11. Barr, *Fundamentalism*, 81.
12. Huxtable, *The Bible Says*, 70.

than Evangelicals commit themselves to the historicity of the *Chronicles of Narnia* when they say, reverently, that "Aslan is not a tame lion." A preacher may confess from the pulpit that after his visit to Las Vegas, he knows what Frodo must have felt like carrying that ring, but no one assumes the preacher has confused fantasy and reality. Factual theological claims are made all the time by reference to fictional narratives, and no one gets in trouble for it. Jesus may simply have been working within the assumptions of his tradition, even if he knew better. On the other hand, he may not have known better; in all likelihood, Jesus assumed the traditions with which he was raised.

The Heresy of Inerrancy

Nevertheless, the Chicago inerrantists disallow these possibilities by fiat, as stated in article fifteen of the CSBI: "We deny that Jesus' teaching about Scripture may be dismissed by appeals to accommodation or to any natural limitation of His humanity."[13] In other words, Jesus is not allowed to condescend to our own assumptions, even if he knows better. (Why this is disallowed is not clear.) He is further denied permission to assume the traditions into which he was born. According to the logic of fundamentalism, if Jesus assumed traditions that were wrong, then Jesus himself would have been wrong—and the whole religion (apparently) collapses in on itself. But this point of view cannot be sustained; it essentially denies Jesus the right to be human.

Luke 2:52 tells us that "Jesus grew in wisdom and in stature." But according to the inerrantists, this is impossible. To "grow in wisdom" implies that one must begin with a lesser degree of wisdom. Was Jesus *all-wise* and *all-knowing* when he was lying in the manger? Did Jesus make mistakes when he was learning to speak Aramaic, or would that necessitate that he was an imperfect being who could no longer be trusted? Inerrantists seem to think that any mistake or faulty assumption held by Jesus threatens the notion of his perfection. They believe that Jesus was sinless, based on Heb 4:15 and 1 Pet 2:22, and think that this must imply his perfection in every facet of human existence.[14] If Jesus had a faulty assumption, then he must have been deceived; and if he propagated that faulty assumption, then Jesus must have been a *deceiver*.

Yet this does not follow. If I am told that the world is flat, I am not a sinner, any more than I was a sinner when I tried to force the square peg into the round hole the first time around. If Jesus is to be human, then he must be allowed to operate under faulty assumptions until the point at which those

---

13. Henry, *God Who Speaks,* 214.

14. See, for instance, the false analogy made between Jesus' sinlessness and biblical inerrancy in article two of the CSBH.

assumptions are corrected, either by experience or by instruction. If we grant that Jesus must have operated under the normal faulty assumptions, later to be corrected, when he was a child learning how to navigate language and the world, why can we not grant that there were still some lingering faulty assumptions into his adulthood? At *what* point, exactly, did Jesus cease to be human and become omniscient?

In reality, it is absurd to posit any such point in time. To do so would be to commit oneself to a heretical position: denying Jesus the right to have faulty assumptions is just another form of Docetism. It is a denial of Jesus' humanity, because an indispensable part of being human is being a product of one's own time and place. I do not first believe the world is spherical because I am a superior being; I first believe it is spherical because that is what I was taught. In the same way, if Jesus believed the world was flat, and that Daniel wrote Daniel, it is not because he was an inferior or imperfect being; it's because he was fully a *human* being, which is precisely what the Council of Chalcedon affirms about him. If we take the Council of Chalcedon to be a standard of orthodoxy (see: a conditional clause), then we must deem the Chicago Statement on Biblical Inerrancy to be a heretical document.

The Double Standard

In the last chapter we saw that the Chicago inerrantists appeal to "the mainstream of church history" in order to legitimize their insistence that orthodox Christianity necessarily entails a commitment to biblical inerrancy. We saw, however, that despite their appeal to church history, the reality is that much of church history, including much of "the mainstream" of it, does not live up to the standards for inerrancy set by the Chicago Statement. However, even if they could legitimately claim church history for their cause, what would such an argument entail? For all intents and purposes, the claim is this: we are justified in our belief in inerrancy because church history expresses a belief in inerrancy. What this essentially amounts to is a *dogmatic* claim; it is not an appeal to reason or to evidence. But this raises the question: why should we care what was believed throughout church history? What weight should such a fact hold for us in our process of reasoning? This is a legitimate question, for even if we grant that "the mainstream of church history" affirmed the doctrine of inerrancy, as expounded by the Chicago inerrantists, we must also acknowledge the reality that the mainstream of church history has not always held to justifiable beliefs.

The mainstream of church history has also been outrageously anti-Semitic. The mainstream of church history upheld the institution of slavery.

It propagated patriarchy, and with it misogyny. The mainstream of church history believed it was appropriate to punish or even to execute those with dissenting views. For instance, John Calvin, the arch-hero of many Chicago inerrantists, was not only responsible for but also *relished* in the execution of Michael Servetus, a Christian theologian who did not accept the doctrine of the Trinity and who taught against the baptism of infants. After the murder of Servetus, Calvin was criticized by some Christians. He responded that "whoever shall now contend that it is unjust to put heretics and blasphemers to death will knowingly and willingly incur their very guilt."[15] Calvin's modern-day apologists will often attempt to minimize this by saying that Calvin was merely "a man of his times," but the fact that some Christians from "his times" opposed the execution of heretics exposes the calloused deception in such claims.[16] Nevertheless, if they can claim that the church's willingness to murder dissenters was just a "reality of the times," why then can they not conclude their church's alleged espousal of inerrancy was just an embarrassing product of a bygone era? The fact is that, if anything, it was the assumption of biblical infallibility that contributed to such savagery in the first place.

In this chapter we have looked further at the fallacious claim of the Chicago inerrantists that "the whole Bible" affirms the doctrine of inerrancy. We have seen that this is not the case, but let us grant for the moment that this were true. What would such a claim amount to? Essentially this: the Bible is inerrant because the Bible says that it is inerrant. This is of course the very definition of circular reasoning. It is a dogmatic claim, and not a rational one. It is not a claim that can be supported by any external evidence. It begins with the assumption that the Bible is a direct word from God, and then concludes that it must be a direct word from God because that is what it says about itself. To question the veracity of some biblical text is seen as sheer arrogance. By denying that this particular text is accurate, I am setting myself up against God, declaring that I myself know more than God. But this is pure sophistry, and it quickly becomes a flagrant double standard: it is rebellious pride when one questions the Bible; it is common sense when one questions the Qur'an. Yet the Qur'an similarly claims to be inerrant. *Surah* 4:82 says that if the Qur'an had come from anyone other than God, then most certainly many discrepancies would have been found within its pages. According to the logic of the Chicago inerrantists, that *must* mean that the Qur'an is inerrant. After all, it *says* it is.

15. From Calvin, *Defense of Orthodox Faith,* reproduced in Schaff, *History of the Reformation,* 2:791.

16. Greg Boyd makes similar criticisms of Calvin's defenders in Boyd, "Did Calvin Kill Servetus?," paras. 6–7.

But Christian apologists will argue that the Qur'an is full of contradictions and lies. On the other hand, Muslim apologists will argue that the Bible is full of contradictions and lies. And in point of fact, Muslims do a splendid job of pointing out precisely what those contradictions in the Bible are. It is much more difficult to find contradictions in the Qur'an, predominantly because it was written over a very short period of time and almost exclusively by one person; whereas, the Bible was written over a period upwards of a thousand years, at minimum by dozens of different authors. As a result, if internal coherency constitutes evidence for the divine origins and inerrancy of a sacred text, as the Chicago inerrantists claim, then the Qur'an wins over the Bible hands down.

At this point, Christian apologists will begin a campaign of character assassination against Mohammed: he was a liar, he was violent, etc. Again, this introduces a double standard. After all, Moses (the alleged author of the Pentateuch) was a liar and an extraordinarily violent man. In fact, if the Bible is accurate, then Moses was exceedingly more violent than Mohammed. Moses killed women and children in the name of God, whereas Mohammed condemned the killing of women and children for any reason. It does no good, either, to argue that many of the traditions in the Qur'an are dependent upon traditions from the Bible. The same thing is true of many of the traditions in the Bible. The story of the flood depends upon much older traditions, such as the Epic of Gilgamesh. The laws of Moses depend upon the earlier Code of Hammurabi. The vision of the "one like a son of man" in Daniel 7 borrows closely from the Ugaritic Baal cycle, and so on. Much of the Bible is a patchwork pastiche of broader ancient Near Eastern lore. Pointing out the differences between the Bible and these earlier traditions is irrelevant, since there are also differences between the Qur'anic traditions and their predecessors in the Bible.

In sum, therefore, in their criticisms of other sacred texts outside of Judaism and Christianity, fundamentalists display that they do not accept their own arguments in favor of biblical inerrancy. In fact, the same arguments work much better in favor of the Qur'an than they do of the Bible, since the Qur'an is by far the more internally coherent document. Their arguments would also work better for me, if I were to claim that this particular book is inspired by God, and that it is without discrepancy. The latter claim could easily be verified (since I do not tend to contradict myself), and by fundamentalist logic would count as evidence for the former claim. In fact, I'll state as much: this book is inspired by God and is without error in everything it affirms. Now then, if the Chicago inerrantists reject the legitimacy of my "argument," they are obliged to reject the legitimacy of their own. If they refuse to abandon their argument, then they must accept mine, which would lead to a paradox since I affirm that the Bible is not inerrant. What a profound divine mystery!

Discrepancies Notwithstanding

Speaking of profound divine mysteries, we recall that in the last chapter we learned that for the inerrantist, the "best" interpretation of a given passage is not the best *historical-grammatical* interpretation, but the best of the available options left over after any contradictory readings are ruled out by fiat. Given that there are thousands of discrepancies and contradictions within the pages of the Bible, it is to be expected that in some cases, it is impossible to come up with a "best" explanation which would resolve a discrepancy. It is bound to happen that after thousands of attempts, the inerrantist will run out of excuses. In such cases, the inerrantists have a trump card: the profound divine mystery. Essentially, what the claim becomes is that, *discrepancies notwithstanding*, there are no discrepancies in the Bible. This principle was stated some time ago by B. B. Warfield: "Every unharmonized passage remains a case of difficult harmony and does not pass into the category of objections to plenary inspiration."[17] In other words, if there is a discrepancy that we are not able to harmonize, it cannot be used as evidence against inerrancy; it merely moves into the category of "difficult" texts.

This underhanded tactic is stated even more brazenly in article fourteen of the CSBI and in its exposition. After affirming the unity and internal consistency of the scriptures, the article flatly denies "that alleged errors and discrepancies that have not yet been resolved vitiate the truth claims of the Bible."[18] Somehow, according to the Chicago inerrantists,

> The truthfulness of Scripture is *not negated* by the appearance in it of . . . seeming discrepancies between one passage and another. *It is not right to set the so-called 'phenomena' of Scripture against the teaching of Scripture about itself.* Apparent inconsistencies should not be ignored. Solution of them, where this can be convincingly achieved, will encourage our faith, *and where for the present no convincing solution is at hand we shall significantly honor God by trusting His assurance that His Word is true, despite these appearances, and by maintaining our confidence that one day they will be seen to have been illusions.*[19]

17. Warfield, *Inspiration and Authority*, 220.
18. Henry, *God Who Speaks*, 214.
19. Ibid., 217–18, emphasis added.

Put more bluntly: despite all reason and evidence to the contrary, we will continue to affirm the inerrancy of scripture. Even when we find discrepancies in the text, we will salvage our belief that they do not exist by classifying them as "unsolved mysteries." Inerrantists claim that in the afterlife God will explain to them how, for instance, all of the Egyptian livestock was completely destroyed by God *twice* (Exod 9:6, 25), or how Jesus was in the desert for forty days *immediately* after his baptism (Mark 1:12–13), and how simultaneously he was at his home in Bethany the day after his baptism, and in Galilee the day after that, and at a wedding the day after that, and subsequently in Capernaum for a few days with his mother, brothers and disciples (John 1:35–39, 43; 2:1, 12). If these discrepancies (and thousands along with them) do not make sense to us now, we are reassured by article fourteen of the CSBI that it will all make sense in heaven.

Notice also the claim that "it is not right to set the so-called 'phenomena' of Scripture against the teaching of Scripture about itself." In other words, one is not permitted to use the content of the Bible as evidence against the inerrancy of the Bible. In short, the doctrine of inerrancy is a hypothesis that cannot be falsified. It is a basic axiom of science that a hypothesis that cannot be falsified is a useless hypothesis. Yet fundamentalists *feign* commitment to scientific standards of exegesis.

Once again, the inerrantists depend on a double standard. They refer to obvious discrepancies as "alleged" discrepancies, or put the word "discrepancies" in scare quotes, as if those who identify them as such are hostile prosecutors who should be laughed out of court. Yet they refuse even to abide by the processes of the trial, disallowing the very *possibility* that such discrepancies might exist within their own text. Of course, when it comes to apparent discrepancies in the Qur'an or in the book of Mormon, the normal prosecutorial standards are put back into effect; any "alleged" discrepancy counts as evidence against the inerrancy of *those* texts. When Mormon apologists use the same harmonization tactics exercised by mainstream Christian apologists, Mormons are just evading the obvious in order to justify their rebellion against God and the truth of scripture. When Christians do it, they are being faithful. Errors notwithstanding, the Bible is obviously inerrant.

Controlling Presuppositions

When all else fails for the Chicago inerrantists, there is always character assassination. A frequently employed last-ditch stratagem is to accuse critical scholars of possessing nefarious motives. They will claim that "opponents, in arguing from empirical evidence, are in fact not motivated by a zeal for the empirical evidence but by a theological hostility to the true gospel."[20] According to the Chicago inerrantists, any reading of the text that posits a contradiction must begin with some type of faithless presupposition. Article nineteen of the CSBH, for instance, identifies "naturalism, evolutionism, scientism, secular humanism, and relativism" as "alien preunderstandings" that inevitably result in the misreading of the text.[21] "When these un- and anti-biblical principles seep into men's theologies [note the gender bias] at [the] presuppositional level, as today they frequently do, faithful interpretation of Holy Scripture becomes impossible."[22] In other words, the inerrantists accuse non-inerrantists of operating under *controlling presuppositions* that distort accurate readings of the text.

If, for instance, the critical scholar sees a conflict between Matthew and Luke's theology, or between Ecclesiastes and Daniel, it is not because such a conflict actually exists, but because the scholar is imposing his own theological ideas upon the text. He *wants* to see a conflict, because it serves his own agenda. Likewise, if the critical scholar at some point *ceases* the attempt to harmonize two conflicting passages, it is not because that scholar is being honest with the material; it is because she is arrogant, or because her poor presuppositions do not require her to continue the search for a harmonizing interpretation, thus allowing her to engage in sloppy exegesis. Such scholars are seen no longer as historians or as linguists but as halfwits and enemies.

But as James Barr reminds us, the accusation of controlling presuppositions "is of course no very original criticism, since most theologies have said the same of other theologies for centuries; and certainly fundamentalism is in no good position to use that criticism, since it is in fact a uniquely effective device for doing just this, for imposing upon the Bible the fundamentalist religious pattern and preventing anyone from getting anything else out of it."[23] As we have seen frequently throughout this chapter and the last, it is the *inerrantists* who are guilty of allowing their controlling presuppositions to interfere with the proper processes of historical-grammatical exegesis. Before the interpretive process even begins, the inerrantists rule out the possibility that the text can be wrong, *in any way*. This is the very definition of a controlling presupposition. Though the exposition on article nineteen of the CSBH "demands that all preunderstanding be subject to 'correction' by the teaching of Scripture,"[24] the inerrantists refuse to allow the teaching of

20. Barr, *Fundamentalism*, 71.

21. Radmacher and Preus, *Hermeneutics*, 886.

22. Henry, *God Who Speaks*, 218.

23. Barr, *Fundamentalism*, 66.

24. Radmacher and Preus, *Hermeneutics*, 900.

Scripture to correct the "alien preunderstanding" of biblical inerrancy. As we saw earlier in this chapter, the Bible *does not* teach the inerrancy of every text in the canon; rather, it is their alien and controlling presupposition of inerrancy that causes them to misinterpret texts in order to support their position. Moreover, when one scripture teaches, for instance, that there is *no* afterlife, and another scripture teaches that there *is* an afterlife, then the divergent teachings of scripture should correct the alien presupposition of inerrancy; but they do not allow scripture to interfere with their own ideas. Instead, their controlling presupposition of inerrancy *requires* them to misinterpret one text so that it will comply with other texts.

On the other hand, as James Barr rightly explains, "the critical approach to biblical literature is the one in which it becomes (for the first time!) possible to understand the literature without having to use the category of 'error.' It is only within the fundamentalist world-view that it seems as if critical scholars are primarily concerned with the imputation of 'error' to scripture. It is the fundamentalist doctrine, and not any other, that insists on pressing the category of error to the forefront of the discussion."[25] In reality, the vast majority of critical scholars are not motivated by any hostility to the Christian faith. Most critical scholars of the Bible in fact are *devout adherents* to the Christian faith.

Inerrantists accuse critical scholars of rejecting inerrancy so that they can believe whatever they like; but the truth is that inerrantists have no problem believing whatever they like and forcing their view onto the text. Inerrantists acknowledge that this happens, but stipulate that it should not occur in principle; yet then again, so do non-inerrantists. Although it is possible for a critical scholar to ascribe an error to the text where there is none, *there is no reason in principle why the critical scholar is required to ascribe error to the text.* Critical scholars regularly point out when and where the text is accurate, or is supported by external evidence. Conversely, *it is the inerrantist who in principle is required to deny the existence of errors.* Although both sides sometimes fail to live up to their own ideals, the ideal of the critical scholar is a degree of objectivity; the ideal of the inerrantist *is* bias.

In the end, when the Chicago inerrantists call out "naturalism, evolutionism, scientism, secular humanism, and relativism"—the "usual suspects" of crimes against inerrancy—they are throwing up a whale of a red herring (not to mix marine metaphors). In reality, *none* of these presuppositions are necessary in order to conclude that the Bible contradicts itself. For instance, a Muslim is not any of these things; the Muslim believes in supernatural revelation, miracles, creation, absolute truth—all the essentials. But the Muslim can still detect errors in the Bible. Moreover, *so can the Christian.* I speak

25. Barr, *Fundamentalism*, 55.

here from experience. I was an inerrantist, until I wasn't. I never doubted the supernatural; I never doubted the possibility of special revelation; I never doubted that some things are just objectively true. In fact, it was *precisely because* of my faith in the Bible that I came to recognize that it was not inerrant. I believed that because it was inerrant, it could certainly survive a little critical scrutiny. Based on *that* assumption, I proceeded to scrutinize the text, and found that given consistent principles of exegesis, the construct of inerrancy could not be sustained. I neither wanted nor expected to discover what I discovered, but my faith in the Bible's inerrancy contained within it, as they say, the seeds of its own destruction.

The Inerrancy Tax

I have been arguing that the doctrine of inerrancy as articulated particularly by the Chicago inerrantists implodes in upon itself; the very arguments used in its defense display how untenable a doctrine it is, as we see when those selfsame arguments are put to work to defend the inerrancy of other sacred texts. Yet not only does inerrancy undermine itself, it also undermines basic theological tenets of mainstream Christianity. I call this the inerrancy tax. If you want to buy into inerrancy stock, it's going to cost you in other ways. In order to sustain its bureaucracy, the Inerrancy Revenue Service will levy a tax on your favorite brand of theism—and the inerrancy tax cuts deep into the theological pocket book.

Taxing Human Freedom

Article nine of the CSBI asserts that "inspiration, though not conferring omniscience, guaranteed true and trustworthy utterance on all matters of which the Biblical authors were moved to speak and write."[26] Put a different way, when God inspired scripture, God prevented the authors of scripture from making mistakes, and from including their own, less-than-inspired ideas in the mix. A free will theist is generally someone who believes that because of God's love for humanity and God's desire to be freely loved in return, God has granted human beings the freedom to make volitional mistakes, to attempt to usurp God's authority, to deny God's will—in sum, the freedom to be self-determining moral agents on their own terms. Free will theists believe that the history of God's involvement with the world is a *messy* history—not a straight line so much as a spiral or a zigzag. This is because God chooses to work with and through human beings, and human beings are imperfect.

26. Henry, *God Who Speaks*, 213.

The problem: the doctrine of inerrancy denies the human authors of scripture that free will. Farther on down the line, it also denies those who formed the various biblical canons those same freedoms. The doctrine of inerrancy *rejects out of hand* the possibility that the human authors of scripture were permitted to exercise their God-given free will in the writing of what would eventually become scripture; it denies the possibility that the scriptures could be just as messy as salvation history, and for the same reasons.

A free will theist could potentially respond that God did not *override* their free will; rather, the authors of scripture voluntarily *subjected themselves* to the suspension of their free will. But in that case the inerrantist's faith would not be in God, but in each individual writer of scripture. The inerrantist is obliged to put her confidence in dozens, perhaps hundreds of fallible human beings (authors, editors, canonizers, etc.), trusting *in them* that they chose to suspend the exercise of their free will for the purposes of creating what they may or may not have known would eventually become "sacred scripture." For my part, I know human beings too well (having been one myself) to entrust such confidence to them. I would scarcely put such confidence in *one* human, let alone in *all of hundreds*, which is what would be required to affirm inerrancy.

The only alternative to putting one's faith in all of hundreds of individual human beings, then, is to assent to the proposition that God *overrode* human free will in order to provide us with a perfect book. But for the free will theist, this is no easy claim. It is not like the temporary powers given to a head of state in a time of crisis. Free will theists believe that God's issuance of free will is an extension of God's very nature—God could not have done otherwise than to give free will; for to do so would mean that God was not perfect in love. Therefore, to say that God overrode the free exercise of human will is to say that God overrode God's own nature. Free will theists believe that God gave human beings the power *not to listen to God's voice*; they therefore have no recourse to claim that human beings could not have erred, held back, gone too far, or even lied, when writing scripture. One can be an inerrantist only at the expense of one's commitment to free will theism.

Taxing Divine Sovereignty

Yet the Chicago inerrantists are adamant that human free will could *not* have interfered with inerrant inspiration. Article nine of the CSBI goes on to "deny that the finitude or fallenness of these writers, by necessity or otherwise, introduced distortion or falsehood into God's Word."[27] How are they able to

27. Ibid.

deny this? They are able to deny this possibility because the majority of the drafters and signers of the CSBI are *not* free will theists—they are Calvinists, or Reformed theologians, who believe that the specific activities and ultimate destiny of all human beings were mapped out by God in advance, predestined since the time of the fall of humanity depicted in Genesis 3. These theologians believe that free will theism *diminishes* God's sovereignty. They believe that God's sovereignty is such that God has total control over every aspect of human history. Since the fall, nothing has ever been done that has not been foreordained by God.

The problem: the doctrine of inerrancy denies God the right and the power to intentionally inspire error, falsehood, or even *evil* in the text of scripture in order to achieve God's own purposes. Initially this may sound like a strange thing for God to do, but not if you are a Calvinist. Generally speaking, Calvinists believe either that God decreed and ordained evil (in other words: *is responsible for its existence*), or at the least that God *uses* the evil that already exists in order to achieve certain objectives. The former, stronger view is stated emphatically by eighteen-century Reformed theologian Jonathan Edwards:

> Thus it is necessary, that God's awful majesty, his authority and dreadful greatness, justice, and holiness, should be manifested. *But this could not be, unless sin and punishment had been decreed;* so that the shining forth of God's glory would be very imperfect, both because these parts of divine glory would not shine forth as the others do, and also the glory of his goodness, love, and holiness would be faint without them; *nay, they could scarcely shine forth at all. If it were not right that God should decree and permit and punish sin,* there could be no manifestation of God's holiness in hatred of sin, or in showing any preference, in his providence, of godliness before it.
>
> There would be no manifestation of God's grace or true goodness, if there was no sin to be pardoned, no misery to be saved from. How much happiness soever he bestowed, his goodness would not be so much prized and admired. . . . *So evil is necessary*, in order to the highest happiness of the creature, and the completeness of that communication of God, for which he made the world.[28]

Put succinctly, the God of Jonathan Edwards *ordered evil into existence* in order to glorify himself; the reason for this is apparently that without evil this God's goodness would not be quite as apparent. Commenting on this excerpt from Edwards, Calvinist theologian and megachurch pastor John Piper writes that "God is *more glorious* for having conceived and created and governed a

28. Edwards, "Divine Decrees," 528, emphasis added.

world like this with all its evil."[29] Elsewhere, Piper further expounds his version of divine glory and sovereignty. After remarking that the 9/11 attack on the World Trade Center was *ordained by God*, on the grounds that God did not miraculously prevent the planes from crashing into the buildings, Piper explains why this conception of divine sovereignty brings him comfort:

> The answer is because there are 10,000 orphans who wonder if they have a future. Will they have a future if God isn't powerful for them? I'm coming to those families and I'm saying when they ask me, "Do you think God ordained the death of my daddy?" I say, "Yes. The Lord gives and the Lord takes away. Blessed be the name of the Lord. But the very power by which God governs all evils enables him to govern your life. And he has total authority to turn this and every other evil in your life for your everlasting good. And that's your only hope in this world and in the next. And therefore, *if you sacrifice the sovereignty of God in order to get him off the hook in the death of your daddy, you sacrifice everything.* You don't want to go there."
>
> The sovereignty of God, while creating problems for his involvement in sin and evil, is the very rock-solid foundation that enables us to carry on in life. *Where would we turn if we didn't have a God to help us deal with the very evils that he has ordained come into our lives?* So yes, absolutely, I believe in the sovereignty of God and I believe in its comforting effects.[30]

My intention in displaying these quotations from Edwards and Piper is not to analyze them or to test them for any semblance of coherency, but only to point out that according to the Reformed understanding, the notion of the sovereignty of God entails that God either decrees evil (as with Edwards and Piper) or merely directs and employs evil (as with the more moderate Reformed theologians and with Calvin himself) in order to accomplish some purpose, whether manifestly good or "profoundly" mysterious. Unfortunately for every Christian, the perspective of Edwards and Piper is not too far off from some perspectives inscribed in our own scriptures. For instance, in 1 Kgs 22:19–23, Yahweh had determined to kill Ahab, the king of Israel, and accomplished this purpose by sending a "lying spirit" to Ahab's 400 prophets. Yahweh's lying spirit told the prophets that Ahab would be victorious in battle at Ramoth-gilead; as a result, Ahab went up to battle and was fatally wounded. Yahweh *lied*—or commissioned a lie—in order to kill.

29. Piper, *Desiring God*, 351, emphasis added.

30. Piper, "How Can Evil Have a Good Purpose," paras. 7–8, emphasis added. I am indebted to Halden Doerge for bringing these quotations from Edwards and Piper to my attention.

Even more significant is the claim made in Ezekiel 20. The setting is the wilderness period, between the exodus from Egypt and the entrance into the Promised Land. In this case, Yahweh's objective is to punish the Israelites for their disobedience. Yahweh accomplishes this by *intentionally giving Israel bad commands*. The specific bad command that Ezekiel refers to is found in Exod 22:29: "The firstborn of your sons you shall give to me." According to Ezekiel, Yahweh commanded Israel to sacrifice their firstborn sons to him, in order to punish them for their disobedience. In Ezek 20:25–26, Yahweh says, "I gave them laws that were not good and rules by which they could not live; I corrupted them through their very gifts, when they offered up all their firstborn, so that I might make them desolate, so that they might know that I am Yahweh." We will look much more closely at this passage in chapter 5, but for now suffice it to say that, according to Ezekiel, Exod 22:29 contains a command that is expressly evil; Ezekiel's explanation for that fact is that Yahweh intentionally issued the evil command as a form of punishment for Israel's sins.

And this brings us back to the problem for inerrantists who are committed to Reformed conceptions of divine sovereignty. If Yahweh's sovereignty entails the use of evil means to accomplish his undisclosed objectives, if Yahweh sent lying spirits in order to deceive, if Yahweh intentionally commanded the Israelites to sacrifice their children in order to punish them, if he intentionally gave them bad commands (at least one of which we know to be recorded in Exodus 22, where it is depicted deceptively as a *good* command), then what is to prevent God from intentionally giving us *other* bad scriptures, intentionally obfuscating revelation as a form of punishment, or as some sort of examination, to test our mettle? (Is this not what he did with Abraham?) If all of these things are true of Yahweh, and if this is what his sovereignty entails, then it is clear that a doctrine of inspiration not only *does not* but *cannot* necessitate a corresponding doctrine of inerrancy.

We recall that article nineteen of the CSBH demands that "any preunderstandings which the interpreter brings to Scripture should be in harmony with scriptural teaching and subject to correction by it."[31] Yet it is clear that the Chicago inerrantists themselves are in violation of this axiom, since they continue to *insist* that scripture must be inerrant regardless of the "scriptural teaching" in Ezekiel 20 that Yahweh has intentionally inspired errant scripture, resulting in "inspired errors," if you will. If God "authored" evil, he can also author a flawed book, and still be sovereign. By insisting on the inerrancy of the scriptures, the Reformed articulators of the Chicago Statement are limiting God's sovereignty by denying God the right to use error, decep-

31. Radmacher and Preus, *Hermeneutics*, 885.

tion, and evil to accomplish God's own undisclosed purposes. In the words of John Piper, "if you sacrifice the sovereignty of God in order to get him off the hook in the [inspiring of errant scripture], you sacrifice everything. You don't want to go there." The doctrine of inerrancy can only be maintained at the expense of divine sovereignty. The IRS always collects.

Inerrancy Stunts Your Growth

But inerrancy is not content with taxing your favorite brand of theism; it also taxes you. It taxes your development as a moral agent; it taxes the process by which the discernment necessary for moral agency is achieved. As I concluded at the end of chapter 1, the doctrine of inerrancy is a human concoction designed to aid in the exercise of political control over moral agents. It effectively does this by shortcutting the processes of moral enlightenment. In cultures where scripture is considered to be inerrant, those who control the interpretation of scripture control the behavior of the people.

For example, in first century Palestine, the scribes and teachers of the law were able to exercise political control over the population by setting standards for interpretation of the laws of Moses. However, if the inspiration and unified Mosaic authorship of the entirety of the Pentateuch were not accepted by the populace, then the official interpreters of the law would have been powerless to exercise control over the behavior of the people. Similarly, in the United States, political control over the behavior of the populace is vested in lawmakers and judges, *on the assumption* that the Constitution of the United States is an authoritative document. If the majority of the population did not share that assumption with lawmakers and judges, then any exercise of political control over the population would not be considered legitimate.

Yet the doctrine of biblical inerrancy seeks a more totalizing control over human behavior than does the Constitution of the United States, which guarantees certain moral freedoms that the laws of Moses do not. In order to support the established authorities (in Jerusalem, in the synagogues, in the churches), the doctrine of inerrancy claims that the Bible was, in effect, dropped from heaven, as an answer to all the "essential" questions humans have to ask. It purports to give us infallible answers to moral and ethical questions. In doing this, it militates against intra-communal diversity, which the elites tend to see as a potential threat to the stability of the minority religious culture in a pluralistic environment; it is also in this way enabled to preserve the community's peculiar identifying marks *as a given*, as a part of the "order of nature," as it were.

For example, because of certain portions of Deuteronomy (portions which critical scholars for good reasons believe were added by King Josiah and the high priest Hilkiah in the seventh century BCE), it is taken for granted by Jews that sacrifices to Yahweh are to be made in Jerusalem only. Despite centuries of tradition to the contrary, the construct of infallibility ascribed to these portions of Deuteronomy (see Deut 12–14) gives the policy of centralization an appearance of *naturalness* in the eyes of later, unsuspecting generations, an appearance of naturalness that it did not always possess. A Jewish man's assumptions about the infallibility of the text thus forbid him from asking the obvious question, "Why can't I worship Yahweh in my own backyard?"

In the same way, to complicated questions like, "What is the moral significance of homosexuality?" the Bible gives a definitive answer: it is an abomination. Because of the assumption of infallibility, and because of the structural norms of a community ordered around that infallible text, abominating homosexuality seems perfectly natural. Because the Bible is inerrant, there is no room for moral discernment here, no room for discussion. We can debate how to *treat* homosexuals, but not what homosexuality's moral significance is. The answer to that question is quite literally etched in stone. But this is a shortcut—a dangerous shortcut—around the processes of moral discernment that are necessary in order to make humans with the potential for moral agency into *bona fide* moral agents.

This is what I call the moral argument for the existence of errors. An infallible set of scriptures is ultimately just a shortcut through our moral and spiritual development. To have a book dropped from heaven, the likes of which is beyond the reach of all human criticism—that is a shortcut. It is no wonder humans have always attempted to create these kinds of foundational texts; and it is a revelation of God's character, from my perspective, that cracks have been found in each and every one of those foundations. A good teacher does not issue orders one after the other and demand assent from her students; a good teacher shows the students how to come to the right conclusions on their own. If God were to have given us an infallible set of answers to our moral questions, God would have been consigning us to moral immaturity and ignorance. That kind of unassailable source of moral knowledge at our fingertips is a way of evading the kind of moral struggle that produces virtuous people and virtuous communities. A book dropped from heaven takes all of the hard work out of it for us. That construct promises us certainty, it promises us hard and fast solutions to moral enigmas, but what it delivers is dependence, lethargy, and self-righteousness. This construct is held up as God's very word to us, but it is a cheat sheet; it is the answers in the back of the book. Precisely by offering us an unassailable set of moral axioms—ready-made—it removes the necessity of the only thing that can make us moral and virtuous people: struggle.

Don't mistake me. I am not saying that the scriptures themselves do this to us. I am saying that the *construct* of an infallible book does this to us. Freedom from this construct, freedom to examine the scriptures, freedom to subject them to critique—that is the freedom to engage in moral struggle, the freedom to *commit* oneself to the struggle to find God, to find the truth, to find justice, even if that means struggling against some of our own traditions and sacred texts. It is not a rejection of God, but the freedom to choose not to take the shortcuts that the powerbrokers of the past have concocted to keep the rabble in line and the so-called heretics disempowered. It is the freedom to *reengage* in the Argument; the freedom to read the scriptures as they were read before the Argument was eclipsed by the Word. To engage in that argument is what it means to be a part of the religious tradition. We need to be allowed to hear the distinct voices in the argument; but inerrancy wants to homogenize those voices. The struggle is essential; and it is perpetual. There is no easy road to moral maturity. The scriptures have a lot of guidance to offer us along that difficult road, but they are not the destination. If they were, we would not have to walk the road. The scriptures are a great source to work with throughout the struggle, but they are not an infallible alternative to it.

* * *

The next five chapters will be devoted to displaying how and why our scriptures are fallible (and fallible in significant ways). This is just to establish that something needs to be done about the traditional reading strategies; but these five chapters will not attempt to answer the question of what to do with these fallible texts, if they are to be preserved within our canons of scripture. I will not attempt to answer that question until chapters 9 and 10. I only ask the reader not to shortcut their path to understanding by skipping over the next five chapters in order to find the answers in the back of the book.

4 YAHWEH'S ASCENDANCY
WHITHER THOU GOEST, POLYTHEISM?[1]

THE TRADITIONAL READINGS OF THE SCRIPTURES WE HAVE inherited are monotheistic, but that has not always been the case. As I will argue in this chapter, there is conclusive evidence scattered throughout the Hebrew Bible that the worldview of Israelites prior to the Babylonian exile—just like that of Israel's Canaanite and ancient Near Eastern neighbors—was thoroughly polytheistic. Obviously, the Bible attests that Israelites frequently worshiped gods other than Yahweh, for which they came under censure by Moses and the prophets. We read this condemnation of the worship of other deities (epitomized in the first commandment) through the lens of our monotheistic theology as a condemnation of the worship of *false* gods. But there is an important difference between the condemnation of the worship of *false* gods and the condemnation of the worship of *other* gods. It makes little sense why Israelites would have oscillated between the belief that Yahweh is the only God on the one hand, and the worship of gods they otherwise believed did not exist on the other. To make clear what my claim is here, it is not that the commoners held a polytheistic worldview while the religious leaders were consistently monotheistic. The evidence I am about to present will show that the narrators themselves, the writers of our own sacred scriptures, assumed a polytheistic worldview.

Yahweh's Inheritance

The Song of Moses in Deuteronomy 32—alongside the Song of Miriam in Exodus 15—is considered by scholars to be some of the oldest material in the Hebrew Bible, dating back roughly to the mid-thirteenth century BCE. The Song of Moses tells the story of Yahweh's victory over the Egyptians and his deliverance of his people Israel, and in verses 8–9 we learn something about how Israel originally came to be a people belonging to Yahweh. In

1. For the basic structure and many of the main points of this chapter, I am indebted to Rollston, "Rise of Monotheism."

order to tease out the most primitive form of this story, we are going to look at these verses from three different sources—the Masoretic Text (MT), the Septuagint (LXX), and the Dead Sea Scrolls (DSS).[2] Deut 32:8–9 in the MT reads as follows:

> When Elyon divided the nations,
> when he separated the sons of Adam,
> he established the borders of the nations
> according to the number of *the sons of Israel.*
> Yahweh's portion was his people,
> Jacob his allotted inheritance.

The LXX renders the same two verses this way:

> When the Most High divided the nations,
> when he scattered the sons of Adam,
> he established the borders of the nations
> according to the number of *God's angels,*
> and his people Jacob became a portion for the Lord,[3]
> the land of Israel his inheritance.

I have highlighted the significant difference between the two in *italics.* The MT says that Elyon[4] divided up humanity according to the number of the

2. For those who are unfamiliar with these terms, the Masoretic Text refers to the Hebrew manuscripts of the Hebrew Bible which were copied and preserved by the Masoretes, a group of scribes who lived and worked between the seventh and tenth centuries CE. Until the late 1940s, the MT represented the only Hebrew manuscripts of the Jewish Bible. Between 1947 and 1956 the Dead Sea Scrolls were discovered in the caves of Qumran, several miles outside of Jerusalem. Among these scrolls were numerous biblical manuscripts which antedated the MT by close to a thousand years. The Dead Sea Scrolls were copied and preserved between the second century BCE and the mid-first century CE. They are by far the oldest Hebrew manuscripts extant. The Septuagint is a Greek translation of the Hebrew Bible, originally translated between the third and second centuries BCE. Extant fragments of the Septuagint date back as early as the second century BCE. (The Septuagint is abbreviated LXX because of a tradition about the seventy scribes responsible for its translation.) Between the MT, LXX, and DSS there are numerous differences, some more significant than others. A scholarly discipline called "textual criticism" is concerned in part with analyzing these differences and attempting to determine which version may reflect the most primitive textual tradition.

3. The LXX translates the divine name Yahweh with the Greek word *kyrios,* meaning "lord." This is unfortunate, because Yahweh does not mean "lord." Yahweh originally meant "he who creates," and was probably short for the fuller divine name Yahweh Sabaoth, meaning "he who raises armies."

4. Elyon is Semitic word, a divine name meaning "Most High." I have left it untranslated because it is a proper noun in Hebrew. I rendered it "Most High" from the LXX because in the Greek it had already lost its value as a proper noun.

sons of Israel, while the LXX says that the Most High divided up humanity according to the number of *God's angels*. That is certainly an intriguing difference. How do we explain this? And what does this have to do with polytheism?

Until the discovery of the DSS (1947–56), there was no good explanation for this divergence, but the discovery of the Deuteronomy scroll in the fourth cave of Qumran (the scroll is referred to as 4QDeut^q) has shed some light on this conundrum. It should be pointed out that the DSS antedate the MT by about a thousand years. The passage in 4QDeut^q reads as follows:

> When Elyon divided the nations,
> when he separated the sons of Adam,
> he established the borders of the nations
> according to the number of *the sons of the gods.*
> Yahweh's portion was his people,
> Jacob his allotted inheritance.

The Hebrew text says, "according to the number of the *běnêy hāĕlōhîm,*" which means, "the sons of the gods." This phrase, *běnêy hāĕlōhîm*, is a common Semitic phrase that refers to the junior deities in the divine pantheon. It is well attested in the ancient Near Eastern literature. *'Ēlōhîm* is morphologically plural (gods) but can sometimes be semantically singular (god). In this case it matters little, because it is the *sons* of *'Ēlōhîm* that are at issue.

The NRSV takes some interpretive license and translates this phrase, "according to the number of the gods." As it happens, this interpretation is fairly accurate. As already noted, throughout the ancient Near Eastern literature, the Semitic phrase *běnêy hāĕlōhîm* occurs frequently, always meaning the same thing—*junior deities of the divine pantheon.* The notion of a divine pantheon—with a chief deity at the top, a consort (wife-deity), and their progeny, all comprising the "council of the gods"—was widespread throughout the ancient Near East, not least in the Canaanite mythologies. In the literature, this council convenes to talk politics, as it were—to determine the order of things.

Interestingly, in the Canaanite literature, one deity is typically considered to be the head of the pantheon. This deity's name is El Elyon. El Elyon is the god served by the priest-king Melchizedek in Genesis 14. El is the generic term for god, but El Elyon—God Most High—is the king over all gods in the region of Canaan. Upon Elyon's mountain is where these (political) councils of the gods are said to convene.

Now we can look again at Deut 32:8–9 and get a clearer sense of what is going on:

> When Elyon divided the nations,
> when he separated the sons of Adam,

he established the borders of the nations
according to the number of *the gods.*
Yahweh's portion was his people,
Jacob his allotted inheritance.

In this early piece of Israelite poetry (remember that Israel is in Canaan!), we have a picture of one of these councils of the gods. These verses reflect an etiological narrative[5] explaining the division of nations. In it, Elyon, the mountain god, head of the divine pantheon, divides humankind according to the number of his children, the junior members of the pantheon, so that each gets a people group as an inheritance. Yahweh, one of Elyon's sons, is given Israel as his inheritance.[6] Thus Yahweh becomes Israel's patron deity. That is what is envisioned here in the oldest extant Hebrew text of Deuteronomy 32.

So what happened? Why does the LXX say "angels" and the MT "sons of Israel"? The answer is quite simple. The LXX and the MT both reflect time periods *after* Israel had become monotheistic. This text poses a problem to monotheism, and they both attempt to deal with the problem in different ways.

The LXX's solution is to interpret the *běnêy hāʾĕlōhîm* as "angels." The "sons of god" is taken as a metaphor for the celestial beings of second temple lore. There are two problems with this. First, the phrase "sons of god" does not mean angels. Hebrew has a perfectly good word for angels—*malʾăkîm.* The second problem lies in the meaning of the word "angel" itself. Angel simply means "messenger." It can be used just as appropriately of a human messenger as of a celestial messenger. Yet in the ancient world, these "angels" were *not* considered *non-divine* celestial beings; they too were gods. They were not necessarily members of the pantheon, but they served the pantheon. Recall Acts 14:12. There is mention of a messenger from Greek mythology. "They called Paul Hermes because he was the main speaker." Hermes in Greek mythology is an "angel" because that is the Greek word for messenger, but Hermes is an angel-god. This may sound confusing to us, but it simply means messenger-god. In the ancient Near Eastern literature the *malʾăkîm* were likewise considered divine beings, but of lesser status

5. An etiology is a story told about the past to explain some phenomenon in the present. For instance, Genesis 3 is an etiological narrative explaining, among other things, why snakes do not have legs, why child birth is painful, and why everything dies.

6. Some scholars argue that Elyon and Yahweh are the same god here, but the most straightforward reading of the text does not permit this. First, it is said that Yahweh is given an inheritance. A father does not give an inheritance to himself, but to his child. Second, the text says that Elyon divided up humankind according to the number of his children, not according to the number of his children plus himself. Thus, Yahweh is portrayed here as the son of Elyon.

than the direct progeny of the great gods, like El Elyon. The *mal'ăkîm* were messenger-gods.

Sometime after the Babylonian exile and the shift of the Jews to monotheism, the strategy of at least some groups was to demote these messenger-deities to non-divine or significantly lesser divine status while flatly denying the existence of other national deities such as Kemosh, Baal, Asherah, etc.[7] In this fashion, the LXX simply changes *běnêy hāělōhîm* (sons of the god/s) to *angelōn theou* (messengers of god). There is zero exegetical warrant for this alteration. The Hebrew does not say *mal'ăkêy hāělōhîm*; it says *běnêy hāělōhîm*. Yet there was good theological warrant for it—the translators of the LXX were monotheists.

Centuries later, some devout Jewish scribes, probably motivated to preserve theological orthodoxy, altered the text yet again, changing *běnêy hāělōhîm* to *běnêy yiśrāēl*, and this is the reading preserved in the MT. This solved the problem of the text's polytheistic implications better than the LXX rendering, because it does not leave room for divine interpretations of the angels. Perhaps more significantly, however, it reflects an Israel-centric worldview. Israel is not just one nation among many, albeit the one the Most High (conflated with Yahweh on this reading) chooses for himself. Rather, the whole of humankind is, we might say, *Israelform*. Humankind is divided up according to the number of the tribes of Israel. This does not actually make sense as a literal claim, but what does make sense is why the scribes felt they had to change the text. They had to change the text because the text reflected a polytheistic worldview that was no longer theologically acceptable.

Yahweh's Prowess

As we have seen above, Yahweh is depicted in the Song of Moses as a young deity, a son of El Elyon, the Most High God. The principal theme of the poem is Yahweh's victory over the Egyptians. Yahweh is portrayed as an up-and-coming warrior deity who is making a name for himself among the nations. His exploits in battle are recounted in graphic detail. Yahweh's arrows are "drunk with blood," and his sword "devours flesh" as he takes vengeance upon his enemies (Deut 32:42). Because of this, the poet calls upon the heavens to give honor to the people of Israel, and upon the other gods to kneel before Yahweh, a warrior who has proven himself in battle. Verse 43 of 4QDeut[q] reads:

7. It was not necessary to deal with Elyon since he was conflated with Yahweh prior to Israel's transition to monotheism, as we shall see below.

> Praise, O heavens, his people
> Kneel before him, all you gods

Here again is an unambiguous reference to deities other than Yahweh. Moreover, as one might expect, these lines read differently in the LXX and in the MT.

> O heavens, rejoice with him
> Worship him, all you angels of God (LXX)
>
> O nations, rejoice [with] his people (MT)

Here we see the same two strategies as before. The LXX sees "gods" and changes it to "angels of God." The MT just deletes any reference to other gods altogether, and changes "heavens" to "nations." Michael Heiser concludes that "the Masoretic text originally had [two lines], a pairing that was deliberately eliminated to avoid the reference to other 'divine beings.'"[8] The most primitive reading of verse 43 is certainly preserved in the DSS. Yahweh is depicted as an up-and-comer among the gods, whose prowess in battle commands the respect of his fellow divine beings.

Interestingly, a casual reading of verse 39 might seem at first to reflect a monotheistic view, but actually reinforces our case. "See now that I myself am he," Yahweh says. "There is no god besides me." To our ears this may sound like a denial of the existence of other gods, but we know that just a few verses later other gods are called upon to acknowledge Yahweh's distinction. In fact, the expression "there is no one besides me" is a common Semitic idiom for the idea of superiority. In Isa 47:8, the city of Babylon says of itself, "I am, and there is no one else besides me." Nineveh says the same thing of itself in Zeph 2:15. Obviously, Babylon and Nineveh are not claiming to be the only cities in the world. They are claiming to be without equal. In the case of Deut 32:39, it means, "No god's prowess in battle compares to mine." It is the boast of a young god seeking to establish himself among the pantheon,[9] and it mirrors the boast of a young nation (Israel) seeking to establish itself among the nations.

A similar claim is made about Yahweh in another early song, ascribed to Moses and his sister Miriam.

> Who is like you, O Yahweh, among the gods?
> Who is like you, majestic in holiness,
>   awesome in grandeur, doing marvelous things? (Exod 15:11)

8. Heiser, "Deuteronomy 32:8 and the Sons of God," 59.

9. See Bembry, *YHWH's Coming of Age*, who shows that early Israelite traditions portrayed Yahweh as a young deity; he did not become the "ancient of days" until Daniel 7.

Some traditionalists argue that Moses did not indicate belief in the existence of the other gods here. Rather, Moses is asserting Yahweh's superiority over the false gods of other nations. Of course, this raises the question of how Yahweh is glorified by being compared to nonexistent entities. The whole logic of this acclamation of superiority requires the existence of inferior gods. If Moses intended to praise Yahweh for being greater than nonexistent gods, Moses must not have thought much of Yahweh. Next to nothing, a nanobe is quite impressive. Next to nobody, Steven Seagal is a great actor. Who is like him among nobody?

Yahweh's Jealousy

Inevitably, whenever I broach this subject of polytheism in ancient Israel, somebody asks, "But what about the first commandment?" Well, here is the first commandment: "I am Yahweh your God, who brought you forth from the land of Egypt, out from the house of slavery; you shall have no other gods in my presence" (Exod 20:2). And here is what it does *not* say: "I am Yahweh your God, who brought you forth from the land of Egypt, out from the house of slavery; you shall not worship *false gods*, but only me, *the one true God*."

The first commandment in reality does not deny the existence of other gods; it simply says other gods are not to be worshiped by Israel. Why not? Because *other gods* did not bring Israel out of Egypt. Yahweh was the one who did that, and therefore Israel owes its worship to him. Yahweh is Israel's patron deity. That Yahweh is a jealous deity (Exod 20:5) in fact assumes the existence of real competitors for Israel's affections. There is no claim here, yet, about Yahweh being the god of creation, or a universal god. That understanding of Yahweh is further along in Israel's theological development, as we will see below. For now, Yahweh remains Israel's tribal god, a second-tier deity in Elyon's pantheon. Every nation in the ancient Near East had a tribal deity, a god who took care of his or her people, fought on their behalf, in exchange for their unconditional allegiance.[10] What we see here in the first (and second) commandments is just that—a contract between one god among many and one people among many. There is nothing very unique about Israel's relationship to Yahweh as reflected in these commandments. It is standard ancient Near Eastern religion.

---

10. This is why the distinction between henotheism and polytheism is essentially useless.

The Sons of God and the Daughters of Men

> When men began to multiply upon the face of the earth, and they had daughters, the sons of God saw that they were beautiful. So they took women for themselves as they saw fit. Then Yahweh said, "My spirit shall not abide in men forever, since they are flesh; their days shall be one hundred twenty years." In those days, the Nephilim were on the earth—later as well—when the sons of God slept with the daughters of men and impregnated them. Their offspring were the mighty men of yore, men of renown. (Gen 6:1–4)

There are generally four interpretations of the "sons of God" in this passage:

(1) The most common interpretation is one we might expect, namely, that the *běnêy hāĕlōhîm* are "angels." This interpretation is of course attested in the LXX. It is also attested in 1 Enoch, a Second Temple (i.e., "monotheistic") document, and is generally the line taken in late Second Temple Judaism.[11] Yet, as noted above, Hebrew has a perfectly good word for "angels" (*malʾākîm*). The word *malʾākîm* is used elsewhere in Genesis, but not here. There is no exegetical warrant for this interpretation. These are not divine *messengers* enjoying conjugal relations with mortal women. These are the progeny of the gods.

(2) Walter Kaiser interprets the *běnêy hāĕlōhîm* as the ancient Near Eastern potentates—the kings of the earth. This reading is also attested in one of the Aramaic Targums[12] (post 70 CE). But this reading does not adequately explain the significance of the Nephilim, the progeny of the *běnêy hāĕlōhîm* and the daughters of men. Kaiser argues that the Nephilim are not giants—as Num 13:33 would indicate—but "princes" or "aristocrats."[13] (It would seem that the principle, "let scripture interpret scripture" takes a back seat to orthodoxy.) But if the Nephilim are merely princes or aristocrats, why do we need to be told that they were "on the earth in those days," that they were the "mighty men of yore"? Were there no princes or aristocrats on the earth at the time Genesis 6 was written? The passage speaks about the existence of these Nephilim in the past tense, yet Kaiser believes the passage was written by Moses, who was certainly still alive when the Nephilim were spotted in Numbers 13. It is also difficult to understand why kings taking wives is an event worthy of special report like this (except in the context

---

11. The Second Temple period ranges from 515 BCE to 70 CE, at which time the second temple was destroyed by the Romans.

12. The Aramaic Targums are simply translations of the Hebrew Bible into the Aramaic language.

13. Kaiser et al., *Hard Sayings of the Bible*, 108.

of a royal biography). More problematic still is the image of all the kings of the earth going out *en masse* with the aim of taking wives—something like a foxhunt. The report seems to portray the *běnêy hāĕlōhîm* as a collective acting in concord.

(3) An unusually popular interpretation is to understand the *běnêy hāĕlōhîm* as the "righteous descendants of Seth," and the daughters of men as the "unrighteous descendants of Cain." But neither Seth nor Cain is named here, even though both are named earlier in Genesis. Moreover, the word "men" appears in verse 1 and has the generic sense, referring to all humankind. There is no indication that the same word in verse 2 should be restricted to the line of Cain. Also, the contrast is not between good men and bad men, but expressly between the divine and the mortal. Finally, Job 38:7 says that when the stars were created, the *běnêy hāĕlōhîm* shouted for joy. This would seem to indicate that the "sons of God" existed prior to creation; therefore, they can hardly be the descendants of Seth, or ancient Near Eastern potentates for that matter.

(4) The most natural interpretation is to understand the *běnêy hāĕlōhîm* here as the junior (second, third, fourth generation) deities of the divine pantheon. Our monotheistic lens forbids us from seeing this, but it is quite clear if we can take those goggles off for a moment. The same phrase (*běnêy hāĕlōhîm*) appears in Ugaritic, Phoenician, Akkadian, and Aramaic inscriptions; and in all of these cases it means, unequivocally, "junior deities." Moreover, the "sons of Elyon" in Ps 82:6 are explicitly identified as gods and, as noted above, the *běnêy hāĕlōhîm* in Job 38:7 are said to have been present when the stars were put in their place. Finally, this reading of the account closely parallels other ancient myths about the heroic children of gods and humans (e.g., Hercules); this explains the prowess of the Nephilim. In all likelihood, this little narrative is a very early etiology explaining the origins of "giants."[14]

Yahweh vs. Kemosh[15]

Further evidence for the polytheistic worldview of the writers of Hebrew scripture can be found in 2 Kgs 3:4–27. In this account, an alliance of three kings, headed by Jehoram, king of Israel, conspires to defeat the Moabite king Mesha and his army in battle, with Yahweh's help. At first, the three kings are afraid that they might not be victorious over Mesha, so they seek out a

---

14. By ancient Near Eastern standards, someone is considered a giant if they are over six feet tall. (People were shorter back then.)

15. On this episode, see Rollston and Parker, 2 *Kings*, 331–32.

prophet to pronounce a war oracle.[16] Elisha happens to be among their ranks, and after seeking Yahweh, he offers the kings this oracle: "This is a trivial thing as far as Yahweh is concerned. He will deliver Moab into your hands. You will destroy every fortified city and every fine city; you will chop down every fruitful tree, you will plug up every spring of water, and every productive piece of land you will riddle with stones" (2 Kgs 3:18–19).

Victory is assured to Israel, Judah and Edom, against Moab, according to Yahweh's prophet Elisha. Thus they proceed to set a trap for Mesha. Employing an optical illusion, Yahweh leads Mesha directly into an ambush. When it is clear that the Moabites are losing the battle, Mesha makes a covenant with his god Kemosh, and offers up his firstborn son, successor to his throne, as a sacrifice in exchange for victory in battle. "When the king of Moab realized that the battle was not going his way, he attempted to break through the ranks against the king of Edom with seven hundred swordsmen; but they could not. Then he took his firstborn son who was meant to succeed him as king, and offered him as a burnt sacrifice on the wall" (2 Kgs 3:26–27a). What happens next is startling. It is apparent from the narrator's perspective that Kemosh accepts the human sacrifice: "And great wrath came against Israel, so the coalition withdrew from him [Mesha] and returned to their own land" (3:27b).

Here it is clear that the narrator assumes not only the existence of Kemosh, but that Kemosh was strong enough to defeat Yahweh in battle, which is precisely what happens. The allied forces are routed and forced to retreat, because of the "wrath" that "came upon" them. The clear implication is that the wrath that came upon Israel is the wrath of Kemosh, who accepted Mesha's sacrifice.[17]

Some have raised objections to this interpretation, arguing either that the wrath that came upon Israel was the wrath of Yahweh, or that the wrath refers to the force of the Moabite soldiers who, after Mesha's sacrifice, became emboldened and fought harder on account of their belief that Kemosh was now appeased. The problem with the first alternative is obvious. Why would Yahweh pour out his wrath on his own soldiers in response to Mesha's sacrifice to Kemosh? This would make Yahweh capricious. If Yahweh was so appalled by the sacrifice of Mesha's son, one would think Yahweh would pour out his wrath on Mesha, not on the Israelites and their allies who bore no responsibility whatsoever.

16. All ancient Near Eastern peoples had prophets that functioned in this way.

17. In the ancient Near East—not excluding the Hebrew Bible, as we will see in the next chapter—it was a common belief that a nation's patron deity would fight on their behalf in exchange for human sacrifice.

The other alternative deserves more consideration. Could the wrath simply refer to the wrath of the Moabite soldiers against Israel, who were emboldened based upon their belief that the sacrifice of Mesha's son to their god was efficacious? A look at the use of the word *qesep* ("wrath") in the Hebrew Bible will help clarify its meaning. In its noun form, *qesep* occurs only twenty-eight times. Of those twenty-eight occurrences, only three do not refer to the wrath of a deity. In Esth 1:18 and Eccl 5:17 it simply means "anger." In Hos 10:7 it is used metaphorically for the "froth" on the surface of water. However, the vast majority (twenty-four of twenty-eight) of the occurrences refer to the wrath of a deity, usually that of Yahweh.[18] Of those twenty-four, eighteen instances refer to the wrath of a deity upon an army, congregation or nation. The remaining occurrence is our text here in 2 Kings 3. Note that not once does the word *qesep* refer to the wrath of an army.

Since it would make no sense for Yahweh to pour out his wrath upon his own armies for the sin of their enemy, it is clear that the wrath referred to in this narrative is that of Kemosh, the Moabite god. Likely what we see here is an attempt of the historian to provide an explanation for the reality of their defeat in battle. Through Elisha, Yahweh had promised them victory. They believed that Yahweh was stronger than Kemosh. Such a dramatic turn in the tide of the battle, resulting in the retreat of a coalition of three nations, would certainly have produced cognitive dissonance. The story of Mesha's sacrifice to Kemosh provides a suitable explanation for the defeat. Under ordinary circumstances, Yahweh would have defeated Kemosh, but in this case, Kemosh was specially empowered by the blood offering of the king's son—a sacrifice greater than which none could be conceived.

I will have more to say about this passage when I move onto the subject of human sacrifice in ancient Israel, but for the time being, suffice it to demonstrate further evidence for Israel's belief in the existence and potency of deities other than Yahweh. Clearly, this is not just a "popular belief," but one represented by the authors of our own scriptures.

Yahweh's Ascendancy

If Israel began with a polytheistic worldview, how can we account for its shift to monotheism? There are several passages throughout the writings and the prophets that help us to recognize a pattern of development from polytheism to monotheism. We have just finished looking at a handful of passages

---

18. Num 1:53; 16:46; 18:5; Deut 29:28; Josh 9:20; 22:20; 1 Chr 27:24; 2 Chr 19:2; 19:10; 24:18; 29:8; 32:25, 26; Ps 38:1; 102:10; Isa 34:2; 54:8; 60:10; Jer 10:10; 21:5; 32:37; 50:13; Zech 1:2; 7:12.

that represent early Israel's polytheism. Deuteronomy 32 represents probably the earliest period, when Yahweh is portrayed as a son of El Elyon, a junior member of the divine pantheon, who receives Israel as an inheritance from his father.

But as Israel grew in strength as a nation, developed a monarchy and a military power, we see evidence that Yahweh received a promotion in Israel's mythology. In the ancient Near East, a nation's strength was thought to mirror the strength of its patron deity. This is a common idea in the ancient Near Eastern mythologies, perhaps best represented in the *Enuma Elish* creation myth, which tells of Marduk's rise to supremacy among the gods, after his defeat of the goddess Tiamat. This myth parallels Babylon's own ascendancy as an imperial power. So it is not surprising, after the rise of the monarchy in Israel and with various attempts to consolidate political power, to see Yahweh ascend to the head of the pantheon in Israel's own theology. We see this very clearly in Psalm 82:

> God has established his place in the divine council;
> in the midst of the gods he judges. (82:1)

Here Israel's god is said to set himself up on the throne, indicating that Yahweh has made a power play. In this psalm, Yahweh goes on to critique the gods of other nations for their many injustices. In the ancient world one of the fundamental duties of a monarch was to uphold justice. Israel's god is thus portrayed here as "king" of the gods. He says to them,

> You are gods,
> all of you are sons of Elyon;
> but surely you will die like men,
> and fall like one of the princes. (82:6–7)

Here again is a clear reference to the divine pantheon. Yahweh has now ascended to the top, but in this psalm he is still distinct from Elyon. Here he pronounces judgment, declaring war against the gods because of their injustice, despite their ancestry. This motif of one god declaring war against the others has numerous parallels in the ancient Near Eastern mythologies.

In Psalm 29 again we see Yahweh at the top of the pantheon of deities:

> Give to Yahweh, O sons of gods,
> give to Yahweh glory and strength.
> Give to Yahweh the glory of his name;
> worship Yahweh in the splendor of holiness. (29:1–2)

Once more in Psalm 89, a clear reference to the divine council, and Yahweh's ascendancy to its throne:

> May the heavens acclaim your marvelous deeds, O Yahweh,
> your faithfulness in the assembly of holy ones.
> For who in heaven can be compared to Yahweh?
> Who among the sons of the gods is like Yahweh,
> a god who terrifies the council of the holy ones,
> who is feared by all that are around him? (89:5–7)

Yahweh is depicted in Job 1 and 2 in the same way: "On a certain day the sons of God came to present themselves before Yahweh, and the Adversary was also among them" (1:6). "On a certain day the sons of God came to present themselves before Yahweh, and the Adversary also came among them to present himself before Yahweh" (2:1). Here he is depicted as the head of the pantheon, presiding over the divine council of the gods. This image is reminiscent of numerous ancient Near Eastern and Greco-Roman epics in which the gods deliberate over the righteousness or prowess of a man or group.[19]

Psalm 87 reflects a significant shift. Here Yahweh is identified as El Elyon (God Most High):

> And it will be said of Zion,
> "This man and that man were born in her";
> and Elyon himself will establish her.
> Yahweh recounts, as he registers the people,
> "This man was born there." (87:5–6)

This reflects a time period in which El, the god of the patriarchs, is beginning to be identified with Yahweh. This shift is also reflected in Exodus 3, when Yahweh identifies himself to Moses as the God of Abraham, Isaac, and Jacob. It is at this point that Yahweh begins to be identified as the creator God, but this is still not monotheism.[20]

A major shift toward monotheism does not come until the late seventh century BCE, just a few decades before the Babylonian exile.[21] Perhaps conveniently, it also coincides with the Josianic reforms, in which the high places

19. The Adversary (the *Śāṭān*) is not yet seen as a rebellious enemy in the Israelite mythology. The Adversary here acts as an agent of Yahweh whose concern is to ensure that God's people are righteous. This is the same role the Adversary plays in Zechariah 3, in which he is concerned to preserve the purity of Yahweh's temple. It is not until the Second Temple period that Satan becomes an enemy of Yahweh, and only then is he identified by some apocalyptic thinkers as the serpent in Genesis 3. (Here I am indebted to Christopher Rollston.)

20. Note in Gen 14:19, Melchizedek refers to his deity El Elyon as the "maker of heaven and earth." Now that Yahweh is being conflated with El Elyon here in the late monarchical period, the status of creator god is inevitably ascribed to Yahweh as well.

21. For a more complex yet concise breakdown of the development from polytheism to monotheism in Israel, see Smith, *Early History of God*, 182–99, especially 189–94.

of worship (which were normative from at least the time of David on) are torn down, their priests slaughtered *en masse* by Josiah and his military, and strict religious centralization (a novelty in Judean religion) is imposed. We see this reflected in Jeremiah, a sympathizer with the Josianic reforms who characterized foreign deities as the concoctions of artisans. In Jer 10:1–16, for instance, the gods of other nations are said to have perished. They are no more. In fact, they are merely the work of human hands; they are not gods at all. This idea is further solidified during the Babylonian exile, as reflected in Second Isaiah:[22]

> All who make idols are nothing, and the things they delight in do not profit; their witnesses neither see nor know. And so they will be put to shame. Who would fashion a god or cast an image that can do no good? Look, all its devotees shall be put to shame; the artisans too are merely human. Let them all assemble, let them stand up; they shall be terrified, they shall all be put to shame. The ironsmith fashions it and works it over the coals, shaping it with hammers, and forging it with his strong arm; he becomes hungry and his strength fails, he drinks no water and is faint. The carpenter stretches a line, marks it out with a stylus, fashions it with planes, and marks it with a compass; he makes it in human form, with human beauty, to be set up in a shrine. He cuts down cedars or chooses a holm tree or an oak and lets it grow strong among the trees of the forest. He plants a cedar and the rain nourishes it. Then it can be used as fuel. Part of it he takes and warms himself; he kindles a fire and bakes bread. Then he makes a god and worships it, makes it a carved image and bows down before it. Half of it he burns in the fire; over this half he roasts meat, eats it and is satisfied. He also warms himself and says, "Ah, I am warm, I can feel the fire!" The rest of it he makes into a god, his idol, bows down to it and worships it; he prays to it and says, "Save me, for you are my god!"
>
> They do not know, nor do they comprehend; for their eyes are shut, so that they cannot see, and their minds as well, so that they cannot understand. No one considers, nor is there knowledge or discernment to say, "Half of it I burned in the fire; I also baked bread on its coals, I roasted meat and have eaten. Now shall I make the rest of it an abomination? Shall I fall down before a block of wood?" He

22. Scholars generally divide the book of Isaiah into three parts: (1) chapters 1–39 represent First Isaiah, written by Isaiah himself or transcribed by his scribes from his original oracles more than one hundred years before the Babylonian exile; (2) chapters 40–55 represent Second Isaiah, written toward the end of the Babylonian exile by an anonymous poet in the school of Isaiah; and (3) chapters 56–66 representing Third Isaiah, written by anonymous disciples of Isaiah in the years immediately after the Babylonian exile.

feeds on ashes; a deluded mind has led him astray, and he cannot save himself or say, "Is not this thing in my right hand a fraud?" (Isa 44:9–20, NRSV)

This satirical polemic[23] represents a point-of-no-return in the official theology of Israel. Now that other national deities have been exposed as *false* gods, no gods at all, there is no turning back. Israel would never again struggle, as it did so often in former times, with the worship of foreign deities, now that the very notion of deities other than Yahweh has become laughable (Yahweh's extensive network of divine retainers notwithstanding).

How can this development be explained? We may be inclined to attribute it to divine revelation, and that may very well be. But there are historical factors to consider as well. It certainly is a very small jump from the middle period—outlined above, in which Yahweh is seen as the king of the gods—to monotheism. Yahweh is said to be so much greater, so much more powerful than all other deities, eventually it becomes incoherent even to speak of these other beings as gods at all—so vast is the expanse between their strength and that of Yahweh. Yet this feature is not exactly unique to Israel. All great nations believed their patron deity possessed immeasurably greater strength than the gods of their enemies. Nevertheless, Israel (remarkably) is the only nation ever to make that small leap over to thoroughgoing, sustained monotheism.

Their experience in exile certainly had something to do with it. The idea that oppression by a foreign nation was the punishment of an unhappy patron deity is a common one throughout the ancient Near East. The Mesha Stele attests to this. According to the Mesha Inscription, the Moabites had been oppressed by the Israelite dynasty of Omri for several generations. Mesha interprets this oppression as punishment from his god Kemosh for their sins against him. This idea, so thoroughly attested in the Hebrew prophets, is not unique to Israel. It seems to reflect a common explanation ancient peoples gave for the reality of suffering.

The Babylonian exile was such a jarring experience for Israel that it could not but have had an influence on their theology. Usually, it was be-

---

23. As scholars of the ancient world are well aware, Jeremiah and Second Isaiah's language is purely polemical; it is not an accurate representation of ancient Near Eastern religion. The cultic images that were crafted by human hands were not considered to be gods; they were merely representations of the gods which were believed to have existed beyond human comprehension. Thus, when Jeremiah and Isaiah mock worshipers of other gods for bowing down to wooden objects, they are fundamentally misrepresenting the religions they are attacking. This misrepresentation may reflect inter-cultural ignorance on Jeremiah and Second Isaiah's part; more likely, the tendentious representation of foreign religion is intentional and serves the polemicists' own nationalist agendas.

lieved that a nation was as great as its deity. Victory in warfare meant the superior strength of their patron god. Defeat meant his or her inferior strength. This was often symbolized in warfare when the victors would confiscate the palladium of their defeated foes (e.g., 1 Sam 4:11). But the belief in Yahweh's supremacy over the other gods had become so firmly established in Israel's theology by the time of the exile that they could not interpret their experience as Yahweh's defeat without unraveling the very fabric of their national identity. The religious ruling elite, therefore, had a vested interest in sustaining Yahweh's supremacy. Thus the exile could not be attributed to the strength of Marduk (the Babylonian god). It was necessary to credit it to Yahweh. It is interpreted as Yahweh's punishment for Israel's sins. Yahweh's supremacy is therefore amplified, and this is reflected in the solidification of the belief that Yahweh alone is God. The jump to monotheism is still unprecedented in the ancient Near East,[24] but it is not without historical explanation.[25]

* * *

This brief look at the development in Israelite religion from polytheism to monotheism reveals a significant crack in the doctrine of inerrancy. We may not blame early Israel for being a product of its culture's mythological interpretation of history, but blame is not the issue here. The issue is the claim of inerrantists that the Bible possesses perfect theological unity. In contrast to such a presupposition, it is difficult to reconcile a polytheistic worldview with monotheism. Much simpler than the many attempts of committed inerrantists to reconcile these vastly diverse biblical ideas is the recognition that the Bible contains different ideas about God—different ideas that reflect the dif-

---

24. A single, irrelevant exception being an Egyptian foray into monotheism that lasted only a single dynasty, before Israel even came into existence.

25. To this explanation, Smith, *Early History of God*, 194, adds that "new reflections developed out of Israel's new social circumstances as well as its new political situation on the international stage from the seventh century on. The loss of family patrimonies due to economic stress and foreign incursions contribute to the demise of the model of the family for understanding divinity. With the rise of the individual along with the family as significant units of social identity came the corresponding notion on the divine level, namely of a single god responsible for the cosmos. Judah's reduced status on the world scene also required new thinking about divinity. Like Marduk, Yahweh became an 'empire-god,' the god of all the nations but in a way that no longer closely tied the political fortunes of Judah to the status of this god. With the old order of divine king and his human, royal representation on earth reversed, Yahweh stands alone in the divine realm, with all the other gods as nothing. In short, the old head-god of monarchic Israel became the Godhead of the universe." Smith develops these points further in *Origins of Biblical Monotheism*, 77–79, 163–66.

ferent cultures and circumstances in which the various biblical writers found themselves. In a very real way, the texts we have looked at in this chapter reveal how Israel's theology mirrored the various theologies of their neighbors, and how it was adapted over time in order to accommodate the changing socio-political fortunes of Israel.

5 MAKING YAHWEH HAPPY
HUMAN SACRIFICE IN ANCIENT ISRAEL

HUMAN SACRIFICE WAS AN ORDINARY PART OF ANCIENT NEAR Eastern religion. It was generally believed that the gods fed off of the blood of humans, that they could be satiated (satisfied) by human sacrifice, and that in exchange for human sacrifice the gods would give favor to their worshipers, usually in the form of victory in battle or in increased rainfall and crop productivity. Virtually every ancient Near Eastern cult practiced sacrifice. Animal sacrifice was acceptable, but human sacrifice was considered more efficacious for obvious reasons—humans were the more valuable, thus the greater sacrifice.

It is clear that in various times and places human sacrifice was practiced in Israel. The practice was fairly widespread, as the later prophetic denunciations of the practice indicate. At least one King—Manasseh—sacrificed his son, heir to the throne, according to 2 Kgs 21:6. Ordinarily we read instances like this through the lens of the later prophetic denunciations of human sacrifice (seventh and sixth centuries BCE). We assume that human sacrifice was always considered idolatrous, that it deviated from official, orthodox Israelite religion. But there is good evidence (much of which is internal to the Hebrew Bible canon itself) that human sacrifice was considered not only efficacious, but commendable in official Israelite religion.

In this chapter, we will be taking a tour of a number of legal, narrative, and prophetic texts. Some of these texts have been read as criticisms of human sacrifice, but I will show that these readings are anachronistic, that rather in every case belief in the efficacy and virtuousness of human sacrifice is upheld. This will be an exercise in re-reading. We will need to temporarily suspend our disbelief in order to look at these familiar texts using a different paradigm. If we can do this, I believe we will come to see that in the case of human sacrifice, pre-exilic Israel held largely the same beliefs as their Canaanite and ancient Near Eastern neighbors.

Human Sacrifice in the Mosaic Law[1]

Evidence for the general acceptance of the ideology of human sacrifice per-
vades the Hebrew Bible. We will begin by looking at two pertinent texts in
the legal code of the book of Exodus (22:29b and 34:20b).

Exod 22:29b represents this ideology in the starkest of terms: "Your
firstborn sons you shall give to me." The demand is unequivocal. The traditional solution is to read the provision for the redemption of the firstborn
sons found in Exod 34:20b back onto the unqualified command in 22:29b.
This provision reads: "All your firstborn sons you shall ransom. You shall not
come before me empty-handed." In other words, Yahweh demands the blood
of the firstborn sons of Israel as satiation, but allows Israel to sacrifice an
animal instead of their sons. Some interpreters believe this settles the matter.
No human sacrifice is actually envisioned here. Yet several considerations
disqualify this strategy as an easy solution to the problem.

First, the logic of the requirement of the firstborn is not repudiated
in 34:20b. Yahweh still demands the blood of the firstborn, but is willing to
accept an animal substitution as satiation. This is more significant than we
might think. If human sacrifice is abhorrent to Yahweh, why does Yahweh
not simply say so? Yahweh does not say, "I am not like other gods. I do not
demand the blood of your firstborn sons." On the contrary, Yahweh does
indeed demand their blood, but is willing to accept a lesser sacrifice in their
stead. The logic of human sacrifice is not repudiated here, but sustained.

Second, the archaeological record indicates that other ancient cultures,
cultures that certainly practiced child sacrifice, also allowed for the substitution of animals in a child's stead. Archaeological digs in the ancient Near
East have discovered the remains of children who had been the subjects of
sacrifice, buried in the same fashion and on the same site as the remains of
animals that had been sacrificed.[2] Child sacrifice was considered a nobler
sacrifice than mere animal sacrifice for the obvious reason that one's children
were more valuable than one's livestock. Thus it is clear that the provision
for the redemption of the firstborn in Exod 34:20b is not evidence that child
sacrifice was forbidden.

Third, Exod 34:20a indicates very plainly that the motivation for the
redemption of a sacrifice is not moral in nature, but utilitarian. The full verse
reads, "The firstborn of a donkey shall be ransomed with a lamb, or if you
will not ransom it, break its neck. All your firstborn sons you shall ransom.
You shall not come before me empty-handed." In the first case, the firstborn

---

1. My argument in this section is indebted to Levenson, *Death and Resurrection*,
3–4.

2. See for instance, Stager and Wolff, "Child Sacrifice at Carthage," 31–51.

of a donkey is demanded to satiate the deity, but it is to be substituted with a lamb. Is this because a donkey's life is intrinsically more valuable, in a moral sense, than that of a lamb? Not exactly. A donkey is a more useful animal in an agrarian society, and thus its substitution serves a clear utilitarian function. In the same way, a child laborer is more valuable in an agrarian society than any animal. The utilitarian logic prevails here as well. No moral motivation is offered for the redemption of the firstborn sons.

Finally, and most significantly, as we will see below, later texts indicate that ancient Israelites interpreted Exod 22:29b as a command to offer their firstborn sons to Yahweh, and that many indeed carried out these instructions. The provision for substitution in 34:20b was not interpreted as a normative provision, or else the practice of child sacrifice which was so widespread in ancient Israel could not have claimed any legal basis. The most significant of these later texts is perhaps Ezek 20:18–26, which we will discuss in more detail below.

Human Sacrifice in the History Books

Abraham and Isaac

> And he said, 'Now take your son, your only son whom you love, Isaac, and go to the land of Moriah and offer him there as a sacrifice on one of the mountains which I will point out to you. (Gen 22:2)

We are familiar with the story. Abraham takes Isaac to the place of sacrifice, binds his son upon an altar, and just as he is about to strike Isaac dead, Yahweh's messenger calls to Abraham from the heavens and stops his hand. Abraham had passed the test of loyalty to Yahweh. A ram is discovered in a nearby thicket, and Abraham offers it to Yahweh in Isaac's stead.

This account of the near-sacrifice of Isaac is commonly read as a repudiation of child sacrifice, but this is an anachronism. At least since Kierkegaard, moreover, the drama of the narrative has been understood to revolve around an ethical crisis: obedience to Yahweh is pitted against ethical norms that condemn child sacrifice.[3] But the crisis for Abraham does not revolve around the ethics of child sacrifice; child sacrifice was an ordinary part of Abraham's culture. The crisis revolves around the fact that Yahweh's promise to Abraham was put in jeopardy by Yahweh's command to Abraham. A careful reading of the account will reveal that the logic of child sacrifice is never repudiated in the narrative. On the contrary, Abraham is held up as the archetypical model of faithfulness precisely because of his willingness to

3. See Levenson, "Abusing Abraham," 268–69.

do what by later standards is considered one of the most heinous, morally depraved acts imaginable. As Jon Levenson comments, "It is passing strange to condemn child sacrifice through a narrative in which a father is richly rewarded for his willingness to carry out that very practice."[4] The account ultimately sustains the logic of child sacrifice.

Jephthah and His Daughter

The account of Jephthah's vow in Judg 11:29–40 is even more relevant. A vow is made by the warrior Jephthah to the war-god Yahweh; a human sacrifice is offered in exchange for victory in battle. If Yahweh will make Jephthah victorious in battle, Jephthah vows to sacrifice to Yahweh the first person to greet him upon his return home.[5] Traditional readings of this account usually revolve around the rashness of Jephthah's vow, but the narrative itself is a tragedy, not a polemic. Upon his victorious return, Jephthah is greeted by his virgin daughter, and Jephthah must offer her up to Yahweh as satiation, in keeping with the vow.

Unlike the account in Genesis 22, in this case Jephthah goes through with the sacrifice, which makes the lack of censure in the text all the more striking. The narrator affirms the logic of human sacrifice. Indeed, even Jephthah's own daughter, the tragic victim of a battle-vow, affirms the system: "My father, if you have opened your mouth to Yahweh, do to me according to what has gone out of your mouth, since Yahweh has taken vengeance against your enemies on your behalf" (Judg 11:36). The logic of the narrative implies that a man's vow to a god was more valuable than a human life. Indeed, "Jephthah's actions are intelligible only on the assumption that his daughter—he had no son—could legitimately be sacrificed as a burnt offering to YHWH."[6] No repudiation of the sacrifice is found here. Nor does Yahweh intervene to spare the life of Jephthah's daughter. The mood of the narrative "is one of great pathos rather than moralistic judgment."[7] Jephthah is portrayed as a tragic hero here. Even in the Christian scriptures, Jephthah

---

4. Levenson, *Death and Resurrection*, 13.

5. Some commentators argue that Jephthah could have been envisioning an animal sacrifice, because the Hebrew word does not necessarily mean "person," but simply, "the one coming forth." This argument is a bit tenuous, however, since it was not common practice in those days—or in ours—for a man's livestock to come out of his house to greet him.

6. Levenson, *Death and Resurrection*, 14.

7. Ibid.

is praised as a champion of Yahweh, who "through faith . . . became mighty in battle and sent foreign armies running scared" (Heb 11:33, 34).

King Mesha and His Son

In the last chapter we looked at 2 Kings 3, the account of the Moabite King Mesha's battle with the allied armies of Israel, Judah, and Edom. Mesha, losing the battle, makes a covenant with his god Kemosh and sacrifices his firstborn son, heir to his throne, in exchange for victory in battle. The narrator tells us that after Mesha sacrificed his son, the tables turn, a "great wrath" came against Israel, and they were forced to retreat. We have already noted how this constitutes evidence for the assumption of the existence of other deities (in this case Kemosh) on the part of the biblical narrator. Here we cite it as evidence for the biblical narrator's belief in the efficacy of human sacrifice. Let's look at the text again:

> When the king of Moab realized that the battle was not going his way, he attempted to break through the ranks against the king of Edom with seven hundred swordsmen; but they could not. Then he took his firstborn son who was meant to succeed him as king, and offered him as a burnt sacrifice on the wall. And great wrath came against Israel, so the coalition withdrew from him [Mesha] and returned to their own land. (2 Kgs 3:26–27)

The most natural reading of the text here would seem to indicate that Mesha's sacrifice worked—that Kemosh was satiated and in return kept up his end of the bargain. Kemosh's wrath was leveled against Israel, Judah, and Edom and they were forced to retreat. Let us look again briefly at two alternative readings of this passage.

(1) The narrator does not necessarily believe in the efficacy of human sacrifice, but the Israelite armies did so believe. When they learned of Mesha's sacrifice they were overcome with fear and retreated. There are two damning problems with this reading. First, the text never indicates that the Israelites knew about the sacrifice of Mesha's son. Second, the text does not say they were overcome with fear (an internal force); it says that great wrath came upon them (an external force).

(2) The "wrath" that came against Israel was not the wrath of Kemosh but the wrath of the Moabite armies. This explanation follows this logic: Mesha sacrificed his son in exchange for victory, a superstition in which the Moabite armies believed. Thus they were emboldened after so great a sacrifice, assuming the aid of Kemosh was now with them. Their renewed

boldness in combat is what the text refers to when it says that "great wrath came upon Israel."

To the extent that an actual historical battle is recorded here (its historicity is debated by scholars), this reading is probably valid as a sociological explanation for the dramatic shift in the course of the battle. Not many of us would profess belief in the Moabite deity Kemosh. Accordingly, most of us would assume that a human sacrifice to Kemosh could not be in any way efficacious. Yet the soldiers believed in both Kemosh and in the efficaciousness of the sacrifice, and therefore were emboldened to fight fearlessly, thus turning the tides of the battle. We can accept this as a demythologizing interpretation of the text.

The problem of course is that the narrator of the book of Kings does not so demythologize the text. As discussed in the previous chapter, the Hebrew noun *qeṣep* (wrath) occurs twenty-eight times in the Hebrew Bible. Of those twenty-eight occurrences, twenty-four refer to the wrath of a deity. Two refer to human anger in a very general sense. One is somewhat poetic and refers to the froth (i.e., *wrath*) on the surface of the sea. The final occurrence is here in 2 Kgs 3:27. Not one of the twenty-eight occurrences refers to the wrath of an army or of any sort of warrior. Thus it is clear that the most natural reading is to see this as a reference to the wrath of a deity, in this case Kemosh. The word is associated with deities twenty-five out of twenty-eight times. That is 89 percent of the time.

It is clear, therefore, that the biblical narrator does not himself demythologize these events. The strongest reading indicates that the narrator was attributing Israel's defeat to the power of the Moabite god Kemosh, and indirectly to the efficacy of human sacrifice. This reading coheres with the ideology of human sacrifice we have seen represented in the accounts of the binding of Isaac and the sacrifice of Jephthah's daughter. The latter account in fact closely parallels the logic here, for in both cases the belief is that deities are willing to offer aid in battle in exchange for human sacrifice.

Sacrificing the Spoils of War

Another form of this arrangement between warriors and their gods can be seen in the ancient practice of *herem*, a Semitic term referring to the devotion or consecration of objects to a divine being, sometimes called "the ban" in warfare contexts. As an alternative to the sacrificial offering of a loved one, as with the warrior Jephthah, it was also possible to exchange the spoils of war for the promise of victory. "The ban as sacrifice is an ideology of war in which the enemy is to be utterly destroyed as an offering to the deity who has made victory possible. Implicit in this ideology is a view of God who appreciates human sacrifice."[8] The Moabite Stone, a ninth century BCE victory stele detailing the aforementioned King Mesha's exploits, offers an example of the ancient Near Eastern belief that the sacrifice of human spoils could be offered to the gods in exchange for victory in battle. "And Kemosh said to me, 'Go, seize Nebo from Israel.' So I went at night and I attacked it from the break of dawn until noon when I seized it and I slew everybody in it—seven thousand men, boys, ladies, girls, and maidens—for to the warrior Kemosh I devoted them."[9] Here the deity issues an order to attack an enemy, and, in exchange for victory, the spoils of war (wives and slave-laborers) are offered as a sacrifice to satiate the deity. They are devoted (*herem*) to the warrior-god Kemosh.

A biblical parallel to the sort of thing we see in the Mesha Inscription can be seen in Numbers 21. Here, Israel is facing a Canaanite enemy, the king of Arad and his armies. Israel (collectively) makes a vow to Yahweh: "'If you will indeed give this people into my hands then I will devote their cities to destruction.' Then Yahweh listened to the voice of Israel, and handed over the Canaanites; and they devoted them and their cities to destruction" (21:2–3).[10] Here again, the sacrificial nature of the *herem* is clear. Yahweh promises victory to the Israelites against Arad's forces, and in exchange Israel promises Yahweh the sacrificial offering of the cities' inhabitants (noncombatants). The "sacrifice" entailed the forfeiture of virgin wives and potential slaves out of gratitude to the deity for the victory. Similar sacrificial arrangements can be seen in Josh 6:17–21 and 8:2, 24–29.

---

8. Niditch, *War in the Hebrew Bible*, 151. In his critique of scholars who argue that an ideology of human sacrifice lies behind the earliest forms of Israelite holy war, Paul Copan misleadingly quotes Susan Niditch (*War in the Hebrew Bible*, 46) when she writes that the "dominant voice in the Hebrew Bible treats the ban not as sacrifice in exchange for victory but as just and deserved punishment." Copan fails to mention that Niditch had already made the case that the "dominant voice" on this matter was not the *earliest* voice in the Hebrew Bible. Whereas the later, "dominant voice" condemned human sacrifice, the "earliest voice" approved of it. Intentionally or not, Copan pulls the wool over his readers' eyes by using Niditch selectively to reinforce a similarly selective reading of the biblical data, one that she herself exposes. See Copan, "Yahweh Wars and the Canaanites," 2.

9. The Mesha Stele, lines 14–17. This is the translation of Stern, *Biblical Ḥerem*, 55.

10. This is the translation of Niditch, *War in the Hebrew Bible*, 32.

Human Sacrifice in the Prophets

It is clear from the texts we have looked at so far that human sacrifice played at least some role in the religion of early Israel. This is evinced, especially, in the fact that in the seventh and sixth centuries BCE—just prior to and during the Babylonian exile—the practice began to be roundly condemned by the prophets. We will now look at three important texts in this regard. The first text (Mic 6:6–8), composed during the reign of Hezekiah, is significant not because it represents a condemnation of human sacrifice—as it is frequently understood—but because it shows the persistence of the logic of human sacrifice as late as the eighth century. The second and third texts (Jer 19:5–6 and Ezek 20:18–26) are significant because they reflect two different strategies, strategies clearly at odds with one another, for explaining the phenomenon of human sacrifice in Israelite religion, and for condemning it.

Micah 6:6–8[11]

> With what shall I come before Yahweh,
> bowing myself before the high God?
> Shall I come to him with burnt offerings,
> with one-year-old calves?
> Will Yahweh be satisfied with thousands of rams,
> with ten thousand of rivers of oil?
> *Shall I offer my firstborn for my transgression,*
> *the fruit of my loins for the sin of my soul?"*
> He has told you, O mortal man, what is good.
> What does Yahweh demand of you?
> Only to do justice, and to love covenant loyalty,
> and to walk humbly with your God?

This famous passage is often read as a condemnation of the practice of child sacrifice. The only basis for such a reading seems to be Micah's claim that child sacrifice does not please God; only justice, loyalty, and humility please God. But this is an arbitrary reading of the text. The logic is quite clear. It is not only child sacrifice that is said not to please God, but also the sacrifice of calves and rams and offerings of oil. And why is it said not to please God? Not because the acts in themselves are inherently immoral, but because Israel performs them *in lieu* of justice, loyalty, and humility. The point of the text

---

11. For this and the subsequent two sections I am beholden chiefly to Levenson, *Death and Resurrection*, 4–12.

is not that sacrifice is abhorrent, but that sacrifice without repentance from structures of injustice is useless.

Moreover, a closer reading of the text will show that human sacrifice is held up as the greatest type of sacrifice. There is a progression in three parts from the least to the greatest sacrifice. The first is year-old calves. The second is "thousands of rams, ten thousand of rivers of oil," an example of Hebrew parallelism. This is clearly a step up from a year-old calf. The crescendo culminates in the sacrifice of the firstborn child—the greatest of all the sacrifices, for obvious reasons.

Rather than a condemnation of child sacrifice, the logic of child sacrifice is upheld. It is seen in the text as the epitome of sacrifice—the greatest gift to be given. The "shock" of the text comes when even the greatest of sacrifices (child sacrifice) is said to be of no value without justice. Micah's rhetoric in fact depends upon the common assumption that the sacrifice of one's child is noble. If that assumption was not shared by his audience, his rhetoric would fall flat. The text does not condemn child sacrifice, or else it must necessarily also represent a condemnation of the sacrifice of calves and rams, and of the offering of oil. This is clearly not the intent of the text. Micah is simply making the point that Israel's sacrifices are meant to lead them to repentance, and that when they do not repent, the efficacy of such sacrifices is nullified. It is a progressive critique of the sacrificial system, to be sure, but a condemnation of the logic of sacrifice, even human sacrifice, it is not. As late as the time of Hezekiah, the logic of human sacrifice is still basic to Israelite religion.

Jeremiah 19:5–6

> They have built shrines to Baal, to put their children to the fire as burnt offerings to Baal—which I never commanded, never decreed, and which never came into my mind. Assuredly, a time is coming— declares [Yahweh]—when this place shall no longer be called Topheth or Valley of Ben-hinnom, but Valley of Slaughter.[12]

This is a beguiling text. On the surface it appears to be a simple, clear-cut condemnation of the practice of sacrificing children to a false god—Baal. But there are several problems with this reading. At the very least, the text testifies to the practice of child sacrifice in Israel. The question then becomes, what is the nature of this practice, and to which god are the Israelites sacrificing their children?

12. This is the translation of Levenson, *Death and Resurrection*, 4.

It is important to note that the divine name Baal originally was just a generic Semitic term for "lord." It was frequently applied to Yahweh and only began to be equated *in every case* with a distinct Canaanite deity in the eighth century, with the ministry of Hosea. This is reflected in the names for Saul's son and grandson. In the book of Chronicles their real names are preserved: Ishbaal and Meribaal. The first name simply means "man of Baal" and should just be understood as "the Lord's man," not as an indication that Saul's son worshiped a deity other than Yahweh. But the Deuteronomistic Historian (the author of the book of Kings), who was not favorably disposed toward Saul's dynasty, changed the names of these two sons of Saul to Ishbosheth and Mephiboshet. *Bōšet* means "shame," thus turning "the Lord's man" into a "man of shame."

Jeremiah, a contemporary of the Deuteronomistic Historian, shared Hosea's predilection to associate "Baal worship" with idol worship. But it is clear that there is a long history in Israelite religion of identifying Baal with Yahweh. By the seventh century, when Jeremiah writes, the identification of Baal as a false deity was quite well established among the elites, though not necessarily in the popular or mainstream religion.

This complexity is reflected in the text cited above; there are a number of semantic tensions. For instance, Jeremiah has Yahweh saying that he "did not command or decree" the practice of sacrificing children to Baal, that such a thing "never entered my mind." But this strains against credulity. If Baal is not Yahweh, and all worship of gods other than Yahweh has *always* been condemned from the earliest times, even in polytheistic Israelite religion, why then would Yahweh need to point out that he never decreed the practice of sacrificing children to another god? This is a classic case of "methinks thou dost protest too much."[13] Taking into consideration what we have outlined above with regard to the original semantics of "Baal" as an honorific epithet for Yahweh, it seems that beneath the surface of the text we can discern a situation in which popular Israelite religion is sacrificing Israelite children to "Baal," i.e., Yahweh, but the religious elites equate Baal with a foreign deity, a god other than Yahweh.

This seems to me the only way to make sense of the text. What Jeremiah's language comes down to, then, is an early attempt to equate child sacrifice *in general* with idolatry. It is clear from the legends of the binding of Isaac and from the sacrifice of Jephthah's daughter, as well as from the traditions represented in Exod 22:29 that child sacrifice was performed *for Yahweh*. Jeremiah's strategy for condemning child sacrifice, then, is (following Hosea)

13. So Levenson, *Death and Resurrection*, 4.

to depict "Baal" as a foreign god, and thus to relocate the practice of child sacrifice under the theological category of idolatry.

In short, Jeremiah is faced with a tradition of child sacrifice in popular Israelite religion, and his strategy for condemning it is to deny that Yahweh ever decreed it. Whence came the idea that Yahweh decreed child sacrifice? Perhaps it came, as we have seen, from Exod 22:29: "Your firstborn sons you shall give to me"—from the law of Moses itself. Additionally, Yahweh commanded Abraham to sacrifice his only son—the ultimate sacrifice—in a tradition which, as I have argued, remembers Abraham as the archetype of faith precisely on the point of his willingness to kill his son in order to satiate Yahweh. Jeremiah flatly denies that this was ever Yahweh's intention for Israel, and does so by attempting to depict all human sacrifice as a form of idolatry, precluding the very notion—a notion simply assumed by the prophet Micah just a few generations past—of a human sacrifice to Yahweh.[14] Yet the most significant attempt to condemn child sacrifice would not come until the following century, during the Babylonian exile, with the prophet Ezekiel.

Ezekiel 20:18–26

> I said to their sons in the wilderness, "Do not obey the laws of your fathers, nor follow their rules, nor defile yourselves with their idols. I, Yahweh, am your god. Obey my laws. Follow my rules. Keep my sabbaths holy, that they may be a sign between me and you, so that you may know that I, Yahweh, am your god." But the children defied me. They did not obey my laws. They did not follow my rules, my life-giving rules. They desecrated my sabbaths.
>
> So I said to myself, "I will pour out my wrath on them and exhibit my anger toward them in the wilderness." Nonetheless, I withheld my hand, for my name's sake, so that my name would not become disreputable in the sight of the nations, after they had watched me deliver Israel. Yet I raised my hand and took an oath be-

---

14. An identical strategy to that of Jeremiah is reflected in Deut 12:31, which associates all human sacrifice with idolatry. Although this portion of Deuteronomy is set during the Mosaic period, the scholarly consensus is that it was actually composed around the time of Jeremiah, and its legal material reflects religious and political concerns contemporaneous with Josiah. An obvious example of this is Deuteronomy 17 which gives detailed regulations restricting the powers of the monarch, more than two hundred years before Israel had a monarchy! One of the restrictions placed on the monarch is that he is not to acquire many wives. In 2 Sam 12:8, however, it is said that Yahweh blessed David with many wives. Especially given the religious problems that arose as a result of Solomon's political marriages, it is clear that this stipulation in Deuteronomy 17 reflects a time period after the monarchy in Israel has been well established.

fore [Israel] in the wilderness, that I would scatter them throughout the nations, and toss them into foreign lands, because they had not followed my rules, but had rejected my laws and desecrated my sabbaths, with their eyes fixed on the idols of their fathers. *Moreover, I gave them laws that were not good and rules by which they could not live; I corrupted them through their very gifts, when they offered up all their firstborn, so that I might make them desolate, so that they might know that I am Yahweh.*

If Jeremiah's strategy for dealing with the reality of the institution of child sacrifice in Israelite religion was to deny that Yahweh ever ordained it, Ezekiel's was precisely the opposite. Like Jeremiah, Ezekiel wants to condemn the institution of child sacrifice, but unlike Jeremiah, he does not think the institution's roots in the law of Moses (Exod 22:29) can be so easily denied. Particularly noteworthy about the above passage from Ezekiel is that the prophet just assumes that Yahweh did command Israelites to sacrifice their firstborn sons as a burnt offering. Ezekiel's strategy, therefore, is to interpret that command as a form of punishment for Israel's unfaithfulness in the wilderness.

Now some have argued that, rather than giving Israel bad commands, Yahweh *gave them over* to their depraved *interpretations* of Yahweh's good commands. This understanding of the text is reflected in the translation of the NIV: "I *gave them over* to statues that were not good" (emphasis added). The NIV intentionally mistranslates the verb here, probably in a well-intentioned attempt to protect Yahweh's character from the implications of scripture. The Hebrew verb is *nātān*, "to give." In the Hebrew, the indirect object of the sentence is "them" and the direct object of the verb is "statutes." The NIV, however, makes "them" the object of the verb and makes the statutes the recipients of the action. The NIV does this with zero exegetical warrant. It is a purely theologically motivated distortion of the text—a distortion of the text with which many of us could certainly sympathize. Nevertheless, the grammar is not ambiguous here, as much as we would like it to be. In no uncertain terms, Ezekiel claims that Yahweh gave bad commands to Israel, and the "bad command" Ezekiel specifically has in mind is the command to offer male children as a burnt offering to Yahweh.

According to Ezekiel, somehow Yahweh's bad command was given as a punishment, which was meant to have two effects upon Israel: to make them desolate (i.e., without firstborn sons) and to reveal to them who Yahweh is ("so that they might know that I am Yahweh"). Ezekiel's logic here is difficult to grasp, and we are left to conclude that Ezekiel, with the best of intentions, is struggling (stretching) to explain away the Mosaic institution of child sacrifice.

What are we to do with Ezekiel's claim? We can accept it as the reality, that Yahweh in fact did *intentionally* command Israel to sacrifice their firstborn sons as a form of punishment, that he intentionally gave them evil commands in order somehow to reveal his glory. Is this not the god that both Jeremiah and the Deuteronomistic historian reject, the one who punishes the son for the sins of the father (Jer 31:29–31; Deut 24:16)? This paints a portrait of a Yahweh who commands the violent, anguished death of children in order to punish the parents of those children. Here the old theological dictum that what God does is just simply because God is just is put to the test and, I am afraid, found wanting. This also raises further questions. If Yahweh gave his people one bad command as a form of punishment, how many other bad commands did Yahweh give?

In the end, I think the best explanation is to conclude that Ezekiel, with the best of intentions, was simply struggling with earlier biblical ideas about Yahweh in light of his convictions regarding the moral reprehensibility of human sacrifice, in an attempt to salvage Yahweh's character. Ezekiel may not have done a splendid job salvaging Yahweh's character, but we can commend the motivation driving the attempt. Human sacrifice is evil. Ezekiel knows that. We know that. Nevertheless, this text is extremely important because in it Ezekiel tells us in no uncertain terms that Yahweh did in fact command child sacrifice. This certainly puts our traditional readings of Exodus 22 (via Exodus 34) at odds with the text itself, especially given Ezekiel's interpretation of it. Once again, a commitment to biblical unity is seen here not only to be forcing itself on a text that cannot accept it, it puts those who hold such a commitment in the rather awkward position of having to affirm that Yahweh commanded something we know to be, quite simply, evil.

* * *

In this chapter we have seen how Israel's theology—at least as reflected by the writers of scripture—changed and developed over time. Once again we have seen how Israel's theological ideas mirrored the various theologies of their neighbors, in this case with reference to their belief in the nobility and efficacy of human sacrifice. In fact, the remnants of this belief may still be detected as late as the second temple period, when early Christians began to interpret the crucifixion of Jesus of Nazareth as a sacrificial death capable of satiating the wrath of Yahweh.

6 BLESSING THE NATIONS
YAHWEH'S GENOCIDES AND THEIR JUSTIFICATIONS

IMAGINE YOUR LOVED ONES. PICTURE THEIR FACES—YOUR MOTHER and father, your brothers and sisters, your husband or wife, your sons, your daughters. Picture yourselves sharing a meal together around a common hearth. Each of you cooperates each day to prepare the meal. Everyone does their part—some happily, others begrudgingly. Imagine the hugs. Imagine the laughter. Imagine the shouting and the scolding. This is your life.

Now imagine that one day a swarm of sword-wielding savages descends upon your town in an instant, raping, pillaging, killing, and destroying. Imagine seeing your grandmother cut down by a thug with a dark sword while another one forces your grandfather to watch. Imagine looking on while your brothers are dismembered as they attempt to protect the women and children. Picture yourself being forced to watch as your pregnant sister is shoved to her knees and beaten. Picture the man who calmly thrusts his blade into her womb before locking her in her home and setting it alight. You can hear her screams as the house burns down upon her, but you are powerless to do anything about it. Imagine watching as your sons, who are trying not to show their fear, are cut in half, one by one. The last one, the youngest, finally loses control and calls out to you in desperation, just before he is killed. His executioner mutters thanksgiving to some god as your boy falls lifeless to the ground. Imagine that the last thing you see is your daughters, bound with ropes and dragged off into the horizon. As their silhouettes become smaller and smaller against the dusty sunset, you realize you are face down in a pool of blood, bleeding to death from a wound you were not aware of until now. As your daughters fade into the horizon, your eyes close. You pray your girls die from heatstroke before being assigned as concubines to the men who slaughtered your people, your people's unborn children. This was your life.

There are countless stories much like this one, told by the black Africans of Darfur, the Tutsis and Hutus of Rwanda, Jewish Holocaust survivors, the Armenians of pre-revolutionary Turkey, the Native Americans under European colonization, and on into the deepest recesses of history. This is genocide—the systematic slaughter of a race or group of people in the name of some god or some ideology. Yet it is not just the slaughter of groups, it is the slaughter of individuals—each of whom had mothers and fathers, sisters and brothers, sons and daughters, friends and aspirations.

According to the Bible, this was the experience of hundreds of thousands of Canaanites, Midianites, and Amalekites whose testimony is lost to history, preserved only in the memories of their killers—the Israelites. In the books of Numbers, Deuteronomy, and Joshua, the Canaanites are depicted much like the Jewish people would later be characterized in Nazi propaganda, and much like the Native Americans would be portrayed in the annals of European invaders—unclean, uncivilized, inhuman, hostile, subversive, and godless. History is written by the victors. Like the ancient Israelites, most perpetrators of genocide justify their actions by reference to divine will and belief in a national destiny in which "all the clans of the earth will be blessed" through the hegemony of Israel (Gen 12:2-3), or Rome, or Germany, or the United States.

Of course, now with a single voice biblical inerrantists condemn genocide. They all agree that nothing could be farther from God's will. Yet despite the obvious parallels between the genocides perpetrated by the ancient Hebrews and those of modern day religious and ideological fanatics, biblical inerrantists make an exception for ancient Israel, insisting that the Canaanite genocides were not only wholly justified, but good. Although every genocidal regime claims to have the sanction of some deity, inerrantists insist that in ancient Israel's case, it was true. It had to be true, because it's in the Bible. Yahweh really did command his people to kill every living and breathing man, woman, and child in the land of Canaan—and in the overarching scheme of things, these actions too reveal a God of love.

In this chapter I will evaluate the standard justifications for these genocides that are offered by biblical inerrantists and Christian apologists. I will argue that every attempt to justify these acts fails. They are either contradicted by the biblical data themselves, or reflect a dangerous moral relativism that ultimately undermines the larger Christian theological project. Before concluding, however, I will show that there is biblical and archeological evidence that the accounts of the genocides recorded in the Bible are often highly exaggerated and at times even entirely fabricated. It will also become clear that the ideology reflected in these accounts is at odds with other perspectives that crop up later in the Hebrew and Christian scriptures.

To be clear, my argument is not that God is evil for commanding genocide. I am not claiming "to know better than God"—an accusation Christian apologists often make against Christians who hold my position.

My contention is that God never did command the Israelites to slaughter the Canaanites wholesale. These accounts reflect a standard ideology that Israel shared with many of its ancient neighbors, and I read them as products of ancient culture, rather than products of pure divine revelation. Therefore, my claim is not that I know better than God, but that we all know better than those who wrongly killed women and children in God's name.

I am not interested in some abstract philosophical discussion about the problem of evil. This is not a game of semantics or an exercise in theodicy. This is indiscriminate human carnage, and it involves real people, with real lives, real relationships, and real aspirations. This is what the Sudanese military and the Janjaweed militia are doing to black Africans in Darfur, what the Tutsis and the Hutus did to each other in Rwanda, what the Nazi party did to six million Jewish people all across Europe, what the Ottoman government did to one and a half million Armenians in Turkey. This is what the European invaders did to the Native Americans in the name of Manifest Destiny. And according to the Bible, this is what the Hebrews did to the Canaanites in the name of Yahweh Sabaoth—He Who Raises Armies.

Justifying Genocide

Eradicating the Cancer

One of the more common justifications for the Canaanite genocides comes straight out of the Bible. It says that the Canaanites needed to be utterly destroyed or else the survivors would propagate their own gods and their idolatrous practices would begin to permeate Israel, causing Israel to turn away from Yahweh. This rationale is seen most clearly in Deut 7:1–6:

> When Yahweh your God brings you into the land that you are
> about to enter and possess, and he casts out many nations before
> you—the Hittites, the Girgashites, the Amorites, the Canaanites,
> the Perizzites, the Hivites, and the Jebusites, seven nations more
> powerful and more populated than you—and when Yahweh your
> God delivers them up to you and you overpower them, then you
> must devote them to utter destruction. Do not enter into any
> covenants with them. *Show them no mercy. Do not intermarry
> with them, giving your daughters as brides to their sons or tak-
> ing their daughters as brides for your sons. If you did that, your
> children would be raised to serve other gods, and they would turn
> away from following me. Then, in Yahweh's anger against you, he
> would obliterate you in a heartbeat.* Thus, this is what you need
> to do them: destroy their altars, smash their monuments, chop

down their sacred poles, and burn their graven idols to dust. For you are a people holy to Yahweh your God. Yahweh your God has chosen you as his special possession out of all the peoples on the face of the earth.

What was so wicked about the Canaanites? Deuteronomy says that they practiced child sacrifice, but condemnation of child sacrifice cannot be the original justification for the massacres. As we saw in the last chapter, child sacrifice was practiced by Israel as well, ostensibly with Yahweh's blessing. When we compare the kinds of cultic rites performed by the Canaanites with those of Israel, we are hard pressed to find many substantial differences. The issue was not so much with the *form* of the cultic rites, but with the *objects* of worship. Canaanite worship was abominable to Israel because Yahweh was not its object. They worshiped other gods, and Yahweh was jealous for Israel's affections. The danger supposedly posed by any surviving Canaanites is that they would influence Israelites away from pure Yahweh worship.

We can grant this much, but there remains a significant problem with this rationale. Why was it necessary to slaughter the children and infants? According to prominent Christian apologist William Lane Craig, "God knew that if these Canaanite children were allowed to live, they would spell the undoing of Israel. The killing of the Canaanite children . . . served to prevent assimilation to Canaanite identity."[1] Yet this is hardly a plausible scenario. Are infants going to teach faithful Israelites to worship false gods? If Israel took the surviving infants and young children, adopted them, and raised them to worship Yahweh, is it likely these children would revert to their parents' idolatrous ways once they reached maturity? That is like saying that an Iranian baby raised in the U.S. would suddenly begin speaking Farsi on its eighteenth birthday. This rationale does not explain why the children had to be killed, and it betrays an untenable ethnic essentialism in Craig's thinking.

Yet this is not the only problem with such an approach. The rationale is contradicted elsewhere. Num 31:7–18, for instance, tells a different story:

They fought against Midian, as Yahweh had ordered Moses, and they killed every last male. They executed the kings of Midian—Evi, Rekem, Zur, Hur, and Reba, the five kings of Midian—alongside their men. They also cut down Balaam son of Beor with the sword. *The sons of Israel captured all the Midianite women and their children*, and they took all their cattle, their flocks, and all their goods as spoil. They burned to the ground all their cities where the Midianites had lived, and all their encampments. But they seized all the spoil and all the booty, both human and animal. And

1. Craig, "Slaughter of the Canaanites," para. 27.

they brought the captives and the booty and the spoil to Moses, to Eleazar the priest, and to the congregation of the sons of Israel, there at their encampment on the plains of Moab by the Jordan River at Jericho. So Moses, Eleazar the priest, and all the chiefs of the congregation met them outside the camp. And Moses's wrath flared up against the army officers—the captains of thousands and the captains of hundreds—who had just come from the battle. Moses said to them, "You let all the women live? These women here, on Balaam's counsel, caused the men of Israel to commit treason against Yahweh in the affair of Peor, an act which brought down a plague among the congregation of Yahweh. *Now therefore, separate the children by gender and kill all the male children, and execute every woman who is not a virgin. But all the young girls and women who are still virgins, keep alive for yourselves.*"

What is going on here? The same rationale can be seen in this account. The women of Midian had led Israel astray before, so to prevent them from doing it again, they were to be killed. The boys were to be killed, presumably, to prevent them from growing up and avenging the murder of their families. Yet the virgin girls and young women were spared. For what purpose? They were spared in order to become the wives and concubines—the sex slaves—of the Israelite men. Apart from the serious moral problems inherent in treating women as sex objects and personal property,[2] the sparing of the virgins undercuts the very logic of the rationale for killing those women who had already been "spoiled" by other men. Many if not most of these virgins would have been accomplished practitioners of the Midianite cultic rites, and the Midianites worshiped their local deity Baal of Peor, according to Num 25:1–9.

Here it could be argued that Moses, not Yahweh, commanded the virgins to be kept alive as trophy wives for the Israelite men. If this were the case, the contradiction could be explained away as an error in judgment on Moses' part. But this explanation will not work. Just a few verses later, in Num 31:25–32, Yahweh himself gives explicit instructions about what to do with the remaining virgins. There are 32,000 young female virgins from among the Canaanite "spoil." Out of that number, thirty-two were to be given to Eleazar the high priest, and 320 were to be given to the Levites. The remainder was to be divided between the soldiers (15,968 virgins) and the rest of the congregation (15,680 virgins).

---

2. This understanding of women as personal property is also reflected in the tenth commandment, in which a man's wife is listed in between his house and his slaves and livestock.

So what happened to Yahweh's command? "Do not intermarry with them, giving your daughters as brides to their sons or taking their daughters as brides for your sons. If you did that, your children would be raised to serve other gods, and they would turn away from following me." Did Yahweh forget that his anger was supposed to be ignited against Israel and that he was supposed to obliterate them in a heartbeat (Deut 7:4)? Or is it more likely that this entire rationale for genocide was concocted by those who were writing these accounts hundreds of years after the events took place?

Another important text from Deuteronomy reveals the same fundamental problem with this rationale. Deut 20:10–18 reads:

> When you approach a city to attack it, first offer terms of peace. If the city accepts the terms of peace and surrenders, then the city's inhabitants shall become your slaves. If, however, it rejects the terms of peace, and moves to face you in battle, then you shall besiege the city, and when Yahweh your God delivers it into your hand, you shall cut down every male with the edge of your sword. *But you may take as the spoils of war all the women, the children, the livestock, and everything else you desire. You may enjoy the spoil of your enemies, which Yahweh your God has given you. This is the way you are to treat all the cities that are very far from you, which are not the cities of the local tribes. But as for the cities that Yahweh your God is giving you for your inheritance, you must not let anything that breathes remain alive. You shall devote them to utter destruction . . . just as Yahweh your God has commanded. You must kill them all, or else they may teach you to do all the abhorrent things that they do for their gods, causing you to sin against Yahweh your God.*[3]

Again, the justification for killing the women inside the borders was that those women would lead Israelites after other gods. Yet if the tribe happens to live outside the borders of the land that Israel is annexing from its longstanding inhabitants, then it is permissible to marry their women. Are we to surmise from this that only women inside the allotted borders worshiped other gods? Were all the women outside those borders faithful and orthodox worshipers of Yahweh? Of course they weren't. They worshiped their own tribal deities. Yet despite this, Israelite men were permitted to take them as wives. The message is very clear here. This is further evidence that

---

3. The next verse goes on to say, "If you besiege a city for a long time, attacking it in order to take it, you are not permitted to destroy its trees with an ax. You may take fruit from them, but you must not cut them down. Are the trees human beings that they should be destroyed by you?" To Yahweh, according to this text, trees have more intrinsic value than humans.

the whole rationale of genocide as "theological defense" was merely camouflage for a more nefarious motivation: the acquisition of land and consolidation of political power.

Despite the blatant problems with this sort of justification, renowned apologist and biblical inerrantist Gleason Archer continues to disseminate this piece of ancient propaganda. To Archer, the genocide of the Canaanite tribes was absolutely necessary. He likens it to a medical procedure: "Just as the wise surgeon removes dangerous cancer from his patient's body by use of the scalpel, so God employed the Israelites to remove such dangerous malignancies from human society."[4] For Archer, apparently, the Canaanite children were as cancerous to Israelite society as were their heterodox parents.

Godwin's law notwithstanding, I think it is not without relevance that the same logic was frequently put to work in Nazi propaganda in order to legitimize the extermination of the Jews. For example, Hitler, whose mother Klara died of breast cancer, would later identify the Jews as "a cancer on the breast of Germany."[5] In another place, Hitler attacked the "spinelessness" of those Germans unwilling to do what is necessary in order to save Germany from (perceived) internal threats, without the assurance that their campaign will be successful. "A person suffering from cancer, whose death is otherwise certain, need not first figure out fifty-one per cent [probability of success] in order to risk an operation. And if the latter promises a cure with only half a per cent probability, a courageous man will risk it."[6] Such is the courage of those who would massacre infants in order to save themselves from their own spiritual weaknesses.

Divine Punishment

Another common justification for the Canaanite genocides is that they are to be understood as episodes of divine punishment. Just as Yahweh punished the earth's inhabitants in Noah's day with a great flood, just as he punished Sodom and Gomorrah in Abraham's day with fire and brimstone, so too he punished the Canaanites with the sword and flame of his favored people Israel. Thus, according to biblical inerrantist Christopher Wright, "The action of Israel against the Canaanites is never placed in the category of oppression

4. Archer, *Encyclopedia of Bible Difficulties*, 121, quoted in Avalos, "Creationists for Genocide," para. 63.

5. See Binion, "Hitler's Concept of Lebensraum." On the use of medical rhetoric by the Nazis, see Aly et al., *Cleansing the Fatherland*; Proctor, *The Nazi War on Cancer*, 45–50; also Koenigsberg, "Genocide as Immunology."

6. Hitler, *Mein Kampf*, 625.

but of divine punishment operating through human agency."[7] Wright notes that although the land of Canaan was promised to Abraham's descendants, it was not to be theirs immediately. Not until "the fourth generation will they return, for the wickedness of the Amorites has yet to attain its full measure" (Gen 15:16). As Wright comments, "What that last phrase means is that the Amorite/Canaanite society of Abraham's day was not yet so wicked as to morally justify God's acting in comprehensive judgment on it. . . . But that time would come. Eventually, the Canaanites would be so 'fully' wicked that God's judgment would deservedly fall."[8] God wanted to wait until their punishment was "fully deserved."[9]

Yet this explanation raises at least three significant difficulties. First, if God knew that the Canaanites were going to become even more depraved, why did he do nothing to intervene in their self-destructive course? Abraham was there in the land of Canaan, doing God's bidding. Why did God not send Abraham to preach to the inhabitants of Canaan, at least to offer them the opportunity to repent? Isn't this why God sent Jonah to Nineveh? Bear in mind, Nineveh was the capital city of the Assyrian empire, Israel's greatest enemy at the time, a nation whose wickedness was so great that its stench rose up to the heavenly abode of Yahweh (Jonah 1:2). Despite this, Yahweh sent Jonah to the capital to announce its coming destruction. Nineveh subsequently repented and Yahweh had mercy on them.

After all this, Jonah was not happy with the result. He wanted to see Nineveh burn. As the story goes, even as Jonah was pouting, God provided a bush to shade him from the sun. The next day, however, God caused the bush to wither, and Jonah was exposed. Suffering from the heat of the day, Jonah begged God to kill him. "I would rather die than live," he said. God asked him if he was right to be angry about the loss of the bush, and Jonah retorted that he was angry enough to die. The book concludes when Yahweh chastises Jonah for being so concerned over the life of a bush and so indifferent to the lives of the more than 120,000 human beings and the countless animals in the great city of Nineveh.[10] Now if the book of Jonah accurately reflects the character of Yahweh, why then did Yahweh not send Abraham, or some other prophet, on a similar mission to the Canaanites? But instead of prophets, Yahweh sent spies (Num 13:1–2).

7. Wright, *The God I Don't Understand*, 92.

8. Ibid.

9. Ibid., 93. Note here what Wright implies: even God's actions need to be "morally justified."

10. Contrast these sentiments with Deut 20:19 which values the life of the trees above those of the human beings dwelling in Canaan.

The second difficulty rests in the question of who deserved the punishment. As God says to Abraham in Genesis 15, a time would come when the character of the Canaanites would be so wicked that their destruction would be, in the words of Wright, "fully deserved." This raises the question: at what point is the slaughter of children, infants, and the unborn "fully deserved"? This is a question Wright does not attempt to answer. Those who adhere to the doctrine of "original sin" may respond that all alike are tainted with sin—the old *and* the young. The depravity of children is not a result of anything they have done, but a condition into which they are born—a genetic syndrome, if you will. To proponents of this doctrine, this would explain why Yahweh is justified in the massacre of babies. Yet if babies are sufficiently depraved to be massacred—before they had done anything right or wrong—why then were the Canaanites in Abraham's day not sufficiently depraved? Why did Yahweh have to wait until their wickedness was of a certain magnitude, if they were already deserving of death the moment they exited the womb; indeed, while still in it?

Coherent answers to questions like these are difficult to come by. In fact, I have yet to find any. While we may grant for the purposes of discussion that the utter destruction of the mature Canaanites was a punishment worthy of their crimes, this justification does not and cannot suffice to explain the destruction of the Canaanite children.

The third difficulty for this notion that the genocides were punishment for sin is found in a text we have already examined above. Recall that in Deut 20:10–18 a distinction is made between the way Israel is to treat those *within* "their" land and the way Israel is to treat those *outside* those borders. Those inside the borders are to be utterly annihilated with no exceptions. No peace treaties are to be made with them. Every last living thing that has breath is to be extinguished. On the other hand, those outside the demarcated borders are to be offered terms of peace. Israelite men may take women from outside the borders as wives and concubines, if they so desire. Did it just so happen that only the tribes living inside Israel's borders happened to be sufficiently wicked to annihilate, whereas it also just so happened that everybody outside those borders were only slightly wicked, but not enough to merit annihilation? The convenience of this picture exposes once again that the appeal to "divine punishment" in order to justify the Canaanite genocides is another attempt to conceal the real motivation: the acquisition of land and consolidation of power. If Yahweh wanted to use Israel to punish wicked nations, why did such a crusade conveniently terminate precisely at Israel's borders?

Despite these difficulties, apologists like Wright continue to insist that by putting the Canaanite conquest "within the framework of punishment for wrongdoing, as the Bible clearly does, it makes a categorical difference to the nature of the violence inflicted."[11] Wright understands that this consideration does not make the genocides "nice," yet an action need not be "nice" to be moral. "Punishment changes the moral context of violence. . . . Whatever our personal codes of parental discipline, there is surely a moral difference between a smack administered as punishment for disobedience and vicious or random child abuse."[12] This is correct. There is also a moral difference between smacking a child for his or her disobedience and killing a child for his or her disobedience, just as there is a moral difference between smacking an *offending* child and smacking *every* child for the offense committed by one. In both cases, the latter action is *immoral*, and it is the latter action, not the former, which corresponds to what we see in the wholesale slaughter of the Canaanites.

Nevertheless, in Wright's mind, "the consistent biblical affirmation that the conquest constituted an act of God's punishment on a wicked society, using Israel as the human agent, must be taken seriously by those who wish to take the Bible's own testimony seriously, and it must not be dismissed as self-serving disinfectant for the poison of Israel's own aggression."[13] Wright attempts to suggest that those who find this justification offered by the Bible for these genocides morally problematic are not taking "the Bible's own testimony seriously." Yet as we have seen, it is precisely by taking the Bible's own (conflicting) testimony seriously that we must conclude that the biblical justification of divine punishment is, in Wright's words, a "self-serving disinfectant for the poison of Israel's own aggression." Wright apparently assumes that taking the Bible seriously entails believing every word it says. Yet it turns out that it is Wright who does not take the Bible seriously when one biblical text contradicts another (as we shall see even more clearly below). In my opinion, taking the Bible seriously and taking the Bible to be inerrant are mutually exclusive reading strategies.

Blessing the Nations

Apologists for these genocides will often attempt to argue that these accounts must be understood within the broader framework of God's overarching plan for Israel, expressed in the form of a promise to Abraham—that through his seed all the tribes of the earth will be blessed.[14] Frequently this approach

11. Wright, *The God I Don't Understand*, 93.
12. Ibid.
13. Ibid.
14. See for example Wright, *The God I Don't Understand*, 98–100.

takes the form of the claim that God needed to protect and preserve Israel in order to bring the messiah into the world. As if an omnipotent and omniscient God—who was powerful enough to fashion the world with a few words and to bring the dead back from the grave—could not think of any way to bring a messiah into the world other than to kill helpless Canaanite children. What this is, essentially, is a utilitarian argument: the end justifies the means. It is at this point that the Christian apologist's fervent defense of the idea of absolute, objective morality is tossed aside in the name of biblical inerrancy. The claim is ultimately that although genocide is morally wrong, God had to do it in order to protect the lineage of one Jesus of Nazareth.

This end-justifies-the-means mentality has manifested itself elsewhere in history. An immediate example would be the United States of America. Like ancient Israelites, early European Americans believed they had a special calling from God, a calling to be a light to the nations. To them, their destiny was plainly manifest. God had brought them to this bountiful new land, flowing with milk and honey, and although it was necessary to eradicate the malignancy of the savage natives, in the end, the blessings the United States had to offer the world would far outweigh any necessary evils committed along the way. Thus, John O'Sullivan can say:

> It is our unparalleled glory that we have no reminiscences of battle fields, but in defence of humanity, of the oppressed of all nations, of the rights of conscience, the rights of personal enfranchisement. Our annals describe no scenes of horrid carnage, where men were led on by hundreds of thousands to slay one another. . . . In its magnificent domain of space and time, the nation of many nations is destined to manifest to mankind the excellence of divine principles; to establish on earth the noblest temple ever dedicated to the worship of the Most High—the Sacred and the True. Its floor shall be a hemisphere—its roof the firmament of the star-studded heavens, and its congregation an Union of many Republics. . . . We must onward to the fulfilment of our mission— to the entire development of the principle of our organization— freedom of conscience, freedom of person, freedom of trade and business pursuits, universality of freedom and equality. This is our high destiny, and in nature's eternal, inevitable decree of cause and effect we must accomplish it. All this will be our future history, to establish on earth the moral dignity and salvation of man—the immutable truth and beneficence of God. For this blessed mission to the nations of the world, which are shut out from the life-giving light of truth, has America been chosen.[15]

15. O'Sullivan, "Great Nation of Futurity," 427; 430.

To argue, then, that the extermination of the Canaanites must be seen as part of the larger picture of Israel's calling to bless the nations is, in effect, just a sleight of hand trick: "Don't look over there. Look over here." Or as Barack Obama said when queried about the possibility of an investigation of past U.S. human rights abuses, "I'm a strong believer that it's important to look forward and not backwards."[16] Buried beneath layer upon layer of such rhetoric lie the victims of those who just want to get on with things. But as Obama said when queried about the possibility of an investigation of past *Indonesian* human rights abuses, "We can't go forward without looking backwards."[17]

As with Obama and his version of United States history, Wright and other Christian apologists want us to focus on all the good bits of Israel's history. When faced with the conundrum of Canaanite carnage, Wright insists that "the overall thrust of the Old Testament is not Israel against the nations, but Israel for the sake of the nations."[18] Of course, Wright offers no evidentiary support for this claim. It would be difficult to do so, since texts in which Israel is pitted *against* the nations far outnumber those in which Israel is for them. Nevertheless, even if Wright's claim were true, it misses the point entirely. Imagine the Israelite soldier consoling the young Canaanite girl, just before running her through with the sword: "Not to worry, young lady. In the overall scheme of things, my people are going to be a blessing to people like you."

Hostile Characters

Some justify Israel's genocides by arguing that the people in and around the land of Canaan were hostile people, attacking Israel without provocation. This perspective is explicit in Josh 11:1–5, and can be discerned in Numbers 21, wherein Israel requests permission from Sihon, an Amorite king, to pass through his territory unharmed. In the account in Numbers, Sihon denies their request and without provocation goes out to the desert with his army to wage war against Israel. Israel emerges from the battle victorious and takes possession of the Amorite territories. Yet the book of Deuteronomy tells the story slightly differently—or rather from the inerrantist perspective, it fills in the gaps.

> "See, I have handed over to you King Sihon the Amorite of Heshbon, and his land. Begin to take possession by engaging him in battle. This day I will begin to put the dread and fear of you

16. Quoted in Greenwald, "When Presidential Sermons Collide," para. 4.

17. Ibid., para. 2.

18. Wright, *The God I don't Understand*, 100.

upon the peoples everywhere under heaven; when they hear report of you, they will tremble and be in anguish because of you."
So I sent messengers from the wilderness of Kedemoth to King
Sihon of Heshbon with the following terms of peace: "If you let
me pass through your land, I will travel only along the road; I
will turn aside neither to the right nor to the left. You shall sell
me food for money, so that I may eat, and supply me water for
money, so that I may drink. Only allow me to pass through on
foot—just as the descendants of Esau who live in Seir have done
for me and likewise the Moabites who live in Ar—until I cross
the Jordan into the land that Yahweh our God is giving us." But
King Sihon of Heshbon was not willing to let us pass through, *for
Yahweh your God had hardened his spirit and made his heart defi-
ant in order to hand him over to you, as he has now done.* Yahweh
said to me, "See, I have begun to give Sihon and his land over to
you. Begin now to take possession of his land." So when Sihon
came out against us, he and all his people for battle at Jahaz,
*Yahweh our God gave him over to us; and we struck him down,
along with his offspring and all his people. At that time we captured
all his towns, and in each town we utterly destroyed men, women,
and children. We left not a single survivor.* (Deut 2:24–34, NRSV)

This version paints quite a different portrait. The Israelites offer Sihon
terms of peace, but Yahweh directly intervenes, hardening the king's spirit,
in order to prevent the king from accepting the terms of peace. Why? The
text says it is because Yahweh wishes to give Sihon's land to Israel. (Bear
in mind, this is not even the Promised Land.) In order to give his people
control of yet more land, Yahweh intervened to prevent peace. And who suffered? Not just the king, but all of the "men, women, and children" (Deut
2:34). The people of Heshbon did nothing wrong here. And even if the king
had denied the Israelites passage *without* the forceful hand of Yahweh, he
would have been doing it in the best interest of his people—to protect them
from a strange and potentially violent group of nomads. Yet according to
Deuteronomy, the choice was not even Sihon's to make. If we are to take the
account in Deuteronomy as an accurate description of the events, it is clear
that the Amorites were not aggressors, but the victims of Yahweh's aggressive
campaign for land.

Unfortunately, this is not an isolated incident. These false peace offerings in fact become a pattern throughout the conquest of Canaanite territories, as indicated in Josh 11:18–20: "Joshua waged war against the Canaanite
kings for a long time and in the end *not even one city made peace with Israel*
(except for the Hivites who lived in Gibeon). Israel vanquished every last city

in battle. This is because *Yahweh hardened their hearts so that they could not do otherwise than to meet Israel in battle.* This way they would all be utterly destroyed and none of them would get any mercy. They were to be exterminated, just as Yahweh ordered Moses to do." City after city was offered terms of peace by Israel, and city after city was prevented by divine intervention from accepting those terms, so that Yahweh's armies would have an excuse to implement Yahweh's policy of Canaanite extermination.

Moreover, even if we were to ignore these passages which ascribe Amorite and Canaanite hostility to Yahweh's meddling, what this apologetic strategy implies is that in order to defend themselves against the hostilities of a king and his armies, it was necessary for Israel to kill their children too. Once again, this strategy hardly exculpates Yahweh, as depicted in these Israelite accounts, from moral responsibility for the killing of these women and children. If Yahweh was in fact setting the rules and giving the orders, what prevented him from simply issuing a command to spare the children and to raise them up as faithful Yahwists? Such a command would not be difficult to relay: "To every child you orphan, a father you shall be. For every mother you kill, a mother you shall provide." Instead we get, "Let nothing that has breath remain alive. Show them no mercy."

A final factor to bear in mind in response to the historian's charges of "hostility" is *who is writing the history.* The victors and those with greater power always identify any resistance as "hostility." The Jewish patriots who resisted Greek and Roman occupation were considered hostiles. The Native Americans who fought to protect their lands from invading foreigners were seen as hostiles by the invaders. In the same way, to identify the Canaanites as "hostiles" is to assume uncritically the perspective of the invading armies. What to one side is seen as bald aggression and hostility, to the other side is seen as a defensive fight for freedom.

Everything with an Even Hand

Another strategy Wright employs is to attempt to mitigate the horror of the Canaanite genocides by pointing out that Yahweh did not withhold his punishment from Israel. Wright cites Lev 18:28 and Deut 28:25–68 in which Yahweh warns Israel that if they committed the sins of the Canaanites, they would be treated as his enemies, just as the Canaanites were treated. "The land that had vomited out the Canaanites would be perfectly capable of doing the same with the Israelites, if they indulged in the same repulsive Canaanite practices. . . . The Israelites needed to know (as do we) that the conquest was not some charade of cosy favouritism. Israel stood under the same threat of judgment from the same God for the same sins, if they chose to commit them."[19] Everything with an even hand.

There are two things to say in response to this. First, it isn't true. Yes, Yahweh punished Israel for its sins against him. Yes, Yahweh put Israel through horror after horror to purge Israel of its idolatries. Yes, Yahweh expelled them from their land. But here is the difference between Yahweh's treatment of Israel and his treatment of the Canaanites: Yahweh brought Israel back. Yahweh always restored Israel. Yahweh never allowed Israel to be blotted out. One cannot, therefore, say that Yahweh rewarded Israel with the same punishment as he did the Canaanites. The punishment of the Canaanites was to cease to exist. This is something Yahweh never allowed to happen to Israel, no matter how often he threatened it. And why did he restrain himself from destroying them all? Precisely because they were his special possession. This is the very definition of favoritism. It may not be "cozy favoritism," but it is favoritism nonetheless.

The second thing is this: conceding that Yahweh *did* punish Israel quite severely for their sins against him, this does not erase the problem of the kind of punishment Yahweh administered. In fact, Yahweh's "evenhandedness" only compounds the moral dilemma. Over and over again, Yahweh punishes sinners by punishing their children, and that in horrifying ways. See how the northern kingdom of Israel's punishment was described in Hos 13:16:

> Samaria will bear the burden of her guilt,
> because of her rebellion against her God;
> by the sword they shall fall,
> their infants dashed to pieces,
> their pregnant women torn open.

As repayment for their unfaithfulness, Yahweh determines to send an army to kill their infants and unborn children. Yet it gets worse. One of Yahweh's favorite punishments was to force parents to eat their own children:

> If you refuse to listen to me, and continue to push against me, then I in my wrath will push back. Indeed, I will punish you for your sins seven times over. You will eat the very flesh of your sons. The flesh of your daughters you will eat. (Lev 26:27–29)

> This is what my lord Yahweh says: "I am coming against you my- self. I will execute my judgments upon you before the eyes of the watching world. Because of your abominations, I am going to do something to you I have never done before, the likes of which I will never do again. This will surely happen among you: fathers

19. Ibid., 95.

will eat their sons, and sons will eat their fathers. This is how I
will execute my judgments upon you." (Ezek 5:8–10)

And I will feed them the flesh of their own sons and daughters,
and every man will eat the flesh of his friends and neighbors.
(Jer 19:9)

As we learn in the book of Lamentations, these are not merely idle
threats. According to the record, Yahweh did indeed punish his people in
this way. In Lam 2:20–21, a broken soul cries:

Look at us, Yahweh, and consider
those to whom you have done this.
Should women eat the fruit of their wombs,
the very children they have cradled in their arms?
Should priest and prophet be slaughtered
in the sanctuary of my Lord?

The young and the old lie face down
in the dust of the streets;
my young women and my finest young men
have fallen by the sword;
in the day of your anger you have slain them.
You have slaughtered us without mercy.

Here the lamenter, who has acknowledged Israel's guilt, nevertheless
is able to question the justice of Yahweh's actions. I encourage you to try
not to shy away from these images. If you can, force yourself to imagine
yourself in this situation—having to kill your own child, then to cook and
consume their flesh, bite after bite after bite, for days. This is not something
that happens quickly and then it's over with. Every bite is a hundred memories mutilated. Every swallow is a thousand dreams destroyed. This is how
the text says Yahweh saw fit to punish his people. Punishment is one thing,
but many would be inclined to say that this moves beyond punishment into
the realm of sadism.

Another question to consider is why these children were required to
suffer in order to punish their parents. Were the children idolaters? Were
they culpable for their parents' sins? Not according to Ezekiel 18:20: "Only
the one who sins, that one alone shall die. The child shall not suffer for the sins
of a parent. Nor shall a parent suffer for the sins of a child. The righteousness
of the righteous belongs to the righteous, and the wickedness of the wicked
belongs to the wicked." Yet Yahweh seems to have no compunction about
feeding these children to their parents as chastisement for their parents' sins.
In this "punishment," the lives of innocent children are discarded in order

to teach their mothers and fathers a lesson. They are reduced to a utilitarian function—a ghastly means to an end.

It should be clear, therefore, why the fact that Yahweh punished both the Canaanites *and* the Israelites does not mitigate the horror of the Canaanite genocides. On the contrary, the horror is only compounded. What we have learned is that Yahweh is willing to kill innocent children on both sides of the dividing line, all in the name of justice. Everything with an even hand.

Better Off Dead

Some apologists openly acknowledge the problems inherent in the idea that God kills children. One strategy taken up by a few is to suggest that, in fact, these children are better off dead. According to self-proclaimed fundamentalist R. A. Torrey, "The extermination of the Canaanite children was not only an act of mercy and love to the world at large; it was an act of love and mercy to the children themselves."[20] The underlying thought here is that by putting the Canaanite children to the sword, the Israelites were saving them from being sacrificed by their parents.[21]

The problems with this "solution" are of course manifold. First, if we know anything about child sacrifice in the ancient world, we know that it was rarely practiced. Parents did not want to sacrifice their children. It was considered to be the ultimate form of sacrifice precisely because it was so hard to bring oneself to do. (Recall our discussion of Micah 6:6–8 in the last chapter, in which child sacrifice is depicted as the greatest of all sacrifices.) Thus, by killing *every living child*, the Israelites were killing far more children than would have been put to death by the Canaanite rites of sacrifice. Second, as we have seen, Israelites themselves performed child sacrifices to Yahweh. At this period in Israel's history, this practice was acceptable. Nowhere in the text is the slaughter of Canaanite children justified on the grounds that they were being saved from sacrifice. Third—and this should be quite obvious—it is absurd to say that Israel was saving children by killing children. If Israel wanted to save the Canaanite children from sacrifice, they would have adopted them. What is taking place in the text, rather, is guilt by association. Canaanites are wicked, and no distinction is made between young and old, male and female. Even the cows and sheep were punished for being Canaanite.

20. Torrey, *Difficulties in the Bible*, 60, quoted in Avalos, "Creationists for Genocide," para. 61.

21. However, see Avalos, "Creationists for Genocide," who makes a persuasive biblical and archaeological case that child sacrifice may not have been practiced by the Canaanites.

A variation of this approach is to argue that killing Canaanite children effectively bought them a one-way ticket to heaven. On this mentality, getting them while they're young, before they had been corrupted by their parents' idolatrous ways, was a way to ensure these children would live happily ever after. Christopher Wright alludes to this position when he writes that "it would be quite wrong to assume dogmatically that every Canaanite who perished automatically 'went to hell.'" For Wright, the horrifying nature of these acts of murder is alleviated by his belief that "God knows the hearts of all and his final judgment is discriminating, just, and merciful."[22] Craig states this position clearly and unabashedly: "If we believe, as I do, that God's grace is extended to those who die in infancy or as small children, the death of these children was actually their salvation. We are so wedded to an earthly, naturalistic perspective that we forget that those who die are happy to quit this earth for heaven's incomparable joy. Therefore, God does these children no wrong in taking their lives."[23]

What does this logic resemble? I am reminded of Andrea Yates, the Houston mother of five who was so convinced she was corrupting her children that she drowned them. Yates explained her actions to her prison psychiatrist: "My children were not righteous. I let them stumble. They were doomed to perish in the fires of hell. . . . Better for someone to tie a millstone around their neck and cast them in a river than stumble. They were going to perish."[24] Yates believed God had told her to do this. In order to save her children from hell, and to guarantee their acceptance in heaven, Yates did the very thing Craig commends the Israelites for having done—she executed children.

Of course, Craig would never condone Yates' actions. The distinction for Craig is that Yates was suffering from psychosis whereas in the case of the Canaanites, the command from God was real. Craig knows it was really a command from God because the Bible says it was. Despite this, it seems apparent that Craig would still concede that the children of Andrea Yates are now better off than they were when they were alive. For Craig, the death of the children is really a non-issue. The real victims, from Craig's perspective, are the perpetrators: "So whom does God wrong in commanding the destruction of the Canaanites? Not the Canaanite adults, for they were corrupt and deserving of judgement. Not the children, for they inherit eternal life. So who is wronged? Ironically, I think the most difficult part of this whole debate is the apparent wrong done to the Israeli [*sic*] soldiers themselves. Can you imagine what it would be like to have to break into some house

22. Wright, *The God I Don't Understand*, 96.
23. Craig, "Slaughter of the Canaanites," para. 28.
24. Quoted in Christian and Teachey, "Yates Believed Children Doomed," paras. 2, 6.

and kill a terrified woman and her children? The brutalizing effect on these Israeli soldiers is disturbing."[25]

Disturbing, indeed, is an apt word here. There are a number of things about Craig's perspective that are disturbing—its unapologetic congruence with the psychosis of Andrea Yates being only the first of many. Another problem is Craig's unchecked assumption that children automatically go to heaven. As much sense as that assumption makes to modern-day Christians, it was not always so self-evident. Throughout most of church history, Christians have believed that the souls of unbaptized and pagan children go either to hell or to purgatory after physical death. The Bible itself says nothing about the question, but it is likely that later biblical thinkers believed that a child's fate in the afterlife was connected to that of his or her family, unless there was a significant departure between child and parent resulting in the child's incorporation into another family, or "fictive kinship" (in the language of sociology). The ancient world was not marked by the atomistic individualism that has become so pervasive since the Enlightenment, especially that variety of "rugged individualism" unique to the United States. In the ancient world, individual identities were largely derivative of corporate entities—families, fictive kinships, tribes, etc. There is no indication in any of the texts that the Canaanite children were somehow morally distinguished from their parents, no indication whatsoever that their fates were conceived any differently. This possibility exists only in the wishful thinking of apologists.

This leads us to another problem with Craig's perspective, and this is his apparent naïveté regarding the development of ideas about death and afterlife in Hebrew thought. At the time of the conquests up until about the second century BCE, Jews did not believe in any afterlife, and this is reflected in texts from this period. For instance, the author of Ecclesiastes ascribes ultimate meaningless to human existence, precisely because there is nothing to look forward to beyond death:

> This is an evil in all that happens under the sun, that the same fate comes to everyone. Moreover, the hearts of all are full of evil; madness is in their hearts while they live, and after that they go to the dead. But whoever is joined with all the living has hope, for a living dog is better than a dead lion. The living know that they will die, but the dead know nothing; they have no more reward, and even the memory of them is lost. Their love and their hate and their envy have already perished; never again will they have any share in all that happens under the sun. (Eccl 9:3–6, NRSV)

25. Craig, "Slaughter of the Canaanites," para. 29.

This perspective is the traditional perspective in Judaism, which denies the possibility of any life after the grave—beyond an ephemeral, sleepy existence beneath the earth where all go, both good and bad. As most Sunday-school Christians are aware, this was the perspective of the Sadducees at the time of Jesus. Many assume that the Sadducees were something like ancient skeptics with regards to belief in the afterlife, but in actuality they were the conservatives. Belief in the afterlife was relatively new within Judaism—those who adopted it were "the liberals." Some Hellenized Jews (Jews who were influenced by Greek philosophy and culture) adopted Greek ideas about the immortality of the soul and the dualism of body and soul. Other Jews belonged to a young tradition that had arisen out of resistance to imperial hegemony. Their experience of martyrdom gave rise to belief in the resurrection of the body and belief in a final judgment at the end of history. This is the apocalyptic tradition of which Jesus of Nazareth was a representative (and about which we will have much more to say in chapter 8).[26]

Yet even within apocalypticism, there is still no notion of "going to heaven when we die." The idea in apocalypticism was not heaven and hell as abodes in the afterlife, but a place of torment and a newly regenerated earth, which physical resurrected bodies will be given to enjoy. The ideas of heaven and hell as the habitats of a disembodied afterlife became predominant in Christianity only after it grew apart from its early apocalypticism and began to embrace more and more the Greek doctrines of the dualism of body and soul and of the soul's immortality.

Thus, Craig's naïve and somewhat callous claim about the fate of the Canaanite children—"those who die are happy to quit this earth for heaven's incomparable joy"[27]—stands in stark contrast from the biblical reality, as expressed cogently by the more nuanced Christian apologist N. T. Wright: "Death itself was sad, and tinged with evil. It was not seen, in the canonical Old Testament, as a happy release, an escape of the soul from the prison-house of the body."[28] It is clear that Craig's perspective is informed by the dualistic categories of Greek thought, in which body and matter are temporary and evil and soul and spirit are eternal and good. The biblical perspective, conversely, calls God's creation good, and mourns the loss of life as the greatest of all evils. Again, N. T. Wright expresses the perspective of the biblical writers when he writes that the Israelites believed "in the goodness and god-givenness of life

---

26. A cogent introduction to the development of Jewish ideas about the afterlife can be found in Wright, *Resurrection of the Son of God*, 85–128.

27. Craig, "Slaughter of the Canaanites," para. 28.

28. Wright, *Resurrection of the Son of God*, 91.

in this world."[29] This regard for the sanctity of life, of course, applied more to the lives of Hebrews than it did to the lives of the uncircumcised.

Nevertheless, it should be clear by now why the attempts of some Christian apologists to alleviate the horror of the Canaanite genocides by reference to comfortable ideas about the afterlife fail to do justice to the biblical material itself. While the ancient Israelites may have shared Craig's belief that the Canaanite children were better off dead, it was not at all for the same reasons. For the Israelites, according to their understanding of Yahweh's marching orders, the only good Canaanite was a dead one.

Not a Repeat Offender

Yet another of Christopher Wright's strategies is to argue that the conquest was only a "single episode within a single generation out of all the many generations of Old Testament history."[30] Wright insists that "it is a caricature of the Old Testament to portray God as constantly on the warpath or to portray the conquest as simply 'typical' of the rest of the story. It is not."[31] Yet it is difficult to see how this "clarification" is relevant. A nation does not have to be "constantly on the warpath" in order to be guilty of war crimes. It only takes one war. And in the case of the Canaanite genocides, it was Yahweh who was issuing the marching orders. It is difficult to concede that Wright's argument adequately explains the necessity of child killing.

Another problem with the claim that Yahweh was not a repeat offender is that it simply does not ring true. Although the conquest of Canaan was a limited historical event, it is hardly the only act of violence committed by Yahweh that raises significant moral questions. The laundry list is long and dirty. According to the traditions preserved in Genesis 6–8, Yahweh's first act of genocide was a worldwide flood, killing all but a single family of eight people, chosen by Yahweh because of the righteousness of the family patriarch, who incidentally turned out to be a drunk (Gen 9:21). According to the text, Yahweh looked upon humanity and determined that "their every inclination was always and only evil" (Gen 6:5). Apparently, this was an accurate description of the thousands—perhaps hundreds of thousands—of children and infants on the face of the earth, because Yahweh punished them too. Or perhaps, like Andrea Yates, Yahweh drowned them all to save them.

A few generations later, Yahweh would again determine it was necessary to kill hundreds of children, because of their association with their par-

29. Ibid.
30. Wright, *The God I Don't Understand*, 90.
31. Ibid.

ents—the inhabitants of Sodom and Gomorrah (Gen 19:23–28). Although Abraham and his three angelic companions made a visit to Sodom just prior to its destruction, apparently the angels were not capable of rescuing any children from the onslaught of fire and brimstone with which God was about to burn them alive. In fact, the only two children God saw fit to save from that horrible death would subsequently get their father drunk and take turns having incestuous relations with him.

Again in Exodus 12, in order to punish Pharaoh for refusing to allow Israel to go on holiday, Yahweh determined it was necessary to kill every firstborn child in Egypt. Only this time, the real perpetrators were not punished along with their children—only the innocent were killed. All of this is prior to the conquest of Canaan. After the conquest, Yahweh would punish Samaria for exercising the free will he gave them to worship other gods by sending a savage army to dash their infants into bits and to rip unborn children out of their mother's wombs (Hos 13:16). Later, a heartbroken (yet according to inerrantists divinely inspired) Judean pronounces a blessing upon those who would repay Babylon for their (God-ordained) crimes against Israel by snatching Babylonian infants and smashing their heads against the rocks (Ps 137:9). Although a monstrous and sadistic image of revenge, this would be somewhat understandable coming from a man who probably had vivid memories of Babylonians giving Judean children much the same treatment. Nevertheless, Yahweh apparently thought it was an idea quite worthy of himself, since he sent the following message to Babylon through his prophet Isaiah:

Whoever is found will be thrust through,
and whoever is caught will fall by the sword.
Their infants will be dashed to pieces
before their eyes;
their houses will be plundered,
and their wives ravished.
See, I am stirring up the Medes against them,
who have no regard for silver
and do not delight in gold.
Their bows will slaughter the young men;
they will have no mercy on the fruit of the womb;
their eyes will not pity children.
And Babylon, the glory of kingdoms,
the splendor and pride of the Chaldeans,
will be like Sodom and Gomorrah
when God overthrew them.
It will never be inhabited

or lived in for all generations;
Arabs will not pitch their tents there,
shepherds will not make their flocks lie down there.
But wild animals will lie down there,
and its houses will be full of howling creatures;
there ostriches will live,
and there goat-demons will dance.
Hyenas will cry in its towers,
and jackals in the pleasant palaces;
its time is close at hand,
and its days will not be prolonged.
(Isa 13:15–22, NRSV)

According to Isaiah, Yahweh was going to repay Babylon for their treatment of Israel by sending an army to dash their infants to pieces, slaughter their young and their unborn children, rape their women, and utterly annihilate the people, turning Babylon into an uninhabited wasteland forevermore. If this is not a picture of genocide, then nothing is.

These are only a few of the many examples that could be cited to show that when it comes to child killing and genocide, the Yahweh of the Bible was in fact a "repeat offender." For this reason, I find it difficult to take seriously Wright's claim that our moral apprehensions about the Canaanite conquests can be assuaged by the fact that it was only a "single episode."

Revenge Killings

Thus says He Who Raises Armies, "I remember what the Amalekites did to Israel—how they lied in wait as Israel came up out of Egypt. Now go up and attack the Amalekites. Devote to utter destruction everything that is theirs. Do not spare them, but execute each and every last man and woman, child and infant, ox and sheep, camel and donkey." (1 Sam 15:2–3)

Those familiar with this story will know that these instructions were given to Saul, who carried them out almost completely, sparing only the life of the king—in order to humiliate him—and some of the livestock which Saul took as spoil. For Saul's failure to utterly destroy everything, the prophet Samuel rebuked Saul and prophesied that another would replace him as king of Israel.

In this clear example of genocide, the only justification offered is, quite simply and unabashedly, revenge. But revenge for what? Was it for recent Amalekite aggressions? No. It was revenge for an offense committed just after Moses led Israel out of Egypt and before their conquest of Canaan. You may recall the event in question from Exodus 17. According to the text, the Amalekites attacked the Israelites, and Israel's armies came out to meet them. During the battle, Moses took high ground and raised the staff God had given him into the air. Whenever the staff was in the air, the Israelites would begin to win. If Moses lowered his arms, the Israelites would begin to lose. Ultimately, with Aaron and Hur beside Moses to help him hold up the staff, Israel won the battle.

For this incident, Yahweh determined to destroy the Amalekites, but he put it off until Israel had settled down in Canaan (according to Deut 25:19). If we follow the timespan between the Exodus and the rise of the Hebrew monarchy detailed in 1 Kgs 6:1, it is clear that approximately 400 years had passed between the time the Amalekites attacked the Israelites and the time Yahweh ordered their extermination by the hand of Saul. Think about that—400 years. If a new generation was born every twenty years, that would mean Yahweh took revenge on the Amalekites for something their ancestors did twenty generations ago.

Let's try to put that into perspective. Imagine waking up in the morning to find on the front page of the newspaper that a large number of Cherokee banded together during the night and killed every man, woman and child in Tulsa, Oklahoma, justifying it by citing a battle between their ancestors and European colonizers from 400 years ago. This is precisely how the texts of Deuteronomy and 1 Samuel justify the extermination of the Amalekites. The kicker is that *Israel won the battle* for which they were taking revenge on Amalek! No motivation other than pure revenge is ever proffered in the Bible. To punish the Amalekites who attacked Moses, Yahweh ordered the slaughter of their children's children's children's children's children's . . . (you get the idea). Yet it was supposedly the same Yahweh who said that "parents shall not be put to death for their children, nor shall children be put to death for their parents; only for their own crimes may persons be put to death" (Deut 24:16). Or as Ezekiel puts it: "Yet you say, 'Why should not the son suffer for the iniquity of the father?' When the son has done what is lawful and right, and has been careful to observe all my statutes, he shall surely live. Only the one who sins, that one alone shall die. The child shall not suffer for the sins of a parent. Nor shall a parent suffer for the sins of a child. The righteousness of the righteous belongs to the righteous, and the wickedness of the wicked belongs to the wicked" (Ezek 18:19–20).

It seems clear to me that either Yahweh is contradicting himself, or somebody at some point spoke on Yahweh's behalf without his permission. If I am going to assert that Yahweh is good, then to me it is obvious that the justification for the slaughter of the Amalekites (a justification which flagrantly contradicts the basic moral axioms reflected in Deut 24:16 and Ezek 18:20) was concocted by men with a vested interest in legitimating Israel's political exploits. It is also noteworthy that the pro-Davidic author of 1 Samuel uses this incident to provide a justification for the replacement of Saul's dynasty with that of David—Saul's failure to execute the king of Amalek "displeased Yahweh." Such propagandistic storytelling is simply the nature of royal annals or "official" political records, both in the ancient and the modern worlds. (About this we will have more to say in the next chapter.)

Yahweh's Quiet Reserve

Some Christians who recognize the horror of the Canaanite genocides have attempted to offer scenarios in which genocide was not Yahweh's ideal, but was either a concession he made to ancient standards of warfare or a strategy he employed to create some other more positive effect on Israel. These strategies might be categorized as "moral pedagogy" or "progressive revelation." They suggest that we do not see a complete picture of God in these accounts, and they try to posit valid explanations for why that is the case. To put it bluntly, they suggest that Yahweh's quiet reserve "let it slide" with the intention of correcting the issue later on.

An example of the first strategy, in which the genocides were Yahweh's concession to ancient standards of warfare, is (tentatively) suggested by Christopher Wright:

> Is it possible . . . that in a fallen world where struggle for land
> involves war, and if the only kind of war at the time was the kind
> described in the Old Testament texts, this was the way it had to
> be if the landgift promise was to be fulfilled in due course? If
> anything along these lines can be entertained—that is to say, if
> herem [ritual sacrifice] style warfare can be even contemplated
> in the same moral framework as slavery and divorce (and many
> might reject the thought outright)—then we might be dealing
> with something God chose to accommodate within the context
> of a wicked world, not something that represented his best will or
> preference. In view of his long-term goal of ultimately bringing
> blessing to the nations through this people Israel, the gift of land
> necessitated this horrific historical action within the fallen world
> of nations at the time.[32]

What Wright is doing here is arguing that the genocides can potentially be categorized under a long list of concessions that Yahweh made to ancient

32. Ibid., 89.

culture, concessions that did not necessarily reflect Yahweh's perfect ideal. Wright offers divorce and slavery as examples. Yahweh's ideal for marriage did not include divorce, but he permitted for divorce on account of the "hardness of men's hearts" (according to the interpretation of the law offered by Jesus in Mark 10:5). More problematic, however, is Wright's invocation of slavery as a concession. There is no indication in either the Hebrew or Christian scriptures that slavery is seen as a concession. In the former case, the institution of slavery is strongly sanctioned by the divine laws. According to Lev 25:44–46, Israelites may acquire or purchase slaves, including child slaves, and they are to be considered as property. A sharp distinction is made, however. Israelites were permitted to have foreigners (non-Hebrews) as slaves, yet Israelites owning Israelites was strictly forbidden. That is, except in the case of indentured slavery. A Hebrew male may be a slave to another Hebrew male, but only for a period of six years at most, according to Exod 21:2–6. However, the six-year limitation does *not* apply to a Hebrew *female*, who may be sold by her father into slavery, ostensibly as a concubine, for life (Exod 21:7–11).

According to the Mosaic law, slaves were considered property to the extent that a slave owner is permitted to beat his slave with impunity, so long as the beating does not cause the *immediate* death of the slave. In that case, an unspecified punishment is to be meted out to the slave owner. If, however, the slave dies from the wounds *a day or two after the fact*, the slave owner is not legally liable for the death (Exod 21:20–21). The Christian scriptures do not contradict, but only reinforce the institution of slavery (Col 3:22; Eph 6:5). Paul's statement in Gal 3:28 that there is no longer any distinction between slaves and freemen is not an indictment of the institution of slavery, but is a perspective derived from Paul's conviction that the world was about to end (a subject we will discuss more thoroughly in chapter 8). In Paul's mind, the normal (and ordinarily acceptable) distinctions between races, genders, and social classes were rendered irrelevant since the time of the end was near.

Thus, Wright's assumption that the institution of slavery in the Bible should be seen as Yahweh's concession to culture is anachronistic and reflective of wishful, rather than textual, thinking. Doubly so with the issue of the Canaanite genocides, which are explicitly commanded by Yahweh, according to the text, and not simply permitted by his quiet reserve. Furthermore, Wright contradicts himself when he suggests on the one hand that the genocides may be understood as concessions to culture and on the other hand that (as we will see below) the New Testament does not condemn but assumes the validity of the conquest of Canaan.[33] If, according to Wright, the New Testament *affirms* the logic and validity of the Canaanite genocides, on what grounds can Wright state that they are to be understood as concessionary?

33. Ibid., 81, 93.

Nevertheless, Wright insists that "we must understand the conquest within the context of ancient Near Eastern culture (and not by the standards of the Geneva Convention)."[34] But why is this so? This brings us to the heart of the issue. Inevitably, attempts to justify the genocides committed by the people of Yahweh terminate in moral relativism. Wright equivocates when he insists that the conquest must be *understood* within the ancient Near Eastern context. In fact, Wright does not want us merely to *understand* the genocides; he wants us to *accept* them as morally legitimate given certain conditions. Although it may be painful to do so, it is not difficult to *understand* the ancient mindset that allowed for genocides such as these to be remembered without embarrassment. But the ability to understand the fact that these activities were not necessarily considered immoral in an ancient culture does not excuse us from the responsibility of making moral judgments about them. Moral philosopher and ethicist Jeffrey Stout puts the matter this way:

> We can understand their concept, if we put our minds to it and learn enough about their use of words and their way of life. . . . We can also sensibly say that specific judgments . . . we would not be inclined to make were justified under the circumstances. . . . So the relativity of justification can help us avoid charging such people with irrationality by allowing us to understand the concepts and reasons at their disposal. What, then, about truth and falsity? Can we sensibly say of such people that their judgments about which acts or agents count as abominable were false? Can we meaningfully criticize people and actions in distant cultures or epochs as *truly* abominable, intending by this something more than the idea that *we find them* abominable or that they are revolting *to us*?
>
> I do not see why not. At least some of the judgments of abomination we make seem to fall roughly where judgments about evil do on the spectrum of relativity. When the Nazis made lampshades out of the skins of their human victims, that was truly abominable. I would be prepared to say the same thing about members of some more distant culture if they engaged in similar practices.[35] In saying so, I would be doing more than simply reporting how things seem to me. . . . If members of a distant culture said that their (Nazi-like) treatment of victims wasn't abominable, I could surely judge them wrong. I needn't

34. Ibid., 87.

35. For instance, David collected the foreskins of his enemies and presented them to Saul as trophies in exchange for the hand in marriage of Saul's daughter. See 1 Sam 18:20–27.

simply call attention to differences in sensibility to explain why a practice they find morally indifferent is abominable "for us" and leave it at that, as if truth weren't at issue.[36]

In other words, according to Stout, there is an important distinction to be made between cultural relativity and moral relativity. Although it is true that different cultures will inevitably produce different moralities based on different metaphysical paradigms and different sets of social relationships and economic arrangements, that does not entail that *certain* moral judgments are incapable of transcending those differences. Ordinarily, Christian apologists will be the first to point this out. Yet when the credibility of their doctrine of biblical inerrancy is at stake, they are also the first to throw this axiom out the window. Unfortunately, the excuse, "It was all right back then," cannot be a substitute for a proper moral judgment.

Therefore, to say as Wright and others do that the slaughter of civilians was an ordinary feature of ancient warfare—in effect, that Israelites were not the only ones doing it—is, apart from being an inaccurate historical claim,[37] to confuse cultural description with moral analysis. It is like the ten-year-old boy who, when caught smoking, protests to his mother that "all the other kids are doing it." That excuse does not fly with any halfway decent mother, and I do not know why biblical apologists think it will fly with clear-headed Christians.

Again, when Wright insists that the conquest of Canaan must *not* be understood by the standards of the Geneva Convention, he is effectively throwing the moral question out the window and substituting it with historical description. This is sleight of hand. But what do the Geneva Conventions say? The Fourth Geneva Convention pertains to the protection of civilian persons in wartime. Under the fourth convention, civilians are classified as "protected persons," and article thirty-three states that "no protected person may be punished for an offence he or she has not personally committed. Collective penalties and likewise all measures of intimidation or of terrorism are prohibited." This is a basic axiom that tends immediately to make sense to humans in just about every culture. It is found in the Qur'an (2:190) and in its traditional interpretations.[38] This article of the Geneva Convention even made sense to the

---

36. Stout, *Ethics After Babel*, 160, emphasis added.

37. There is only one other example of *herem* style warfare in the archaeological record. After an examination of the material, Kang, *Divine War*, 81, concludes that "the idea of the ban is not attested in the ancient Near Eastern context except in the Moabite stone and in the Bible." Not all nations killed civilians in battle.

38. *Kitab Al-Jihad wa'l-Siyar* attributes these words to the prophet Muhammad: "Set out for Jihad in the name of Allah and for the sake of Allah. Do not lay hands on the old

ancient Israelites, as we have already pointed out with respect to Deut 24:16 and Ezek 18:19–20. It is precisely because this basic moral axiom is contradicted by the Canaanite genocides that Christians who are raised to believe in biblical inerrancy experience cognitive dissonance, and it is precisely for that reason that biblical apologetics has become a cottage industry.

A second tack along the lines of "progressive revelation" says that the annihilation of the Canaanites was a strategy Yahweh employed to create some other more positive effect on Israel. John Howard Yoder argued that one should not project a later morality back onto the genocide texts but rather ask how the texts relate to the morality that preceded them. Doing this, Yoder suggested, one is able to identify a moral novelty in the traditions. Yoder pointed out what he called an "economic side effect" to the ban on taking a spoil from the Canaanites. For Yoder, "If all the slaves and the flocks of the enemy are to be slaughtered in one vast sacrifice, there will then be no booty. The war does not become a source of immediate enrichment through plunder."[39] This means that by slaughtering what would otherwise be their spoil, the Israelites were being trained to trust in Yahweh for their provisions. Yoder sees in this the beginning of a trajectory that eventually leads to a full blown ethic of nonviolence rooted in a long tradition of absolute trust in Yahweh for protection, provision, and vindication.

One problem for Yoder's reading is that while certainly in some battles wealth and livestock were placed under the ban (e.g., Jericho), in other battles Israel was commanded to divide the spoils of war among themselves (e.g., Ai).[40] They were expressly permitted to take spoil from any battle other than those that took place in the Canaanite territories. This fact reveals that Yoder's reading misses the point. The ban on taking Canaanite booty was not a way for Yahweh to teach them to rely on him. Daily manna from heaven would fall under that description. Providing drinking water from a rock would fall under that description. But the ban on Canaanite spoil, at least according to the text, was ostensibly an expression of Yahweh's revulsion at Canaanite religious culture. Besides that, even if it *were* an attempt to train Israel to trust in Yahweh, that hardly solves the moral problem. Certainly Yahweh could think of better ways to teach Israel to trust him than to have them murder children.

---

verging on death, on women, children and babes. Do not steal anything from the booty and collect together all that falls to your lot in the battlefield and do good, for Allah loves the virtuous and the pious." This is the translation of Siddiqui, "Book of Jihad and Expedition," para. 22.

39. Yoder, *Original Revolution*, 105.

40. On the various codes relating to plundering in the Hebrew Bible, see Kvasnica, "Shifts in Israelite War Ethics," 175–96.

In a similar vein, Millard Lind argued that the earliest traditions of holy warfare espoused an ethic of nonparticipation in combat, based on the conviction that Yahweh fought miraculously on Israel's behalf.[41] Lind takes the Song of the Sea in Exodus 15 as archetypical in this regard. While Lind is correct in taking the Song of the Sea to represent some of the earliest Israelite tradition,[42] it was not until Isaiah's time that the appeal to trust Yahweh is used explicitly to promote political quietism.[43] Moreover, Collins raises reasonable doubt against a nonviolent reading of the Song of the Sea, showing that the poetic imagery of drowning in water is used elsewhere (Ps 69:1–4) to depict the distress of a subject of military attack. Collins argues that the hymn in Exodus 15 "is simply celebrating the defeat of Pharaoh. To say that he and his army sank in the depths like a stone is a metaphorical way of saying that they were completely defeated and destroyed."[44] If this reading of the hymn is correct—and I think it is—Lind's appeal to the Song of the Sea as the archetypical instance of weaponless victory is undermined.

Lind also believes it is relevant that in the conquest narratives Yahweh is depicted as the principle fighter. Yahweh went before them and gave the enemy into their hands even before the battle had begun (Josh 6:2; 8:1; 24:8, 11). To Lind, the principal difference between ancient Israelite warfare and that of other ancient Near Eastern nations revolves around the issue of political power. In Lind's understanding, the political power in other nations was vested in human leaders, whereas in Israel, it was depicted solely in terms of Yahweh's leadership.[45] But this is a gross mischaracterization of Israel's neighbors. All ancient Near Eastern peoples attributed their military victories to the strength and favor of their particular tribal or national deities.

Sa-Moon Kang analyzes battle accounts from Mesopotamia, Anatolia, Syro-Palestine, and Egypt and concludes that the motif of divine intervention in battle was a "universalistic idea that appeared whenever a new empire was established. In this sense the political-military entity was the expression

---

41. Lind, *Yahweh Is a Warrior*, 47–60.

42. On the dating of the Song of the Sea, see Cross, *Canaanite Myth*, 124. The account in Exodus 14 is considered by scholars to be a later reworking of the tradition in a prose form. The miraculous parting of the waters is not envisioned in the earlier poem in Exodus 15.

43. Collins, *Does the Bible Justify Violence?*, 4–5. On the later prophetic appropriation of the holy war tradition in terms of quietism, see von Rad, *Holy War in Ancient Israel*, 94–114. For a critique of pacifist readings of the prophets, see Hobbs, *A Time for War*, 217–27, who (I think) rightly characterizes the prophetic quietism not as pacifism but as pragmatism.

44. Collins, *Introduction to the Hebrew Bible*, 116.

45. Lind, *Yahweh Is a Warrior*, 81–82.

of divine rulership."[46] Ancient tribes, such as Israel, regularly sent worshipers out in front of the army as a representation of the divine presence. "The visible symbols of divine participation in battle were the divine standards or statues" (e.g., the Ark of the Covenant), and according to Kang, these objects were used "in the vanguard motif in the context of a cultic procession to ensure that divine participation in battle was not ephemeral."[47]

Lori Rowlett compares the rhetoric in Joshua to Assyrian war literature. When Joshua is wildly outnumbered, Yahweh orders him not to fear, because victory is assured (e.g., Josh 10:8). Joshua is not to trust in numbers, as the enemy does, but in the strength of his deity. The same polemic can be seen in the Assyrian literature: "I fought with them with (the support of) the mighty forces of Ashur, which Ashur, my lord, has given to me. . . . At that time Hadadezer [of] Damascus, Irhulina from Hamath, as well as the kings of Hatti and (of) the seashore *put their trust in their mutual strength* and rose against me to fight a decisive battle. Upon the (oracle) command of Ashur, the great lord, my lord, I fought with them (and) inflicted a defeat upon them" (*ANET*, 279). Summarizing the Assyrian literature, Rowlett writes that the emphasis is "on trust in the deity's promise of divine assistance rather than superior numbers or strength. The divine promise, given through an oracle, is linked in these examples with the successful slaughter and humiliation of the enemy through divine help. . . . This is juxtaposed to their opponents' reliance on numerical strength through military alliances."[48]

Kang summarizes the standard ancient Near Eastern war ideology: "The victory is attributed to the divine warrior and the spoils also return to god(s). For the victory is ultimately divine victory. From beginning to end the divine war begins with god and ends with god."[49] Thus Lind's attempt to differentiate the theology behind Israelite warfare from that of its ancient Near Eastern neighbors thoroughly fails. The texts cannot responsibly be read as reflective of a progression toward nonviolence.

The Magic Trick

A more popular explanation of the (perceived) disparity between the "God of violence" in the Hebrew Bible and the "God of love" in the Christian scriptures is that prior to Christ's sacrifice on the cross, God was obliged to punish sin with death. However, now that Christ's sacrifice for sins has been made,

46. Kang, *Divine War*, 108.
47. Ibid., 109.
48. Rowlett, *Joshua and the Rhetoric of Violence*, 104–05.
49. Kang, *Divine War*, 110.

God's wrath is relieved until the final judgment and he is able to be patient with sinners. Problems with this explanation are numerous, but pointing out just one of them will suffice here.

The problem here is that this explanation presents the idea of atonement as though it were some sort of magic trick. It is as if, prior to the crucifixion of Jesus, God's hands were tied and he simply *had* to kill to satisfy his wrath. But once the blood of Christ had been spilled, God was suddenly free to be patient with sinners. The shedding of the blood magically changed the way God dealt with humanity. But this is undermined by the Hebrew scriptures themselves. For instance, as we have already seen, Deuteronomy 20 distinguishes between the Canaanite cities and those outside the borders of the territories God was giving to Israel. Those inside the borders were to be annihilated as punishment for their sins. Those outside the borders were to be offered terms of peace. So it is not as though God was incapable of being patient with sinners. The unlucky ones were only those who happened to live where God determined Israel belonged.

Another relevant text is Jonah. As we mentioned above, the wickedness of the Ninevites was so rank that Yahweh could smell it from heaven. He determined to wipe them out, but sent Jonah to warn them first. In response to Jonah's warning, the Assyrians repented, and Yahweh had mercy on them and forgave them. But in the text, no blood sacrifice is offered to Yahweh. The Ninevites put on sackcloth and sat in ashes. They mourned. They fasted. They turned from their wicked ways. Yet no blood sacrifice was offered, and Yahweh forgave them. Moreover, it was *prior* to his crucifixion that Jesus condemned the Jewish elites of his generation for their unbelief and invoked against them the integrity of the Ninevites. Jesus declared that those who repented at the proclamation of Jonah would stand up and judge those who refused to repent at the proclamation of Jesus (Matt 12:41; Luke 11:32).

Thus, it is hardly the case that Yahweh required a blood sacrifice in order to be patient with sinners, or even to forgive them. Christ's death did not fundamentally change the way Yahweh dealt with sinners. Long before the execution of Jesus of Nazareth, Yahweh was forgiving the wickedest of them without demanding a blood sacrifice. Yet in the case of the Canaanites, no opportunity to repent was offered; no prophet was sent to them.

New Testament Approval

Christopher Wright appeals to the witness of the Christian scriptures (or New Testament) in order to defend the moral legitimacy of the Canaanite genocides. To him, it is significant that "never did Jesus or any of the New

Testament writers critique the words or actions of God in the Old Testament or suggest that the stories were immoral in their own context."[50] Wright cites Heb 11:31, which refers to the people of Jericho as "those who were disobedient," as an example of a Christian text confirming as legitimate the justification of divine punishment for the genocides.[51] The problem for Wright is that the book of Hebrews is the *only* book in the entire New Testament that even alludes to the book of Joshua. Furthermore, Hebrews itself only alludes to Joshua in one other place (Heb 4:8), and in that case it is essentially to deny that the entrance into the Promised Land in Joshua's generation was the true fulfillment of God's promise!

Another problem for Wright is that besides the reference to the destruction of Jericho in Heb 11:31, the author of Hebrews alludes to a number of morally problematic episodes from the Hebrew Bible and ascribes moral legitimacy to them. For instance, just a few verses later in Heb 11:32–34, the author cites Jephthah as an example of virtue, who "by faith" was able to "escape the edge of the sword, find strength out of weakness, become valiant in battle, and rout the armies of foreigners." You will remember Jephthah from our last chapter. He was the warrior who made a vow to offer a human sacrifice to Yahweh in exchange for victory in battle. After Yahweh afforded him victory, Jephthah subsequently offered his virgin daughter to Yahweh as a burnt offering. The account in Judges does not condemn Jephthah for the action, and the author of Hebrews praises Jephthah as a man of faith. To say that the author of Hebrews simply *assumes* that Jephthah's human sacrifice is condemnable is to go well beyond what the text actually says.

In fact, the acclamation of Jephthah as a hero of the faith is consistent with a general trend in late and post-Second Temple Judaism in which biblical interpreters, for the sake of community instruction, sought to render morally ambiguous characters from the Hebrew Bible as either unambiguously good or evil. We see this trend with respect to a number of biblical characters, including Lot, Esau, Balaam, and King Manasseh.[52] Therefore, contrary to Wright's claim that the praise of biblical heroes in Hebrews 11 "does not whitewash evil actions done by some of them,"[53] we find that reading the reference to Jephthah in Hebrews 11 in light of this trend and in light of its immediate context makes it clear that the author of Hebrews has

50. Wright, *The God I Don't Understand*, 81.

51. Ibid., 93.

52. On Lot, see Kugel, *The Bible as It Was*, 181–85; on Esau, see ibid., 202–08; on Balaam, ibid., 482–87; on King Manasseh, see Hulbert, "Traditions about Manasseh" and Halpern, "Why Manasseh Is Blamed," esp. 491.

53. Wright, *The God I Don't Understand*, 81.

determined to categorize Jephthah as one of the unambiguously righteous exemplars of the faith. Succinctly put, Hebrews 11 whitewashes Jephthah.

Accordingly, I find it to be a problematic move to suggest that the description of the inhabitants of Jericho as "those who were disobedient" in Heb 11:31 should be read as though it constitutes any serious attempt on the part of the biblical writer to engage in sober and critical moral reflection on the episode. The purpose of the book of Hebrews was not to make such moral judgments about antiquated historical episodes. James Kugel summarizes the approach of Jewish biblical commentators from this period: "The past was not approached in the spirit of antiquarianism but for what message it might yield, and this is necessarily predicated on an interpretive stance, indeed, a willingness to deviate from the texts' plain sense. The words of prophets, the accounts of ancient historians, were to be 'translated' into present-day significance, referred to (and sometimes distorted) in order to support a particular view of the present, or a program for the future."[54]

Earlier biblical ideas were rejected regularly in the Hebrew scriptures themselves and within the literature of post-exilic Judaism, including the Christian scriptures, without the necessity of any explicit statements denying the authority of the scriptures they contradicted. For instance, Jesus outright rejects the understanding of *suffering as punishment for sin* that we see in the traditional wisdom literature and in the Deuteronomistic history books (John 9:3). Also, New Testament writers regularly subverted militant messianic texts such as Psalms 2 and 110 by reapplying them to the Isaianic motif of suffering servanthood as they saw it exemplified in the life and death of Jesus of Nazareth.[55] Explicit reference to and verbal rejection of a text is not the only way to be critical of it, and for that reason Wright is mistaken in his assumption that because the conquest narratives are never directly confronted in the Christian scriptures, they are therefore not challenged or subverted by new ideas.

With that said, I am not making the claim that Jesus or the writers of the Christian scriptures consciously rejected the ideology of genocide we find in the conquest narratives and elsewhere in the Hebrew Bible. In fact, according to the synoptic Gospels, Jesus identified the inevitable destruction of Jerusalem by the Romans as Yahweh's punishment (Luke 19:41–44) and even compared Yahweh's imminent judgment of Jerusalem with that of

54. Kugel and Greer, *Early Biblical Interpretation*, 38.

55. See Enz, *The Christian and Warfare*, 69–80. I do not fully concur with Enz's assessment that the New Testament writers were pacifistic, at least not in the typical Anabaptist sense, but Enz does a fine job of showing how the militant psalms are taken out of context by the Christian writers for their own purposes. Enz calls this "redeeming metaphors" (80).

Sodom and Gomorrah, claiming that the latter two cities would be better off than Jerusalem on the day of divine judgment (Matt 10:15)!

The problem is that Wright appeals to Jesus and the Christian writers as some sort of trump card. It is as though we all assume that the New Testament is more sacred ground than the Old Testament. Wright's logic concedes that the Old Testament may at least be questioned, but if the questionable material in the Old Testament is approved of in the New, that fact automatically settles the matter. What Wright is doing, essentially, is defending inerrancy by depending on the assumption of inerrancy, which is the very point of dispute in the first place. This is begging the question. Appeals to the New Testament's perspective to defend the moral problems in the Hebrew Bible are another example of apologetic sleight of hand. The obvious moral difficulties are not resolved by Wright's pointing out that other writers of scripture did not see them. If that is true (and I do not necessarily disagree with Wright on this), that fact only compounds the problem for inerrancy. No matter how many biblical writers agree on an issue, if what they believe is an error, it is an error. Internal consistency does not make a wrong right.

God Is Good, All the Time

"If God is all the Bible says he is, all that he does must be good—and that includes authorization of genocide."[56] So says biblical inerrantist Eugene Merrill. This statement represents the thinking of a broad swathe of Evangelical Christians and fundamentalist biblical scholars. It is essentially the last resort of those who have tried and failed to defend the Canaanite genocides by appeal to ordinary conceptions of morality. Whatever God does must be good, because good is defined as whatever God does. If what God does does not appear to us to be good, that is only because our mere mortal minds cannot comprehend the complexities of God. So says Daniel Gard: "What appears to the human mind as 'evil' acts of God (such as the genocide commands against the Canaanites) are in fact not 'evil' acts at all since they come from the Lord himself. There simply comes a point in which human reason must bow to the divine and recognize that his ways are truly not ours and his thoughts are truly above our own (cf. Isa 55:8–9)."[57]

At first glance, William Lane Craig seems to take a similar position:

> According to the version of divine command ethics which I've defended, our moral duties are constituted by the commands of a holy and loving God. Since God doesn't issue commands

56. Merrill, "Moderate Discontinuity," 94.

57. Gard, "Response to C. S. Cowles," 55.

to Himself, He has no moral duties to fulfill. He is certainly not subject to the same moral obligations and prohibitions that we are. For example, I have no right to take an innocent life. For me to do so would be murder. But God has no such prohibition. He can give and take life as He chooses. We all recognize this when we accuse some authority who presumes to take life as "playing God." Human authorities arrogate to themselves rights which belong only to God. God is under no obligation whatsoever to extend my life for another second. If He wanted to strike me dead right now, that's His prerogative.[58]

What Craig is essentially saying is that human morality consists of God saying to us, "Do as I say, not as I do." To us, morality is whatever God tells us to do. But since there is no one to tell God what to do, God is, as it were, above morality, and is free to do otherwise than what God has commanded us.

Yet this description of God's morality seems to be in real tension with Craig's language elsewhere, where he maintains that God does not arbitrarily choose what is good and what is evil. Rather, "Christian theologians believe God to have certain essential virtues, such as love, fairness, impartiality, compassion, and so on. These are as essential to God as having three angles is to a triangle."[59] Moreover, the commands that God issues to humankind "are not arbitrary but grounded in the nature of a just and loving God."[60]

Can you spot the contradiction? The first time around, Craig said that God's command prohibits human beings from taking innocent life, but that, since God is not subject to any such command, God is able to take innocent life at will without moral contradiction. Conversely, the second time around, Craig stated that God is loving, fair, impartial, and compassionate *by very definition*, and that any command God issues to humankind is derived from those incontrovertible characteristics of God. If God's commands are derived directly from who God is by definition (as in the second case), how would it be possible for God to go against one of those commands (as in the first case)? This is a logical contradiction.

Despite himself, Craig ultimately comes down on the side of the second scenario: God cannot be other than what God is, and God's commands to humankind are directly derived from what God is. Therefore, God cannot go against God's own commands. If God tells us that we cannot kill an innocent person, then it would be a contradiction of God's very nature for God to kill an innocent person. Craig reveals that this is what he actually believes

58. Craig, "Slaughter of the Canaanites," para. 17.
59. Craig, "Divine Command Morality," para. 13.
60. Ibid., para. 15.

when he concedes that it would be possible to show that a given command is *inconsistent* with God's nature. Referring to God's directives concerning the slaughter of the Canaanites, Craig writes that "the biblical theist needs to show how such commands are consistent with God's nature"[61] by defending the proposition that "God had morally sufficient reasons for what He commanded the Israelis [*sic*] to do, reasons that are not contrary to His nature."[62] Craig then states that, "If such a defense fails, then one will have to either give up the historicity of these stories . . . or else hold that the Jews erroneously thought God had commanded them to drive out the Canaanites."[63]

Therefore, by Craig's criteria, if it *cannot be shown* that God's command to kill Canaanite children *does not* contradict God's inherent properties such as fairness, impartiality, justice, or compassion, then the theist must conclude that God could not have commanded the Israelites to kill Canaanite children. Or, as Craig puts it, "If we Christians can't find a good answer to the question before us and are, moreover, persuaded that such a command is inconsistent with God's nature, then we'll have to give up biblical inerrancy."[64] I couldn't agree more.

So despite initial appearances, it is clear now that Craig is *not* within the company of those who insist that the Canaanite genocides are good simply because Yahweh ordered them. For Craig, if we determine that there is no morally sufficient reason to kill children, then we must conclude that God, by definition, could not have issued such a command and therefore that the biblical accounts are flawed. Craig is not, therefore, a moral relativist—at least in principle.

But Craig does not speak for Eugene Merrill, or Daniel Gard, or A. van de Beek, the latter of whom characterizes the dogmatic inerrantist position in very stark terms: "What goodness is at a specific moment is determined by the action of God at that moment. And if today God acts differently than yesterday, goodness today is different from what it was yesterday. God is the criterion for good and evil. . . . There is no authority above him to which he could be subject."[65] In other words, God is not subject to what we would call morality. God literally *makes* and *remakes* morality with God's every action. This is precisely the position that Craig identifies as moral relativism and therefore rejects.[66] In this picture of God, there is no consistent character. If

61. Ibid., para. 16.

62. Ibid., para. 19.

63. Ibid., para. 17.

64. Craig, "Slaughter of the Canaanites," para. 16.

65. Van de Beek, *Why?*, 263.

66. Craig, "Divine Command Morality," para. 19.

God has no consistent character, then God's self-revelation would be meaningless, because anything we learn about God could potentially be contradicted the moment God chose to be otherwise.

Moreover, to say that God is good when God does precisely what God
has told us is evil is to render the language of good and evil meaningless. If
God commanded genocide, then to say that God is good is to render "good"
utterly unintelligible. C. S. Cowles puts the matter this way: "If the indiscriminate slaughter of human beings for any reason can be called a 'good'
and 'righteous' act . . . then all moral and ethical absolutes are destroyed, all
distinctions between good and evil are rendered meaningless, and all claims
about God's love and compassion become cruel deceptions. It represents the
ultimate corruption of human language and makes meaningful theological
discourse virtually impossible."[67] Echoing Cowles, Eric Seibert writes that "if
God's standard of justice is so fundamentally different from ours that physical abuse and the slaughters of babies can be considered just, then it no longer seems possible to have a meaningful conversation about what constitutes
justice."[68]

Thus it seems clear that, once again, the foremost apologists for an absolute morality rooted in God's nature have chosen to abandon the cause
in the name of biblical inerrancy. Take for instance the issue of abortion. In
most cases, these same apologists take the view that abortion is a damnable
species of murder and that their god condemns it. They believe the Bible
teaches a consistent principle of the sanctity of human life. Yet they also affirm that this same god commanded soldiers to kill pregnant women and
the unborn children inside them. They can't have it both ways. Either their
god condemns the killing of unborn children or he condones it. Yet they are
generally oblivious to the way their modern-day moral and political positions are frequently undermined by the very Bible in whose inerrancy they
profess to believe.[69]

Admittedly, there is a certain element of well-intentioned piety in the
claim that God's goodness is beyond our comprehension. This attitude is
meant to glorify and honor God, and to keep ourselves from arrogantly setting ourselves up in God's place as ultimate moral arbiters. Yet as Seibert
remarks, "Rather than glorifying God, this approach actually dishonors God
by suggesting God sometimes acts in ways that are incongruous with our
most basic beliefs about what is right."[70] It is not that we think our "most ba-

67. Cowles, "Response to Eugene H. Merrill," 100.

68. Seibert, *Disturbing Divine Behavior*, 74.

69. See Avalos, "Creationists for Genocide."

70. Seibert, *Disturbing Divine Behavior*, 73–74.

sic beliefs" are more important than God. It is just that we have good reason to think that it is much more likely that imperfect human beings killed other human beings in God's name than that a God who is somehow good determined that it was necessary to kill children for their parents' misdeeds. One is almost an everyday occurrence: human beings have forever been killing in the name of their gods. The other is a logical impossibility.[71]

Of course, it is at this point that some apologist for biblical inerrancy will resort to the old cliché: "God is mysterious. The answers are not clear to us now, for now we see dimly. But they will become clear on that day, for then we shall see face to face." This is of course partly right. How it is possible to affirm both that God committed genocide and that God is good—that is a mystery. Whether it's a profound mystery or a convenient one is up to you to decide.[72]

Allegorizing Genocide

From the earliest times, Christians have had difficulty managing the conquest narratives. A dominant strategy throughout the first several Christian centuries was to allegorize the texts, so that Israel's conquest of Canaan became a metaphor for the Christian mission to the Gentiles, or for Christ's conquest of the soul. Origen is representative when he writes that "within us are the Canaanites, the Perizzites, and the Jebusites" (*Hom. Jes. Nav.* 1.7). In other words, the conquest account is not to be read literally as the divinely sanctioned slaughter of entire tribes, but as an allegory of the conquest that takes place within the soul of the believer. Significantly, however, for Origen the use of allegory is not merely a hermeneutical option chosen to make a historical text relevant for the building up of the Christian community; rather, the allegorical reading is necessitated by the problematic content of the material itself: "As for the command given to the Jews to slay their enemies, it may be answered that anyone who looks carefully into the meaning of the passage will find that it is impossible to interpret it literally" (*Cels.* 7.19). In his *Homily on Joshua*, Origen reiterates this position. Referring to the genocidal narratives in the book of Joshua, he stipulates that "unless those carnal wars were a symbol of spiritual wars, I do not think that the Jewish historical books would

71. There are at least two other possibilities. (1) God does not exist. (2) God exists but is malevolent and not good. If the latter is true, the issue is whether one thinks such a God is worthy of worship. Would it be moral or immoral to worship a malevolent God simply by virtue of its sheer power?

72. For a more concise survey and critique of apologetic strategies for salvaging the biblical genocide narratives, see Avalos, *Fighting Words*, 159–70.

ever have been passed down by the apostles to be read by Christ's followers in their churches" (*Hom. Ios.* 15.1).[73] Origen averred that the only alternative to allegorizing the texts is to go the way of Marcion!

Yet Origen, who was a pacifist, did not find the content objectionable simply on account of the violence.[74] This is clear because in *Against Celsus* 7.26, Origen explains that it was necessary for the Israelites to make war in order to survive as a nation, but that since the proclamation of the gospel, Christians are not tied to land or any nationality, rendering war among them obsolete. What Origen is displaying in this is that he makes a distinction between Israel's defensive wars and its genocides. The former may safely be taken literally, but the latter must be taken metaphorically.

Over a century later, the Cappadocian Father Gregory of Nyssa—a thoroughly orthodox theologian and Christian philosopher—approached the moral problem of the tenth plague (the slaughter of Egypt's firstborn children) in precisely the same way as Origen. In his *Life of Moses*, Gregory interprets the killing of the firstborn sons of Egypt as an expression of "the principle that it is necessary to destroy utterly the first birth of evil" (*Mos.* 2.90).[75] Referring again to the killing of the firstborn, Gregory asks,

> How would a concept worthy of God be preserved in the description of what happened if one looked only to the history? The Egyptian (Pharaoh) acts unjustly, and in his place is punished his newborn child, who in his infancy cannot discern what is good and what is not. His life has no experience of evil, for infancy is not capable of passion. He does not know to distinguish between his right and his left. The infant lifts his eyes only to his mother's nipple, and tears are the sole perceptible sign of his sadness. And if he obtains anything which his nature desires, he signifies pleasure by smiling. If such a one now pays the penalty of his father's wickedness, where is justice? Where is piety? Where is holiness? Where is Ezekiel, who cries: *The man who has sinned is the man who must die* and *a son is not to suffer for the sins of his father*? How can the history so contradict reason? (*Mos.* 2.91)

Gregory concludes that the only legitimate recourse is an allegorical reading. The solution must be that the murderous events on the night of the first Passover took place "typologically," as a lesson for believers. According

73. Quoted in Swift, "Early Christian Views," 286.

74. *Contra* Swift, *Early Fathers*, 59, who mistakes Origen's objection to the genocides as a general objection to violence.

75. This and subsequent quotations from Gregory of Nyssa are the translation of Mahlerbe and Ferguson, *Life of Moses*.

to Gregory, the lesson is this: "When through virtue one comes to grips with any evil, he must completely destroy the first beginnings of evil" (*Mos.* 2.92). To destroy these "first beginnings of evil" means, in colloquial terms, to "nip the problem in the bud." For Gregory, then, the tenth Egyptian plague is the equivalent of Jesus' teaching in Matthew 5, wherein Jesus is "all but explicitly calling on us to kill the firstborn of the Egyptian evils when he commands us to abolish lust and anger and to have no more fear of the stain of adultery or the guilt of murder" (*Mos.* 2.93).

I will have more to say about the value of the allegorical method later, but for now suffice it to say three things. First, what is good about the strategies of Origen, Gregory of Nyssa, and many others of their day, is that they are fully cognizant of the problematic nature of the text when taken to be literal claims about Yahweh's genocidal commands and actions. They came to grips with the texts soberly and concluded that if they are to continue to be of any use to the church, the literal interpretation must be rejected in favor of a metaphorical reading that produces a message more worthy of God's character and Christian discipleship. Second, the problem with this method is that it does not directly confront the text, and although Origen and Gregory are aware of the moral reasoning behind their adoption of the allegorical method, eventually the historical, literal interpretation will find its way back into the life of the church, precisely as it did later on in church history with the emergence of the Crusades, the Inquisition, Manifest Destiny, and other Christian appropriations of the conquest ideology. Third, in one sense, allegorizing a problematic text is little different from simply discarding it—because the text's original meaning is simply ignored. This can quickly become dishonest and can blind believers to problematic aspects of their faith heritage. These problems will be discussed more fully in chapter 9.

Inventing Genocide

So far we have been examining the conquest narratives on the assumption that what they say happened did in fact happen. On this assumption we've found that the events depicted in the narratives cannot be justified morally, and that the justifications offered by the text for the atrocities committed tend to contradict themselves. Yet apart from the moral difficulties involved with the Canaanite genocides, the conquest narratives face serious problems with regard to historicity. Many of the conquest accounts depicted in the biblical narratives are in fact contradicted both by archaeological and internal textual evidence.

Archaeological Problems

In Num 20:14–21, the Israelites head east across the Negev and arrive at Edom, where, according to the text, they are refused passage by the king of Edom. Yet the archaeological record indicates that at this period, there were only a meager number of nomadic tribes in the region of Edom. Israel could not have been denied access by the king of Edom, since Edom did not attain statehood until the seventh century BCE, approximately 600 years after the events depicted in Numbers. There was no king to deny them access!

Num 21:1–3 narrates that Israel destroyed all the cities of the northern Negev, in the region of Arad. One of the cities they subsequently renamed "Hormah" (meaning "destruction"). Contrary to this, excavations in the 1970s found that no Late Bronze Age occupational levels exist in this entire region. In other words, at the time of the supposed Israelite attacks, nobody was home. With regard to the city of Arad in particular, it was not founded until the tenth century BCE, about 300 years after the events described in Numbers. Furthermore, the tenth century city of Arad was built upon the ruins of an Early Bronze Age settlement, which was abandoned at around 2600 BCE. Thus, at the time the Israelites are said to have destroyed it, Arad had already been a ruin for over 1,300 years.

Recall our earlier discussion of Israel's battle with Sihon, the Amorite king of Heshbon. Israel asked for safe passage through Sihon's territory. In the Numbers account, Sihon refused the peace treaty and attacked Israel unprovoked. In the account in Deuteronomy 2, Sihon refused because Yahweh intervened to prevent him from accepting. From 1968–1976, the site of Heshbon was excavated by a group archaeologists who also happened to be confessing Seventh-day Adventists. They had set out to prove the accuracy of the Bible. What they found instead was no evidence of any Late Bronze Age settlements. In fact, according to their results, the city of Heshbon was not founded until the Iron II period—at the earliest, 250 years after the events depicted in Numbers and Deuteronomy.

According to Num 21:30 (also 32:3), the Israelites sieged and subdued the Moabite city of Dibon. This site was excavated by a group of Southern Baptist scholars in the 1950s, who again were expecting the biblical claims to be validated by the archaeological record. Their excavation resulted in the discovery of the sparse remains of a city from the ninth century BCE, some 400 years after the time of the conquest, and no Late Bronze Age residues. Once again, Israel had sieged a city that wasn't there.

Joshua 2–6 narrates the conquest of the city of Jericho, famous for its tumbling walls. British archaeologist John Garstang excavated the site of Jericho in the 1920s and found the remains of a wall, the destruction of which he dated just prior to the then-accepted period of the biblical conquest. (Garstang's excavation was sponsored by an evangelical foundation.) In the 1950s, however, prominent British archaeologist Kathleen Kenyon excavated the site again and with a superior modern methodology, she concluded that Garstang's wall had been destroyed by the Egyptians during a well-attested campaign in that region during that period. The now accepted date for the biblical conquest, however, is some 200 years later (the mid-thirteenth century BCE),[76] and from that period neither Garstang nor Kenyon found any evidence of occupation in Jericho. Kenyon suggested that it is possible that remains from an occupation during the thirteenth century could have eroded away during the 400 years it was left unoccupied, but it is unlikely that no evidence of occupation would have survived such erosion. After all, strong evidence of occupation from the sixteenth century remains, having survived over 200 years of erosion between the sixteenth and fourteenth centuries, as even Kenneth Kitchen acknowledges.[77] Thus, although it is in theory possible that Jericho was occupied during the period of the conquest, the complete lack of evidence makes it highly unlikely.[78]

Joshua 7–8 describes the destruction of the city of Ai. In the 1930s, the site was thoroughly excavated by Judith Marquet-Krause, a French Jewish archaeologist. She unearthed an Early-Bronze Age city-state, replete with palaces and temples, all of which was demolished in the twenty-third century BCE. Between the twenty-third and the sixteenth centuries, occupations of the city were negligible. From the sixteenth to the twelfth centuries BCE, Ai was entirely unoccupied. In the 1960s, American archaeologist Joseph Callaway, a conservative Christian and a professor at Southern Baptist Theological Seminary, set out to reexamine the site, hoping to vindicate the biblical account against the findings of Marquet-Krause some three decades earlier. Instead, Callaway confirmed her findings and was forced to concede the historical inaccuracy of the account in Joshua 7–8. Callaway wrote, "For many years, the primary source for the understanding of the settlement of the first Israelites was the Hebrew Bible, but every reconstruction based upon the biblical traditions has foundered on the evidence from archaeological remains."[79] (After this, Callaway took an early retirement from the Southern Baptist Theological Seminary.)

76. This date is even accepted by Egyptologist and conservative biblical apologist Kenneth Kitchen. See Kitchen, *Reliability*, 256.

77. Ibid., 187.

78. See Kathleen Kenyon's summary of the data in Kenyon, *Digging Up Jericho*, 256–65.

79. Callaway, "A New Perspective," 72. See also his summary of the relevant data in

These facts seem to be reflected in the name given to the city by the biblical accounts themselves. Ai literally means "ruin." Most scholars believe that the account of the destruction of Ai was an etiological narrative, explaining how the ruin came to be such. That it is known in the Bible by no other name than "ruin" suggests that it was already a ruin by the time the Israelites arrived. This is in fact what the archaeological record shows, a fact that is quite problematic for inerrantists. Conservative biblical archaeologist Alfred Hoerth concludes that "the solution to the 'Ai problem' continues to be elusive."[80]

The next account in the book of Joshua is that of Gibeon. By means of deception, the Gibeonites managed to procure a peace treaty from the Israelites, saving themselves—according to the narrative—from the Israelite invasion. The Gibeonites were spared, but only as slaves to the Israelites. In the 1960s, James Pritchard, an American archaeologist and a devout Christian, excavated the site of ancient Gibeon. Pritchard unearthed some remains from the Iron Age, none of which could be dated prior to the eighth century BCE (500 years after the biblical conquest). Gibeon did not exist during the time of the conquest. The account in Joshua itself indicates the etiological motivation for the story. Josh 9:27 indicates that the Gibeonites were, at the time of the book of Joshua's composition, the slaves of the Judeans. Thus it is probable that the account of the Gibeonites' ruse served to legitimize the servitude of the Gibeonites to the Judeans—their status as slave laborers was depicted as a gesture of mercy on the part of Israel.

One of the few sites at which excavations have shown evidence to corroborate a biblical conquest account is Hazor,[81] which has been excavated by Yigael Yadin and his protégé Amnon Ben-Tor from Hebrew University in Jerusalem. They have found destruction levels dating to the thirteenth century—the period of the conquest. This means that the account of the destruction of Hazor in Josh 11:10–13 is most likely based on a tradition with a historical kernel.[82]

In light of this overwhelming evidence against the historicity of the biblical conquest account, some conservative biblical apologists have begun to attempt to use this to their advantage. For instance, Paul Copan argues

Callaway, "The Settlement in Canaan," 55–90.

80. Hoerth, *Archaeology and the Old Testament*, 212.

81. Hazor and other sites corroborating the conquest accounts are discussed in Mazar, *Archaeology*, 332.

82. The above information is laid out more clearly and summarized more fully in Dever, *Early Israelites*, 23–50. See also the very accessible treatments in Mazar, *Archaeology*, 329–34; and Finkelstein and Silberman, *The Bible Unearthed*, 72–96. Finally, I am deeply indebted to Christopher Rollston for his helpful comments here.

from the archaeological evidence that the Canaanite conquest *did not occur*, thereby exonerating Yahweh and the Israelites from charges of genocide.[83] Yet this is hardly a defensible strategy.[84] Apart from conceding the loss of biblical inerrancy, it continues to ignore two facts. First, such annihilations most likely *did* occur, as the archaeological record at Hazor and some other sites seems to confirm. There is no reason to doubt that early Israelites did engage in such warfare. Although Ai, Jericho, and other genocidal battles probably never occurred, it is not likely that such stories were invented whole cloth. They would have been rooted in the historical memory of similar battles, although probably much fewer in number than the account in Joshua claims. Second, even if the genocides never took place historically, that does not remove the problem that they are presented as Yahweh's ideal in the scriptures. Even if it *is* merely rhetoric, it is *evil* rhetoric. Apologists taking this tack have unwittingly conceded to my own position: that a loving God could not have commanded genocide, and our scriptures are therefore deeply problematic.

Textual Problems

Apart from the archaeological disconfirmations of the biblical conquest narratives, the narratives themselves often tend to contradict their own claims. For instance, Joshua 10–12 claims that Joshua utterly destroyed the kings, armies, and all of the inhabitants of numerous cities, including Aphek, Bethel, Dor, Gezer, Megiddo, and Jerusalem. It is said that Joshua left no survivors, and that he gave these territories over to the various tribes of Israel to inhabit (12:7). Joshua left not a single survivor and completed the task of conquest, doing "everything that Yahweh had commanded Moses" (11:15). After all of the conquered lands were allotted to the Israelite tribes (14:5), "there was peace in the land" (14:15). "The country lay vanquished at their feet" (18:1).

Nevertheless, after the death of Joshua, it is clear that the conquest was far from finished. In Judg 1:21–36, a list of all the Canaanite cities still remaining to be conquered is given, cities still fully inhabited by Canaanites peoples. Among these yet-to-be-conquered cities are Aphek, Bethel, Dor, Gezer, Megiddo, and Jerusalem—six of the cities which Joshua 10–12 claimed were utterly destroyed, their entire populations put to the sword! Moreover, Josh 12:10 names Jerusalem as one of the cities conquered by Joshua and handed over to the allotted Israelite tribe. Yet in 2 Sam 5:6, during the time of David,

---

83. Copan, "Are Old Testament Laws Evil?" Copan's argument follows conservative stalwart Richard Hess in Hess, *Joshua*, 150–57. My thanks to Hector Avalos for bringing these references to my attention.

84. See the criticisms made against this apologetic strategy in Avalos, *Fighting Words*, 162–63.

Jerusalem still belongs to the Jebusites, who are described as "the inhabitants of the land." David proceeds to siege Jerusalem and to take it, later to make it the capital city of Judea. So who captured Jerusalem? Was it Joshua or David?

The same problem presents itself with the account of the annihilation of the tribes of Midian in Numbers 31. The account claims that Israel utterly destroyed all five tribes of Midian, including their kings and their armies. They killed all the male inhabitants of the cities, but took as spoil the children and the women. Moses subsequently ordered the execution of all of the male children and the women who were not virgins. According to the text, all that remained of Midian was its virgin daughters, who were by Yahweh's fiat assimilated into the people of Israel as trophy wives, concubines, and slaves. The destruction of the Midianites by Moses is reiterated as a historical event in Josh 13:21. Nevertheless, Judges 6 tells us that only a few generations later, the Midianites are not only alive but are powerful and numerous enough to have been Israel's oppressors! How did this occur? Did the surviving virgins who were assimilated into Israel's ranks conceive from their Israelite husbands and secretly raise a Midianite army?

Inerrantist biblical scholar Christopher Wright acknowledges these discrepancies, but dispenses with them by claiming that descriptions of the slaughter of "everything that lives and breathes" were "not necessarily intended literally."[85] This of course is a classic example of the unwritten inerrantist hermeneutical principle that historical texts must be interpreted literally unless or until a literal interpretation creates a factual discrepancy, in which case it obviously must be taken metaphorically.

"He struck the city with the edge of the sword and everyone in it leaving no one left alive" (Josh 10:30). "Joshua struck him and his people, leaving alive no survivors" (Josh 10:33). "Every person in the city he destroyed utterly on that day" (Josh 10:35). Joshua "struck it with the edge of the sword, including its king and its cities, and every human in them, leaving no one left alive" (Josh 10:37). According to Wright, this is all metaphorical, a rhetorical exaggeration. *Although it says that Joshua killed every last breathing human being in each town, what it really means is that he killed some of them, but left alive enough of the population that they would be strong enough to continue engaging the Israelites in combat for generations to come.* Does this mean Yahweh was being metaphorical when he commanded the Israelites, time and again, to leave no survivors? "As for the cities that Yahweh your God is giving you for your inheritance, you must not let anything that breathes remain alive. You shall devote them to utter destruction . . . just as Yahweh your God has commanded" (Deut 20:16–17).

85. Wright, *The God I Don't Understand*, 88.

Despite these problems, Wright tenuously insists that "when we are reading some of the more graphic descriptions, either of what was commanded to be done or of what was recorded as accomplished, we need to allow for this rhetorical element. This is not to accuse the biblical writers of falsehood, but to recognize the literary conventions of writing about warfare."[86] Yet this is hardly a satisfactory way to dispense with these contradictions. The purpose of the narratives in Joshua was to present him as the ideal leader, the one who was perfectly obedient to the command of Yahweh. So when Yahweh ordered that not a single survivor from among the Canaanites should remain, Joshua was depicted as *obedient*. "Just as Yahweh had commanded his servant Moses to do, so Moses commanded Joshua. And Joshua did what he was told. He did everything that Yahweh had commanded Moses to do, leaving nothing undone" (Josh 11:15). What command did Joshua fulfill? The verse just prior informs us: "They struck down all the people of the cities with the edge of the sword until they had devoted them all to utter destruction, and they did not allow anyone who had breath to remain alive" (Josh 11:14). But if Joshua only *metaphorically* left no survivors, then he was not obedient to the command to leave no survivors, as the text says he was. Wright's attempt to resolve the textual discrepancies, and thereby to exonerate Yahweh, fails.

Paul Copan also goes to great lengths to persuade us that the command to kill "all that breathes" is a mere rhetorical exaggeration, and that we should not therefore take the text to indicate that the Israelite warriors slaughtered noncombatants, women, or children.[87] First, the comparative evidence undermines such a claim. The language of the ban, of "devoting to destruction all that breathes" is used elsewhere and its meaning is clear. For instance, in the Mesha Stele, king Mesha of Moab boasts of killing all the people of the city (i.e., noncombatants) as a sacrifice to his god Kemosh. The same word that is used in Joshua to describe what the Israelites did to the inhabitants of Canaan is used by Mesha to describe what the Moabites did to a city in Israel. Mesha "devoted to destruction for Ashtar Kemosh" *seven thousand* males, plus all of the females and servant girls. It is difficult to see how this could be a "rhetorical exaggeration." Even if it were an exaggeration, however, what does that leave us with? How many women and children is it acceptable to slaughter before it becomes morally problematic? Perhaps Joshua only put three girls to the sword in each town, even though he claimed to have killed them all. Would the fact that the murders were *exaggerated* get Joshua and Yahweh off the hook?

86. Ibid. Paul Copan also makes the "rhetorical exaggeration" argument in Copan, "Yahweh Wars and the Canaanites," 3.

87. Ibid.

Finally, even if we were to concede that the Conquest narratives are to be read hyperbolically, this argument cannot exonerate Yahweh from the charge of child-killing or lady-killing, since Num 31:17 gives explicit instructions to kill every male child of the Midianites, and all of their non-virgin females, instructions which can in nowise be taken hyperbolically. Neither can the genocide perpetrated by King Saul against the Amalekites be explained away by recourse to hyperbole (1 Sam 15). These texts are conveniently ignored by Copan and others who take this tack. Ultimately, the "rhetorical exaggeration" defense is a red herring.

An Ideological Solution

Wright is partly right, however. The conquest narratives do reflect broader "literary conventions of writing about warfare." Beyond mere literary conventions, in fact, the biblical conquest narratives fit within a genre of ancient Near Eastern literature that may be identified as *national origin myth*. In his monograph on ancient conquest myths, evangelical scholar Lawson Younger compares the chronicles in the book of Joshua to Hittite, Egyptian, and Assyrian conquest literature and concludes that the comparative evidence has shown that "the historical narrative in which Josh 9–12 is cast utilizes a common transmission code observable in numerous ancient Near Eastern conquest accounts, employing the same ideology."[88] According to Younger's careful analysis, "the ideology which lies behind the text of Joshua is one like that underlying other ancient Near Eastern conquest accounts—namely, imperialistic."[89] The literature reflects the attempt of rising empires to express their hegemony through origin stories that crystalize their present-day claims to power. These origin myths present the young nation as an unstoppable force, specially empowered by their deity whose strength far outstrips that of the other tribal deities. The myths serve to crystalize and legitimize the nation's rise to power.

I believe the preponderance of evidence shows us that this is precisely what is going on in the conquest narratives. As is obvious from our review of the archaeological record, a knowledge of thirteenth-century geography is entirely absent from the text; instead, the geography reflects the vantage point of a writer from about the seventh century BCE. A large number of critical scholars believe it is likely many of these accounts were written during

88. Younger, *Ancient Conquest Accounts*, 255. For further parallels between ancient Near Eastern and ancient Israelite holy war literature in general, see Cross, *Canaanite Myth*, 91–144; and Kang, *Divine War*.

89. Younger, *Ancient Conquest Accounts*, 255.

the reign of King Josiah, whose unprecedented (and extremely violent[90]) reforms consolidated religious and political power within Jerusalem.[91] Joshua, the ideal leader, would thus have been read as a type of Josiah.[92] The narrative functions as propaganda, helping to legitimize Josiah's consolidation of power in the name of national unity and faithfulness to Yahweh.[93] Historian Eric Hobsbawm points out that "traditions which appear or claim to be old are often quite recent in origin and sometimes invented."[94] According to Hobsbawm, history demonstrates that often the character of certain political institutions is "so unprecedented that even historic continuity [has] to be invented, for example by creating an ancient past beyond effective historical continuity, either by semi-fiction . . . or by forgery."[95]

Such invented or partly-invented origin myths are of course not anything new to us. We can find them in any Texas high school history textbook, in which we learn about the "hostile Indians" and the brave "Americans" who made the land secure for peace and prosperity. The "othering" of national enemies is a ubiquitous feature in these national origin myths. This kind of history-making is found wherever there is power, and especially where there is militaristic power with imperialistic pretensions. The evidence suggests that much of the history writing in our scriptures falls under this category of ideologically-motivated invented tradition as well.[96]

Reinventing Genocide

As I showed in the previous chapter, until about the seventh century BCE, human sacrifice was most probably a normal and acceptable—though obviously

90. See for example 2 Kgs 23:30: "He [Josiah] slaughtered on the altars all the priests of the high places who were there, and burned human bones on them."

91. The seminal texts are de Wette, *Critical and Historical Introduction*, and Noth, *Deuteronomistic History*.

92. So Rowlett, *Joshua and the Rhetoric of Violence*, 174.

93. Ibid.: "Therefore, Joshua, King's Josiah's stand-in, can appear to be motivated only by loyalty and obedience to the deity, rather than by an attempt to assert his own power. This is one of the rhetorical devices employed to mystify the inequities of the social order and to advance the power of the monarchy. The rhetoric [employs] a kind of false modesty: Yahweh is really in charge. Joshua (and by extension Josiah) poses merely as Yahweh's humble servant, acting as his proxy."

94. Hobsbawm, "Inventing Traditions," 1.

95. Ibid., 7.

96. On invented traditions in the Davidic period, see Hobbs, *A Time for War*, 59–69. On invented traditions throughout the Hebrew Bible, see Coote and Coote, *Power, Politics, and the Making of the Bible*.

somewhat rare—feature of Yahwistic worship in Israel and Judea. We recall also the account of the warrior Jephthah who made an exchange with Yahweh, trading victory in battle for the life of a human being—which tragically for Jephthah turned out to be his beloved daughter. It is quite likely that this ideology of human sacrifice in exchange for victory in battle is what lies behind the earliest accounts of Canaanite genocide. This ideology is seen very clearly in Num 21:2–3, where Israel says to Yahweh, "'If you will indeed give this people into my hands then I will devote their cities to destruction.' Then Yahweh listened to the voice of Israel, and handed over the Canaanites; and they devoted them and their cities to destruction."[97] As I noted earlier, the sacrificial nature of the genocide here is clear. Yahweh promises victory to the Israelites against Arad's forces, and in exchange Israel promises Yahweh the sacrificial offering of the cities' noncombatants. The "sacrifice" entailed the forfeiting of virgin wives and potential slaves out of gratitude to the deity for the victory.

It is possible that other justifications for the genocide accounts (such as punishment for sin and the eradication of the spiritual threat of Canaanite worship) represent later attempts to make the texts serviceable after the ideology of human sacrifice had fallen into disrepute[98] and, in addition, in order to function as a threat to those who resisted Josiah's program of religious centralization (which was against the norm for Yahwistic religion).[99] When Deut 20:17–18 says that Israel is to exterminate the Canaanites in order to protect themselves from Canaan's corrupt cultic rites, Collins thinks the Deuteronomistic historian could be attempting "to rationalize the practice [of the ban] by justifying it."[100] On the other hand, the ideology of genocide as human sacrifice and the justifications of divine punishment and ethnic cleansing are not mutually exclusive; they may have coexisted very early. Needless to say, however, the ideology of genocide as human sacrifice inevitably gave way to the other justifications once human sacrifice in general came to be associated with idolatry.

Concluding Genocide

In this chapter I have evaluated the standard apologetic justifications for the biblical genocides. I have shown that each attempt to justify these acts fails, that they are either contradicted by the biblical data themselves, or that they reflect a dangerous moral relativism that ultimately undermines the larger

97. This is the translation of Niditch, *War in the Hebrew Bible*, 32.

98. For a fuller argument, see Niditch, *War in the Hebrew Bible*, 28–77.

99. So Rowlett, *Joshua and the Rhetoric of Violence*, 173.

100. Collins, *Does the Bible Justify Violence?*, 8.

Christian theological project. In his defense of moral objectivism, William Lane Craig regularly remarks that "Nazi anti-Semitism was morally wrong, even though the Nazis who carried out the Holocaust thought that it was good; and it would still be wrong even if the Nazis had won World War II and succeeded in exterminating or brainwashing everybody who disagreed with them."[101] In the same way, I have argued that the genocides perpetrated by the ancient Israelites were morally wrong, even though the Israelites who carried out the genocides thought that they were good; and they are still wrong even though the Israelites produced scriptures that succeeded in brainwashing objective moralists who would otherwise disagree with them.[102]

I have also mentioned the archaeological evidence which contradicts the claims of many of the conquest stories. Some of the claims made in these stories are also contradicted elsewhere in the Bible itself. But the fact that some, if not many, of these genocides never took place should not bring too much relief to those of us who find ourselves wishing they never happened. We are still at the very least left with the fact that some of the authors of our scriptures thought it reasonable to attribute such atrocities to God. Moreover, the archaeological record suggests that *some such battles did occur*, and I have submitted that an ideology of human sacrifice is likely responsible for instigating at least some of ancient Israel's acts of genocide.

Nevertheless, as I said at the outset, my contention is that God never did command the Israelites to slaughter entire peoples wholesale. These accounts reflect a standard imperialistic ideology that Israel shared with many of its ancient neighbors, and I read them as products of ancient culture, not as products of pure divine revelation. Therefore, my claim is not that I know better than God, but that, by God's design, we all know better than those who wrongly killed women and children in God's name. In chapter 10 I will attempt to show how these texts can still be used by Christians as sacred scripture, without recourse to allegorization strategies or to Marcion's notorious scissor method.

101. Craig, "Meta-Ethical Foundations," 9.

102. Article eleven of the Chicago Statement on Biblical Application (CSBA) denies "that the indiscriminate slaughter of civilians can be a moral form of warfare." Article twelve denies "that any act is acceptable that would harm or diminish another person's natural or spiritual life by violating that person's human rights." It further denies "that age, disability, economic disadvantage, race, religion, or sex used as a basis for discrimination can ever justify denial of the exercise or enjoyment of human rights." Yet somehow the Chicago inerrantists are able to affirm, in article one of the CSBA, "that the revealed character and will of God are the foundation of all morality." See Alliance of Confessing Evangelicals, "Chicago Statement on Biblical Application."

7 THE SHEPHERD AND THE GIANT
GOVERNMENT PROPAGANDA

THERE IS A CANONICAL STORY ABOUT A YOUNG BOY WHO TOOK down a figure as tall as a tree. Maybe you've heard it before. It is the story of a child who was pure in heart, a boy who told it like it was, damn the consequences. The story goes that this young man came into the possession of a sharp new axe, and as boys are prone to do, he thought he ought to try it out. The eager lad took the axe to the base of a certain tree, and before he knew it, down it came. It made a helluva ruckus. Wherefore, along came the boy's father to see what all the commotion was.

"George," the father hollered, "Now who went and cut down muh cherry tree?" Young George gulped; looked his interrogator clean in the eyes.

"I cannot tell a lie, Pa. You know I cannot tell a lie. I did it with muh little hatchet."

As the story goes, the elder Washington beamed a little, and found himself assuaging the guilt of his impetuous but plainspoken son. To a proud father, a son's honesty was more than enough payment for a ruined cherry tree. Of course, the pride of a father would become the pride of a nation, as this boisterous but honest young lad grew up to become the first president of the United States of America. And what a comfort it was to a citizen to know that his fortune rested in the rugged hands of a man who could not tell a lie.

As most of us are now aware, this yarn is pure fiction, a fable concocted by the book-peddler and parson, Mason Locke Weems. It first appeared in his "biography" of George Washington published just one year after Washington's death. This tale is only one of many legendary anecdotes told about the first U.S. president during and not long after his lifetime. Washington was so well loved by his constituents, it is sometimes difficult to tell where the history ends and the legends begin. There was no need for any great passage of time before legends like this one could gain traction among the people. Sometimes, the truth people want is not the truth behind the man, but the truth behind what the man represents.

Just as George Washington represented the hopes and dreams of a nation newly united and liberated from foreign invasion, so too the biblical hero King David, a rugged shepherd boy of humble beginnings, symbolized for a newly united kingdom of Israel—north and south together—the promise of a glorious destiny under the providence of God, free from the tyranny of foreign armies. Just as Americans today look back to that first presidency, immortalizing the man as the model of virtue—everything a president ought to be—so too was King David immortalized from generation to generation, by those who yearned for the kingdom to return to the glory of its rugged youth. Just as legendary tales of Washington's virtue developed independently of the man himself, so it was with King David.

In this chapter we will take a look at another story about a young man who took down a figure as tall as a tree, a story whose significance can hardly be exaggerated. The legend of the epic battle between the giant and the little guy—it has been *the* source of inspiration for countless real life underdog stories. Yet just as the case is with the legend of Washington's cherry tree, we will discover that the legend of David and Goliath may reflect more the truth behind what the man represents than the truth behind the man.

The account of young David's epic victory over the accomplished soldier and giant of a man[1] is found in 1 Samuel 17. It is an amazing story about a young boy who had a simple faith that his god was mightier than the gods of his enemies. When no Israelite soldier would believe, the mere boy David stepped out in faith to face Israel's biggest enemy ever. Because of his faith, and his amazing God-given talent, the shepherd boy would conquer the giant.

Anachronisms and Discrepancies

A Head to Jerusalem

Yet a careful look at the text shows that the story in chapter 17 is an independent block—a tradition that originated independently of the main body of the book of Samuel, later grafted in by someone other than the author. One indication that the story in 1 Samuel 17 developed later is the presence of an anachronism in verse 53. We are told that after defeating Goliath,

1. According to the DSS and the LXX, Goliath was six and a half feet tall, which at the time of David would certainly have been considered a giant stature. Human beings were generally much shorter then than they are now. By the time of the Masoretes in the late first millennium CE (almost two thousand years after the era of Goliath), six and a half feet tall was no longer so impressive. Thus, the Masoretes amended the text, adding another three feet to Goliath's stature, and that is why many Bibles today have Goliath at nine and a half feet tall. See McCarter, *I Samuel*, 286, 291.

David brought Goliath's head with him to Jerusalem, but left his armor in his tent. Of course, at this time, the people of Israel had no relationship to Jerusalem; it was still under the control of the Jebusites. According to the book of Samuel, it would be many years before David conquered Jerusalem (see 2 Sam 5:6–9).

The Absent-Minded Potentate

The independent nature of 1 Samuel 17 is also clear from the obvious discontinuity between 1 Sam 16:21–22 and 1 Sam 17:55–58. In the former passage we learn that "David came to Saul, and entered his service. Saul had considerable affection for David, and David became Saul's armor-bearer. Saul sent a messenger to Jesse, saying, 'Allow David to remain in my service, for he has found favor in my sight.'" As you can see, Saul clearly has intimate knowledge of David, including knowledge of his family background. Yet in chapter 17, after "Saul saw David go up against the Philistine, he said to Abner (his military commander), 'Abner, this boy—whose son is he?' Abner said, 'King, As your soul lives, I do not know.' The king said, 'Find out whose son the youngster is.' When David returned from slaying the Philistine, Abner took him and brought him to Saul, with the Philistine's head in his hand. Saul asked him, 'Who is your father, boy?' And David answered, 'I am the son of your servant Jesse, from Bethlehem.'"

The disparity is obvious. In chapter 16, prior to the events of chapter 17, Saul has intimate knowledge of David and has singled him out as one favored among his servants. Yet in chapter 17, Saul not only does not know who David's father is, he does not even know who David is. It cannot be the case that Saul simply did not recognize David until he summoned him, because Saul and David spoke, at some length, just prior to David's going out against Goliath (17:31–40). Gleason Archer, an avowed inerrantist, attempts to resolve this contradiction by arguing that Saul is not inquiring about David's identity in 17:55–58, but only that of David's father.[2] However, Archer's explanation fails to convince for a number of reasons. First, when David is initially suggested to Saul in 16:18, David is commended to Saul as "a son of Jesse the Bethlehemite." Saul then proceeds to dispatch messengers to Jesse in order to request David's service (16:19). After David came into Saul's service and Saul developed a strong fondness for David (16:21), Saul sent messengers again to Jesse, asking him to allow David to remain in his service more permanently (16:22). Are we really to believe that Saul did not know the identity of David's father in 17:55?

2. Archer, *Old Testament Introduction*, 315.

More problematic still is Archer's basic claim that the issue in 17:55–58 is not David's identity but Jesse's. In the ancient world, a person's identity was not distinguishable from their lineage. This is why when David was first suggested to Saul in 16:18, David is not named but simply referred to as "a son of Jesse the Bethlehemite." Thus, when Saul inquires as to David's lineage, this is actually an attempt to familiarize himself with David. Moreover, nowhere in 17:31–58 does Saul refer to David by name. He refers to him with language indicating their unfamiliarity, i.e., "boy." Are we to believe this is the same "boy" who had recently found such favor in Saul's sight?

It is obvious, therefore, that the story of David and Goliath was not an original part of the narrative of the book of Samuel. What we have in chapters 16 and 17 are two different (and conflicting) accounts of David's initial entrance into Saul's court. The account in chapter 17, the more ostentatious of the two, was a later addition.

The Man Who Killed Goliath

But if David did kill Goliath as a young man, why did that not make it into the original composition of the book of Samuel? Precisely because in the original composition of the book of Samuel, David was not the one who killed Goliath. That honor belongs to an Israelite warrior named Elhanan, and his story remains, however succinctly, in the book of Samuel, standing sharply at odds with that later addition of 1 Samuel 17.

> Then there was another battle with the Philistines at Gob, and Elhanan, the son of Jaare-oregim the Bethlehemite, slew Goliath the Gittite, the staff of whose spear was like a weavers' beam. (2 Sam 21:19)

Here, quite cogently and plainly, with none of the ostentation of that other tale of Goliath's demise, is the original record of the man who killed Goliath.

This is a bit of a problem. Keep in mind that the books of 1 and 2 Samuel were originally one book, separated onto two scrolls simply because of its length. So here we have in the same book two conflicting accounts of the defeat of Goliath. In one account, David did the deed when no one else in all Israel was brave enough even to try. In another account, a virtually unknown soldier named Elhanan killed Goliath, simply in the line of duty. One would think these conflicting accounts would have been problematic, potentially tarnishing David's reputation. One would think someone would have noticed.

The Chronicler's Solution

Well, in fact, someone did notice. The Chronicler noticed.[3] Much like Saul did at first, the Chronicler had considerable affection for David. The Chronicler had so much affection for David's memory, in fact, that he refused to malign David in any way. So, out of reverence for the man after God's own heart, the Chronicler carefully removed any story that put David in a bad light. David and Bathsheba? Never happened. Not a word about it. David's not infrequent murders? Stricken from the record. David's sins? Not his fault. Blame it on Satan.

Accordingly, perhaps one can guess what the Chronicler did when he came across that quiet little sentence in 2 Sam 21:19. He rewrote the text. Here is the original passage again, from 2 Samuel, followed by the Chronicler's version in 1 Chr 20:5:

> Then there was another battle with the Philistines at Gob; and Elhanan, the son of Jaare-oregim the Bethlehemite, slew Goliath the Gittite, the staff of whose spear was like a weavers' beam. (2 Sam 21:19)

> There was war with the Philistines; and Elhanan, the son of Jair, slew Lahmi, the brother of Goliath the Gittite, the staff of whose spear was like a weavers' beam. (1 Chr 20:5)

Now, you might say, this does not prove that the Chronicler rewrote the text. All this necessarily means is that Elhanan killed Goliath (2 Sam 21:19) *and* Goliath's brother Lahmi (1 Chr 20:5). But let's take a look at these two texts in the original Hebrew (remember that Hebrew is read from right-to-left):[4]

וַיַּךְ אֶלְחָנָן בֶּן־יַעְרֵי אֹרְגִים [בֵּית הַלַּחְמִי אֵת] גָּלְיָת הַגִּתִּי וְעֵץ חֲנִיתוֹ כִּמְנוֹר אֹרְגִים :

וַיַּךְ אֶלְחָנָן בֶּן־יָעוּר [אֶת־ לַחְמִי אֲחִי] גָּלְיָת הַגִּתִּי וְעֵץ חֲנִיתוֹ כִּמְנוֹר אֹרְגִים :

The text above is the original from 2 Sam 21:19. The text below is the Chronicler's version, from 1 Chr 20:5. Analyze all the Hebrew text that is not bracketed. Compare the two above and below, outside the bracketed portion, and notice that the sentences are identical. The only difference outside the bracketed area is the absence of "*ōrĕgîm*," the second part of Jaare-oregim's name in the Samuel passage. That just means that the Chronicler shortened his name.[5] (That is where that big blank space is on the bottom side.) Here is what the two lines say when translated:

---

3. The Chronicler is the post-exilic author of the book of Chronicles, writing sometime after the time of Ezra, some 550–700 years after the reign of David.

4. A reading knowledge of Hebrew is not necessary to be able to see what is going on here. As long as you can compare shapes, it will quickly become apparent.

5. We will explain why the Chronicler deleted "*ōrĕgîm*" below.

And Elhanan, the son of Jaare-oregim the Bethlehemite, slew Goliath the Gittite, the staff of whose spear was like a weavers' beam.

And Elhanan, the son of Jair, slew Lahmi, the brother of Goliath the Gittite, the staff of whose spear was like a weavers' beam.

Now. Let's look a closer look at the text inside brackets:

בֵּית הַלַּחְמִי אֶת
אֶת־ לַחְמִי אֲחִי

On the line above, that first word (far right) is *bêt*, which is the word for "house." The word that follows it (to the left) is the word *lahmî*, meaning "bread." Side by side as they are, they mean "house of bread," or as we know it, *Bethlehem*. This form of the word means *Bethlehemite*. It is telling us that Jaare (the father of Elhanan) is from Bethlehem.

Now look at the line below. The first word from the top line (*bêt*) is changed slightly on the bottom to *'et*, which is a word that has no translation value. All it does is mark the next word as the direct object of the sentence (the one to whom the action is done). Now look at the next word (to the left). That first letter (ה) has disappeared, a letter that simply means "the." It has disappeared and we are left with the word *lahmî*, which means "my bread." Thus the two words on the top line meaning *Bethlehemite* have been altered on the bottom to mean, simply, *lahmî* ("my bread"), which is used here as a proper noun—a person's name. Rather than modifying Jaare (i.e., Jaare the Bethlehemite), in the Chronicler's version it has become the object of Elhanan's action. Thus, Elhanan slew Lahmi.

Now let's look at the last word (on the far left) of both the top and bottom lines. You can ignore the lines and dots underneath the letters. They were not written down originally; they were added over a thousand years later, to help with pronunciation. Just look at the letters themselves. The first letter (א) is exactly the same. The second letter (ת and ח) looks almost the same; only a miniscule stroke on the bottom makes the difference. Finally, notice that on the bottom line, a small letter is added (י). So what has happened? On the top line, the word is that untranslatable marker indicating that the direct object of the verb is about to follow. It means that the next word (Goliath) is the one who was slain by Elhanan. On the bottom line, with just a jot and a tittle's difference (literally), we get the word meaning "brother of." So now, instead of Goliath being the object of Elhanan's slaying, we have Lahmi being identified as Goliath's brother.

With just a few tiny strokes of the pen, the Chronicler solved the problem of the two conflicting accounts of Goliath's demise. David gets to be the uncontested champion over Goliath, and Elhanan gets the lesser honor of being the slayer of Goliath's brother Lahmi. Ingenious!

Confused? Here it is in a nutshell: Goliath did not have a brother named Lahmi. The Chronicler took the word "Bethlehem," broke it up, and turned "lehem" into a phony personal name, Lahmi.

Capitalizing on Corruption

At this point, it is probably a good idea to complicate matters even further. How do committed inerrantists deal with this discrepancy? They do so by arguing that the earlier text (2 Sam 21:19) was corrupted by scribal error, and that the Chronicler fixed it. They are able to make their case because of that disappearing word, "*ōrĕgîm.*" In the 2 Samuel version, the father of Elhanan is said to be Jaare-oregim. The Chronicler drops "*ōrĕgîm,*" just leaving Jair. The word "*ōrĕgîm*" actually appears later in the same sentence. It means "weavers." It is used to describe the shaft of Goliath's spear, which apparently resembled the beam of a weaver. So it would appear that a scribe was copying this passage and accidentally wrote "*ōrĕgîm*" twice, once where it belonged, and once where it did not. This is a common scribal error called "dittography." When the Chronicler dropped the word *ōrĕgîm* from his version, most likely he believed he was correcting a case of dittography.

Some inerrantists capitalize on this apparent textual corruption and argue that, since the scribe made an error with the repetition of the word *ōrĕgîm*, then it stands to reason that the text is also corrupt when it names Elhanan as the slayer of Goliath. Archer fairly represents this approach:

> It is quite obvious that a scribal error has marred the transmission of the original text. Fortunately 1 Chr 20:5 affords great assistance in discovering how the error took place. In Chronicles the verse reads: "And Elhanan the son of Jair slew Lahmi the brother of Goliath the Gittite." The copyist of 2 Sam 21:19 apparently mistook the sign of the direct object [*ʾet*] for the word [*bêt*] (probably because the manuscript was smudged or corroded before the final *t*), and thus changed *Lahmi* into "the Bethlehemite" . . . then for a similar reason he misread the word brother [*ʾāḥî*] for the sign of the direct object [*ʾet*], which meant that Goliath himself became the object of the slaying instead of Goliath's brother. . . . Additional evidence that the verse was poorly copied in 2 Sam 21 is afforded by the intrusion of the name *Oregim* after *Jaare*.[6]

6. Archer, *Old Testament Introduction*, 315.

Of course, contrary to Archer, there is no evidence that any other portion of the text is corrupted other than the repetition of ŏrĕgîm. If 2 Sam
21:19 did not contradict 1 Sam 17, there would be no reason to find corruption in any other part of the text. Despite the *prima facie* reasonableness of
this attempt to bring 2 Sam 21:19 into line with 1 Sam 17 and 1 Chr 20:5,
there are insurmountable problems with this argument.

First, it is not necessarily the case that the second ŏrĕgîm is a dittography. It is possible that Elhanan was the descendent of a line of weavers. The
original author may have seen an irony in the fact that the son of a weaver
defeated the giant whose spear famously resembled the beam of a weaver.
Admittedly, it is more probable that ŏrĕgîm is a dittography, but it is not the
only possibility. The attraction of the aforementioned irony may account for
the awkward inclusion of ŏrĕgîm. This explanation also makes good sense of
the fact that a description of Goliath's spear was given in the first place.[7]

Second, and much more significantly, the chances that Lahmi was the
name of Goliath's brother are slim to none. This is so for three reasons:

(1) Lahmi, a word meaning "my bread," is nowhere attested as a personal name.

(2) Lahmi is a Semitic word. Goliath is not a Semitic name. Neither are
the names of the other Philistine giants identified in 2 Sam 21 (Ishbi-benob
and Saph). Other Philistine names such as Achish and Phicol are also non-
Semitic, the evidence pointing to Indo-European origins.[8] It is hardly conceivable that Goliath's parents gave a good, solid Philistine name to the one
son, and a strange Semitic name to the other. One can imagine the anti-Semitic taunts poor Lahmi would have had to endure from his schoolmates.

(3) The probability that Jaare is here being introduced as a Bethlehemite
is very high. Throughout the Hebrew Bible and other ancient Near Eastern
texts, whenever a man is introduced into a narrative for the first time, his
place of origin is almost always given. Also, the construction "name-son of-
name" is usually followed by a geographical reference. Neither Elhanan nor
Jaare had been introduced heretofore in the Samuel narrative, so the probability is high that a geographical or tribal reference is going to follow the
construction. Moreover, when this Elhanan is named among David's mighty

---

7. McCarter indicates that "son of Jaare" should be understood as a gentilic (a geographical identifier). Bethlehem and Kiriath-jearim ("the city of the Jearites") were very
closely associated. So with 2 Sam 23:24 and 1 Chr 11:26, we know that Elhanan's father was
a Bethlehemite. 2 Sam 21:19 should thus be read as "Elhanan the Jearite from Bethlehem"
(with ŏrĕgîm as a dittography). McCarter concludes that there is no warrant for seeing the
Chronicles reading as representing the original. Wryly he identifies it as "a scribal error
with the effect of harmonizing this notice with 1 Samuel 17." McCarter, *II Samuel*, 449.

8. See Bonfante, "Who Were the Philistines," 254.

men elsewhere, his father is said to be a Bethlehemite (2 Sam 23:24; 1 Chr 11:26),[9] thus corroborating the text of 2 Sam 21:19.

Third, there is still the problem of the contradiction between 1 Samuel 16 and 17, which indicates that 17 was spliced in at a later time. Thus the problem with the historicity of the David and Goliath story is not limited to the 2 Samuel / 1 Chronicles contradiction. In fact, the two contradictions reinforce one another.

A Propagandistic Conclusion

The story of David and Goliath in 1 Samuel 17 is thus a hero-worshiping legend which developed late and was (not altogether seamlessly) inserted into the narrative at a later time. Since the book of Samuel tells us both that Elhanan killed Goliath and that Elhanan was one of David's personal guard, it is easy to see how the tradition of David's having killed Goliath began. Because Elhanan worked for David, David got the credit. Over time it evolved into an extravagant tale of David's victory over the giant. Kyle McCarter reminds us that the "deeds of obscure heroes tend to attach themselves to famous heroes." Accordingly, there can be "no doubt that the tradition attributing the slaying of Goliath to Elhanan is older than that which credits the deed to David."[10]

The portion of Samuel referring to Elhanan was written very early, probably no more than a generation or two after David. The Chronicler was of course writing more than 500 years later, leaving ample time for the legend of David and Goliath to develop and to work its way into the book of Samuel, before the legend had to be defended against the original account of Goliath's demise in 2 Sam 21:19. The Chronicler obviously felt it necessary (probably out of a misguided sense of piety) to alter the text in order to preserve what by his time was the well-established reputation of his hero David. This kind of phenomenon is what McCarter calls "royal apologia"[11] and what we in modern parlance tend to call "government propaganda." Or perhaps there was no government conspiracy in this case. There need not have been. After all, we citizens do love to immortalize our national heroes with legends of their *virtù*.

9. In these texts, Elhanan's father is identified as Dodo. It is possible that "Jaare" is some sort of nickname from the root meaning "forest." It is also possible that it should be read as "Jearite" (see note 7 above).

10. McCarter, *II Samuel*, 450.

11. On royal apologia in the book of Samuel, see McCarter, "Apology of David," 489–504.

8 Jesus Was Wrong

or, It's the End of the World as We Know It and I Feel Fine

One of my undergraduate professors used to enjoy stirring up controversy by declaring matter-of-factly in a classroom full of conservative evangelicals that "Jesus was ignorant." Heads would jolt to the left and right, eyebrows would dart up, and my professor would grin from ear to ear, pausing, before going on to quote Mark 13:32: "But about that day and hour no one knows, neither the angels of heaven, nor the Son, but only the Father."

"See! Jesus was ignorant, by his own admission," my professor would quip. "Jesus didn't know the day or the hour he would return."

After carefully studying and scrutinizing Jesus' claims about a final judgment, I have slowly and unhappily come to agree with my professor. Jesus was ignorant. But he was more than just ignorant; he was also wrong. Like the apocalyptic Qumran community before him, and William Miller, Hal Lindsey, and so many others after him, Jesus of Nazareth predicted that the world as we know it would come to an end within his own generation. The big difference between Jesus and those other doomsday prophets is that Jesus was fortunate enough not to be around when his prediction failed. He had already been taken up into heaven, where he has been ever since, observing from above as his followers found ways to adapt in the wake of their upset expectations. Jesus watched from heaven as hundreds upon hundreds of end-of-the-world predictions went unfulfilled throughout the centuries. He watched as the Millerites found ways to adapt to *The Great Disappointment* of 1843 and became the Seventh-day Adventists. He watched Hal Lindsey predict in his worldwide bestseller, *The Late, Great Planet Earth*, that the world would end in 1988. Then he watched Hal Lindsey write the second edition. Jesus is still watching. After 2000 years of his watching from heaven, and 2000 years of our waiting on earth, I think it's time we Christians got together and had a little sit-down.

It was not easy for me, coming to the conclusion that Jesus was wrong. It went against decades-strong conditioning which told me such a thing was impossible—a contradiction in terms almost. But another thing my

Christian faith had conditioned me to believe was that all truth was God's truth, and therefore that we could never get farther away from God in our relentless search for it. Eventually I had to be honest with myself, and with my scriptures, and call it like it is.

In saying this, I want to make it clear that I recognize what a struggle this will be for many Christians. Many may be willing to let go of the inerrancy of the Hebrew Bible, or even of some of the details in the Christian scriptures. But to come to the point of being able to say that *Jesus himself* was wrong! That's a horse of a very different color.

I understand. I've been there. But ultimately we have to decide whether our faith is going to be informed by good evidence and shaped by reason, or determined in advance, prepackaged for us, by women and men just as fallible as we are. I do not see this as a choice between faith and reason, but as a choice between blind faith and reasonable faith. A reasonable faith is mature enough to acknowledge when it needs to be corrected, and it can survive such corrections. In fact, a mature faith learns to thrive on them.

Now with regard to the texts we are going to look at in this chapter, I recognize that they are hotly debated by scholars, theologians and apologists of all stripes. But I tend to think that the primary reason they are so hotly debated is that the question of Jesus' reliability is at stake. I believe the claims Jesus makes in these texts are fairly straightforward, and that there is little wiggle room for differing interpretations. I think in most cases, it's the *unwelcome ramifications of the content* of Jesus' claims that create this sense in the confessing reader that the text simply *must* mean something other than what it says. But I'm convinced that just about anyone with an open mind to the truth of the matter will see how difficult it is not to come to the conclusion that Jesus was wrong. That is to say, providing we are sufficiently informed about the context out of which Jesus spoke.[1]

The Birth of Apocalyptic

Jewish-Christian apocalyptic thought developed out of an experience of cognitive dissonance. Israel was a small nation caught between powerful empires

1. That is also providing one takes the gospels to contain fairly reliable testimony about Jesus' actual claims. In this chapter, the reliability of the synoptic gospels will be assumed. Determining which sayings and deeds of Jesus are authentic and which are not is not unimportant, but is irrelevant to my limited purposes within this chapter. For a great debate on Jesus' apocalypticism between scholars for whom the reliability of the gospels is *not* a basic assumption, see Allison, et al., *Apocalyptic Jesus.* I find Allison's case to be the most persuasive. Against the other contributors to the volume, Allison argues that Jesus was an apocalyptic prophet, much as he is portrayed in the synoptic gospels.

to the north and south. Militarily and economically, whoever controlled Israel and Judea had a strategic advantage. As a result, the Promised Land was constantly under attack. In 722 BCE, the northern kingdom of Israel was conquered by the Assyrian empire. Then in 586 BCE, the southern kingdom of Judea was destroyed by the Babylonians, who subsequently took much of the Judean population into exile in Babylon. During these periods of intense suffering, prophets such as Hosea, Isaiah, Jeremiah, and Ezekiel interpreted Israel's plight as Yahweh's punishment for their sins. Yahweh, who ordinarily fought on Israel's behalf, and who was *certainly* powerful enough to take on Ashur and Marduk, this time was *not* fighting for Israel. In fact, Ashur and Marduk were not to blame for Israel's suffering. Yahweh himself had called in the Assyrian and Babylonian troops to teach his people a lesson. Implicit and explicit in the prophetic interpretation of Israel's plight was the belief that if Yahweh's people repented of the worship of other gods, turned from their injustices, and served Yahweh their God with total devotion, then Yahweh would restore them to their land and establish them as preeminent among the nations. This is what the prophets promised.

The problem is that the prophets were wrong. The Jewish people *did* turn from their wicked ways. They *did* obey the law and devote themselves wholly to the worship of Yahweh (see Ezra for example). But nothing happened. Yes, they were returned to their land, but the land was never restored to their control. One century turned into two centuries, two centuries into three, and so on. Israel continued to be dominated by significantly more powerful nations, and their suffering continued unabated. Out of this experience of cognitive dissonance, apocalypticism developed. The apocalyptic worldview was a way of interpreting the reality of Israel's suffering. In this sense, apocalyptic was a theodicy.

The word "theodicy" comes from two Greek words: *theos*, meaning "God," and *dikē*, meaning "justice." A theodicy attempts to answer the question, "How can God be just (or righteous) given the reality of suffering?" In the case of the Jewish people, the question was not posed about human suffering in general. The question was, "How can Yahweh be just when his *covenant people* are suffering?" The old answer was that Yahweh's covenant people were suffering for their sins. But now they had repented, and their suffering continued. The apocalyptic worldview developed as an answer to that vexing question. "It was not because God was punishing them. Quite the contrary, it was because the enemies of God were punishing them. These were cosmic enemies. They were obviously not making people suffer for breaking God's law. Just the opposite: as God's enemies, they made people suffer for *keeping* God's laws."[2]

2. Ehrman, *God's Problem*, 204.

In chapter 4 we saw how Israel's cosmology began with a polytheistic worldview, in which each nation had their own gods and these gods were at war with one another from almost every conceivable direction. We saw that it slowly developed into a monotheistic worldview, in which all other celestial powers were subordinated to Yahweh, the only one truly worthy of being called God. Apocalypticism represents a further development *within* monotheism, and it entails a sort of *rebirth* of the old rival deities. Only, instead of a cosmology in which many gods are representing many different national interests (something like the United Nations), this time the old gods were retooled and incorporated into a *dualistic* cosmology (something like U.S. foreign policy: *us versus them*). It was the forces of good against the forces of evil, Yahweh and his winged warriors against Belial and his celestial cronies. It was at this period in Israel's mythology that Satan came to be seen as a great enemy. Prior to this point, the Satan was an agent of Yahweh whose task was to ensure that God's people were truly righteous. Now, he came to be identified not as an agent of Yahweh, but as Yahweh's most ancient enemy.

What is important to bear in mind is that the cosmic conflict imagined by Jewish thinkers was reflective of their own experience *vis-à-vis* the nations. During this time, vast angelologies developed which cannot be understood abstracted from Israel's subjection to Hellenistic hegemony in the second century BCE. Larry Hurtado explains:

> Israel's significance seemed marginal. The most powerful realities were the might and structure of the empires that dominated Israel's world. In this period Jews portrayed their God as the great heavenly king with a massive and many-tiered hierarchy of heavenly servants. . . . God's might and awesomeness are portrayed by means of the most impressive model of earthly power known to the writers of these texts, the imperial court and its hierarchy of powerful officers and servants. In other words, the image of the angelic hierarchy was intended as a way of relativizing the earthly structures of authority and power with which Israel had to contend in this period.[3]

It was also at this time, in response to the heavy persecution of Torah-abiding Jews by the likes of the Seleucid king Antiochus IV Epiphanes, that belief in an afterlife found its way into some strands of Jewish theology. The traumatic experience of martyrdom gave rise to the hope of the resurrection and vindication of those who had died for their faithfulness to Yahweh.[4]

3. Hurtado, *One God, One Lord*, 26.

4. Prior to this, belief in any sort of afterlife was denied in scripture. E.g., Eccl 9:3–6, which vocalizes the denial-by-silence elsewhere. See Wright, *Resurrection of the Son of God*, 85–128.

Contiguous with this was the development of a belief in a final judgment after which the course of history would be radically reversed. On this day of judgment it would be said, in the words of the young Jewess Mary, that "he has brought down the powerful from their thrones, and lifted up the lowly" (Luke 1:52).

Summarizing, Richard Horsley writes that the apocalyptic worldview essentially sought "understanding of and consolation in difficult historical circumstances."[5] The fundamental concerns of Jewish apocalypticists were "for the renewal or restoration of the people of Israel, for the eventual divine judgment against their oppressors, and for the vindication of the righteous Jews who endure abuse and even death in their faithful adherence to the traditional covenantal way of life."[6] Stephen O'Leary describes the apocalyptic worldview "as a defense of theism based upon the narrative of the Apocalypse as a 'morally sufficient reason' for the divine sufferance of evil."[7] Another way to put the matter is that apocalyptic asserted that Yahweh's righteousness would be vindicated *when he intervened* to deliver Israel from its undeserved afflictions. The "morally sufficient reason for the divine sufferance of evil" is thus that the end will be restorative. The most important thing to be stressed with regard to this theodicy, however, is that in order for its logic to be sustained, the *end that justified the means* had to be conceived of as *imminent*. If Israel was to continue suffering, world without end, Yahweh's righteousness would *not* be vindicated. Yahweh's righteousness was expected to be displayed in the fact that he could not suffer the suffering of his people for very long.

Apocalypticism and the Jesus Movement

Klaus Koch identifies eight basic features common to various strands of second temple Jewish apocalypticism:[8] (1) urgent expectation of the end of earthly conditions in the immediate future; (2) the end as a cosmic catastrophe; (3) periodization and determinism; (4) activity of angels and demons as explanation for human history; (5) new salvation, paradisal in character; (6) final manifestation of the kingdom of God on earth; (7) a mediator with royal functions; (8) the catchword "glory."[9] Each of these traits is indisput-

5. Horsley, *Sociology and the Jesus Movement*, 96.

6. Ibid., 97.

7. O'Leary, *Arguing the Apocalypse*, 198.

8. Koch, *Rediscovery of Apocalyptic*, 28–33.

9. (1) E.g., Mark 9:1; 13:30; 1 Thess 4:15–17; Rev 22:20. (2) E.g., Mark 13:23–26; 1 Thess 5:2–3. (3) E.g., Acts 2:17; Mark 13:7; 13:32; 2 Thess 2:3. (4) E.g., Matt 13:39; Dan

ably attested within the Jesus movement. To these, Dale Allison adds several features found cross-culturally among apocalyptic or "millenarian" groups, traits that are also found within the Jesus movement. Like other millenarian groups, the Jesus group:

> addressed the disaffected or less fortunate in a period of social change that threatened traditional ways and symbolic universes; . . . emerged in a time of aspiration for national independence; . . . saw the present and near future as times of suffering and/or catastrophe; . . . envisaged a comprehensive righting of wrongs and promised redemption through a reversal of current circumstances; . . . depicted that reversal as imminent; . . . was both revivalistic and evangelistic; . . . divided the world into two camps, the saved and the unsaved; . . . broke hallowed taboos associated with religious custom; . . . replaced traditional familial and social bonds with fictive kin; . . . mediated the sacred through new channels;[10] . . . demanded intense commitment and unconditional loyalty; . . . focused upon a charismatic leader; . . . understood its beliefs to be the product of special revelation;[11] . . . took a passive political stance in expectation of a divinely wrought deliverance;[12] . . . expected a restored paradise that would return the ancestors; . . . insisted on the possibility of experiencing that utopia as a present reality.[13]

The significance of this last point cannot be overstated. Many object to an apocalyptic Jesus because of a misunderstanding of the way in which the standard apocalyptic paradigm was reconfigured within the Jesus movement. The standard apocalyptic paradigm is shown in Figure 01 below. In the standard paradigm, the "old time" of bondage and sin culminates in a period of intense suffering, until it is brought to an abrupt end on the day of Yahweh. At that point, the "new time" of utopia and paradise begins, just as abruptly. But in the Jesus movement, this apocalyptic paradigm was modified to ac-

---

10. (5) E.g., Matt 25:34; Luke 23:43; Mark 12:25. (6) E.g., Mark 9:1; Matt 6:10. (7) E.g., Luke 1:32; Matt 9:6–7. (8) E.g., Mark 8:38; 10:37; Rom 2:10; 8:18.

10. E.g., healings and meals; forgiveness through Jesus rather than the temple.

11. As we saw in chapter 2, this was a characteristic of the Qumran community also. The method of scriptural interpretation at Qumran and in the Jesus movement are remarkably similar. Both believed the ancient texts were speaking of their own time, community, and conflicts. Both adopted this interpretive approach by virtue of their belief that they were living in the last days.

12. The Jesus movement was not the only quietist branch of apocalypticism in Second Temple Judaism.

13. Allison, *Jesus of Nazareth*, 46–48. In his footnotes, Allison lists copious scripture references for each of these features.

count for the fact of Jesus' suffering. The modified, Christian apocalyptic paradigm can be seen in Figure 02. In the modified paradigm, the new time enters the world with the initial arrival of Jesus, and runs parallel to the old time. The new time is present in the ministry of Jesus and his disciples, while the old time, which is hostile to the new, goes on. This conflict between the times culminates in a period of intense suffering, immediately after which the intervention of Yahweh brings an abrupt end to the old time, and the new time is enabled to continue.

Apocalyptic Paradigm
Figure 01

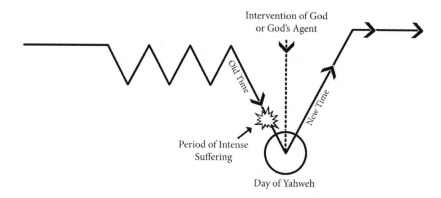

Modified
Apocalyptic Paradigm
Figure 02

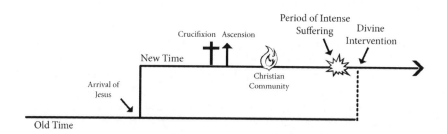

(Diagrams used by permission of Rollin A. Ramsaran.)

Thus, those who appeal to sayings such as Matt 12:28 ("But if I cast out demons by the Spirit of God, then the kingdom of God has come upon you") as evidence against an apocalyptic Jesus fail to understand the modified paradigm.[14] What sayings like Matt 12:28 indicate rather is the idea of a *proleptic* presence of the kingdom through the agency of Jesus. In other words, his ministry was seen as a *sign* that the kingdom would arrive on a cosmic, global scale within a short period of time. This modified paradigm is also seen in the Qumran community, who believed both that the world would end and the new creation would be ushered in by about 40 BCE, *and* that the new creation was already present in their midst. As the harbingers of the kingdom of God, they enjoyed present-day fellowship with the angels and were given special insight into the meaning of the scriptures and the significance of the course of human events.

Given the comparative data, it should be clear that the Jesus movement fits squarely within the apocalyptic paradigm. Jesus was an apocalyptic thinker in a time when apocalyptic strands of Judaism were numerous and dynamic. As noted above, an essential part of this burgeoning apocalyptic worldview was belief in the resurrection. Having emerged at about the time of the Maccabean revolt in the 160s BCE, the notion of the resurrection of the faithful was still relatively very young at the time of Jesus. The Sadducees, who denied a bodily resurrection, were actually the conservative branch, preserving the old beliefs reflected in Ecclesiastes and elsewhere in the Hebrew Bible. The Pharisees, the Zealots, and the Jesus movement (which was closely associated with both groups), would have been seen by the establishment as the young radicals with dangerous ideas. Apart from being theologically "liberal," belief in the resurrection was also politically explosive, for the same reason that contemporary extremist Islamic belief in the resurrection is politically explosive. Belief in the resurrection freed one up to walk a dangerous path of hard-line opposition to Rome and to the puppet temple regime in Jerusalem.

Jesus was one of these fresh, young, dangerous sorts, according to the establishment. Part of his apocalyptic worldview was belief in the resurrection of the body at the end of time. Now, according to the portrait painted by the synoptic gospels, Jesus' peculiar brand of apocalypticism allowed Jesus to see himself as the chief agent of God whose life, death, and resurrection was to herald the imminent end of the present world order and usher in the new age—the kingdom of God on earth, as it is in heaven. According to the synoptic gospels, Jesus believed that his execution at the hands of the authorities would initiate a chain of events that would, within the timeframe of a single

14. This misunderstanding is exemplified quite well in Lohfink, *Does God Need the Church*, 135–39.

generation, lead to the destruction of Jerusalem as divine punishment for the temple regime's rejection of his prophetic message. He believed that immediately thereafter Yahweh would intervene to judge the nations, vindicate Jerusalem, and gather God's faithful from throughout the diaspora. Like most if not all apocalypticists of his day, Jesus believed the final judgment was both inevitable and imminent. Just as the contemporaneous Qumran community saw themselves as the collective divine agent through whom God would restore Israel and judge the nations, Jesus saw himself, and by extension his body of followers, as that agent. Each apocalyptic community had their peculiarities, but the end result was the same—the restoration of Israel and the judgment of the nations.

The main lines of this will be argued below, but I say this at the outset to help us properly situate Jesus within his apocalyptic milieu.[15] There are many things that are original and remarkable about Jesus' thought, but those unique and remarkable elements only appear as developments out of a common apocalyptic matrix within which Jesus and many of his contemporaries viewed the world and Israel's relationship to it. Knowing this helps us not to be shocked when we discover that he expected an imminent final judgment. Jesus was extraordinary in many ways, but not, historically speaking, in terms of his basic worldview. So when we discover that Jesus believed and consequently acted as if the end of the world was imminent, we should not be surprised. Even orthodox faith insists that in addition to being fully divine, Jesus was fully human; and part of being fully human is to be a product of one's time and place.

What Jesus Predicted

Now that we understand a few things about the social and theological context from which and into which Jesus spoke, we are ready to examine Jesus' predictions about the final judgment. Although Jesus spoke of an imminent final judgment frequently,[16] in two of his discourses in particular

15. The original case for an apocalyptic Jesus was made by Schweitzer, *Quest of the Historical Jesus.* The best and most extensive recent case has been made by Allison, *Jesus of Nazareth.* For an excellent, concise, and accessible presentation of the case, see Ehrman, *Jesus.* Finally, the case and the claims made in Loftus, "Failed Apocalyptic Prophet," cannot be ignored by Christians.

16. See Gregg, *Final Judgment Sayings,* who argues that at least ten of the twelve final judgment sayings found in the material unique to Matthew and Luke (material that is called "Q" by scholars) are authentic, and shows that the sayings fit seamlessly within ideas about final judgment found in other apocalyptic groups and texts of Jesus' period. The ten final judgment sayings found to be authentic by Gregg are Q 10:10–12; 10:13–15; 11:31–32; 12:4–5; 12:8–9; 12:10; 12:42–46; 13:29, 28; 17:1–2; 17:33.

Jesus predicts that the final judgment will occur within the lifetime of his disciples. The two discourses are found in Mark 8:34—9:1 (with its parallels: Matt 16:24–28; Luke 9:23–27) and in Mark 13, the famous Olivet Discourse (with its parallels: Matt 24:1–44; Luke 21:5–36). We will first examine the discourse in Mark 8:34—9:1 and its parallels, arguing that Jesus did in fact predict that the final judgment would take place within the lifetime of his generation. I will then address alternative interpretations of this passage and show why they unequivocally fail to do the text justice.

Kingdom Come: The Argument[17]

Mark 8:34–9:1	*Matt 16:24–28*	*Luke 9:23–27*
[34]He called the crowd with his disciples, and said to them, "If any want to become my followers, let them deny themselves and take up their cross and follow me. [35]For those who want to save their life will lose it, and those who lose their life for my sake, and for the sake of the gospel, will save it. [36]For what will it profit them to gain the whole world and forfeit their life? [37]Indeed, what can they give in return for their life? [38]Those who are ashamed of me and of my words in this adulterous and sinful generation, of them the Son of Man will also be ashamed when he comes in the glory of his Father with the holy angels." [9:1]And he said to them, "Truly I tell you, there	[24]Then Jesus told his disciples, "If any want to become my followers, let them deny themselves and take up their cross and follow me. [25]For those who want to save their life will lose it, and those who lose their life for my sake will find it. [26]For what will it profit them if they gain the whole world but forfeit their life? Or what will they give in return for their life? [27]For the Son of Man is to come with his angels in the glory of his Father, and then he will repay everyone for what has been done. [28]Truly I tell you, there are some standing here who will not taste death before they see the Son of Man coming in his kingdom."	[23]Then he said to them all, "If any want to become my followers, let them deny themselves and take up their cross daily and follow me. [24]For those who want to save their life will lose it, and those who lose their life for my sake will save it. [25]What does it profit them if they gain the whole world, but lose or forfeit themselves? [26]Those who are ashamed of me and of my words, of them the Son of Man will be ashamed when he comes in his glory and the glory of the Father and of the holy angels. [27]But truly I tell you, there are some standing here who will not taste death before they see the kingdom of God."

17. Throughout this chapter, scripture quotations in columns will be from the NRSV.

Mark 8:34–9:1	Matt 16:24–28	Luke 9:23–27
are some standing here who will not taste death until they see that the kingdom of God has come with power."		

In each gospel, this discourse is preceded by the "Good Confession," in which Peter answers the question of Jesus' identity with an affirmation that Jesus was indeed the awaited messiah. Jesus then proceeds to predict his own suffering and death at the hands of the authorities. Peter denies the possibility of this scenario, and Jesus rebukes Peter. This rebuke leads to the occasion for the discourse under consideration. The point of controversy was over this notion that the messiah would suffer. Ordinary conceptions of the messiah conceived of him as a triumphant military figure. By very definition, the messiah could not be defeated. Despite this, Jesus speaks to the disciples and crowds, instructing them that just as he was going to suffer, their devotion to him would lead to their own suffering as well. As we saw above, standard paradigms of apocalyptic Judaism believed that faithful Israel would experience an intense period of suffering just prior to their salvation and the last judgment. Just when the suffering was at its worst, the messianic warrior (or Yahweh himself, in some versions) would intervene with an army of angels and liberate Israel from their oppressors. In the synoptic gospels, Jesus is working within this scheme, but altering it slightly. In Jesus' version, the messiah comes prior to the intense period of suffering, and his own suffering initiates that period, which will later be relieved when the vindicated messiah appears to deliver Israel from its enemies. So Jesus does *not* reject the standard picture of the victorious messiah. The only difference is that *the messiah himself suffers* prior to his victory over the enemies of Israel.

In this discourse, Jesus connects the issue of suffering and discipleship to that of the last judgment. Those who are faithful to Jesus, even to the point of enduring suffering, will gain their lives at the end. Those who are ashamed of Jesus, of them the "Son of Man" will be ashamed. In other words, those who do not persevere through the intense period of suffering will be judged and they will lose, not gain, their lives at the end. Matthew's language is slightly different than that of Mark and Luke. Instead of saying the Son of Man will be "ashamed" of the unfaithful, he says that the Son of Man will "repay everyone for what has been done." Matthew's interpretation of Mark's language is therefore that of a final judgment.[18] The language of final judgment is clear

18. Most scholars are persuaded that Matthew and Luke used Mark as a source.

and unequivocal. The Son of Man comes "in the glory of his Father with the holy angels" (Mark), "with his angels in the glory of his Father" (Matthew), "in his glory and the glory of the Father and of the holy angels" (Luke). Then each synoptic gospel follows this description of the final judgment with the prediction that it will happen while some of Jesus' immediate disciples are still alive: "Truly I tell you, there are some standing here who will not taste death before they see the kingdom of God having come with power" (Mark); "Truly I tell you, there are some standing here who will not taste death before they see the Son of Man coming in his kingdom" (Matthew); "But truly I tell you, there are some standing here who will not taste death before they see the kingdom of God" (Luke).

Kingdom Come: Alternative Interpretations

It is obvious why many Christians would have a stake in looking for other ways to read this passage. If Jesus wrongly predicted that the final judgment would occur within the lifetime of his immediate disciples, what does that say about Jesus? What does that say about Christianity? What does that say about our lives? We will address those questions later, but for now, suffice it to point out that this predicament provides some Christians sufficient motivation to find alternative readings of the text, readings which deviate from its plain sense within the context of apocalyptic Judaism.

There are four alternatives frequently proposed by theologians and commentators. Each one attempts to argue that the coming of the "kingdom of God" refers to some event or series of events other than the consummation of the kingdom when the dead are raised and the nations are judged. The four alternatives are the miracles and exorcisms of Jesus, the transfiguration, the resurrection of Jesus, and the outpouring of the Spirit on the day of Pentecost. It is argued that one or more of these events are what Jesus referred to when he said that his disciples would see the "kingdom of God" come before they died. To many, these alternatives seem obvious. The disciples *did* live to see Jesus perform miracles and exorcisms, and those are sometimes described as a coming of the kingdom of sorts.[19] They saw him transfigured. They lived to see him raised from the dead and lived to see the outpouring of the Spirit on that first Pentecost. Nevertheless, despite their obvious appeal to many Christians, these alternatives suffer from the same intractable problems.

First, there's the time problem. All of these events happen within a few months, less than a year at most, of this prediction. In the case of the

---

19. E.g., Matt 12:28: "But if I cast out demons by [the power of] the Spirit of God, then the kingdom of God has come upon you."

miracles and exorcisms, they had already been taking place for some time! Why would Jesus notify his disciples that some of them would not die before seeing the coming of the kingdom, if they had already seen it? Similarly, in each of the synoptic Gospels, the transfiguration occurs directly after this discourse. What kind of prediction is it that? "Surely, some of you will not die before next Wednesday." The same problem applies to the resurrection and Pentecost interpretations. Both of those events would occur no more than a few months after Jesus' prediction (in the case of the resurrection, probably no more than a few weeks).

The second problem is angelic in nature. Mark, Matthew, and Luke each state that when the Son of Man comes with the kingdom of God, he will be accompanied by angels. However, there are no angels accompanying Jesus when he is transfigured on the mount. Moses and Elijah are there (figures who themselves had transfiguration type experiences during their ministries). Yet no angels are there. Neither are there angels at Pentecost. (For that matter, the Son of Man does not show up at Pentecost either.) No angels are seen when Jesus is performing his miracles and exorcisms. On the other hand, angels *are* said to be present at the site of the resurrection. But this leads us to another problem.

In none of these instances does anything like a final judgment take place. It is not merely that angels are present, after all, but that they are present with the Son of Man in power and in judgment.[20] The immediate context in each passage is judgment. Those who have been faithful (by enduring through suffering) will be rewarded. Those who were not faithful, of them the Son of Man will be ashamed. This is a way of saying that they will be shunned, rejected. Matthew makes this clear when he says that "the Son of Man is to come with his angels in the glory of his Father, and then *he will repay everyone for what has been done*" (16:27). Here the scope of the judgment is broad ("everyone"). A more succinct, clearer description of the last judgment is difficult to imagine. The coming of the Son of Man with the angels, in the glory of his Father, is a clear reference to what the antecedent thought suggests—the final judgment. The presence of angels outside Jesus' empty tomb, therefore, does not suffice to fulfill the picture painted by Jesus here. At the tomb, the angels were messengers of the gospel. In this

20. In fact, Mark's phrase, "come in power" is an apocalyptic code word for the end times. James Charlesworth explains that "to 'come in power' is an expression that has special importance for the apocalyptists, like the authors of Daniel, the Apocalypse of John, 4 Ezra, and 2 Baruch. It denotes a total alteration of time and the earth, and an end to normal history." Charlesworth, *Jesus within Judaism*, 19. My thanks to Ed Babinski for bringing this reference to my attention.

discourse, however, Jesus depicts angelic agents of judgment, as seen also in the Apocalypse to John (or book of Revelation).

Finally, each of these attempts at an alternative reading fails to see the clear logic behind Jesus' prediction of the survival of some of his disciples. The question is: *what* is the point behind his claim that some of his disciples would not taste death? A simple reading of the immediate context makes the answer unmistakable. Recall: Jesus tells his disciples that just as he was rejected, they too will be rejected. They must be willing to undergo the sufferings that he would undergo. This is how to be saved. Immediately upon the heels of this statement, Jesus says that the Son of Man will come in God's glory with his angels to judge those who rejected him and reward those who were faithful to him. Then, "Some of you will not taste death before they see the kingdom of God come with power."

Pause and consider this. To say that "some would not taste death" is to imply that others (perhaps most) *would* taste death. Why would they taste death? Jesus had just finished telling them: because they are going to suffer and be rejected too. When does this happen? Does their suffering and rejection take place *before* the transfiguration, resurrection, or outpouring of the Spirit on Pentecost? The answer is unequivocally no. Their suffering and rejection takes place *after* all these things. His faithful disciples will be rejected by the same people who would soon reject him. Some of them will suffer to the point of "tasting death." Those who survive the intense period of suffering will live to see the coming of the Son of Man with his angels—the coming of the kingdom of God—when the faithful will be rewarded and the unfaithful excluded. This also provides a clear motivation for Jesus' promise that some would survive until the end. It is a classic restatement of the basic apocalyptic expectation that the period of intense suffering would be *short*. Yes, they will suffer. Nonetheless, they can find solace in the fact that their suffering will not go on forever, world without end. Jesus comforts them with the knowledge that some of them would live to see Israel delivered from its afflictions.

Kingdom Come: Conclusion

The simplest reading of this discourse, and the reading that fits best with the Jewish apocalyptic context out of which Jesus and his disciples emerged, is also the *only* reading that makes sense of Jesus' claims. This discourse displays in no uncertain terms what the Jesus of the synoptic gospels believed: he believed that he would suffer and die, that he would subsequently be vindicated by Yahweh, that his faithful followers would also suffer for his name's sake, and that some would not remain faithful. He believed that while some of his immediate followers were still alive, the Son of Man would appear in the glory of God, with God's angels (now given to his charge), to judge the earth. Those who were faithful to him are given life, and those unfaithful are shunned, or "repaid." Jesus could not have been clearer if he had said, "I predict that the final judgment will occur within the next forty or fifty years." Two millennia of apologetic attempts to make the text say otherwise have not been successful.

After That Suffering: The Argument

We will now look at Jesus' second prediction that the final judgment would take place within the lifetime of his immediate disciples. This one is made in the famous Olivet Discourse of Mark 13 (with its parallels: Matt 24:1–44; Luke 21:5–36). We will argue, again, that Jesus did in fact predict that the final judgment would take place within his own generation. After a positive argument is made, we will look at common objections to this argument. We will also engage the novel interpretation of this passage put forward by Anglican bishop and biblical scholar N. T. Wright. In the end, however, we will see that the standard objections, as well as Wright's alluring interpretation, fall far short of doing justice to the text.

The discourse begins on the Mount of Olives after Jesus, just having been in the temple court with his disciples, predicted the impending destruction of the temple:

Mark 13:1–2	Matt 24:1–2	Luke 21:5–6
[1]As he came out of the temple, one of his disciples said to him, "Look, Teacher, what large stones and what large buildings!" [2]Then Jesus asked him, "Do you see these great buildings? Not one stone will be left here upon another; all will be thrown down."	[1]As Jesus came out of the temple and was going away, his disciples came to point out to him the buildings of the temple. [2]Then he asked them, "You see all these, do you not? Truly I tell you, not one stone will be left here upon another; all will be thrown down."	[5]When some were speaking about the temple, how it was adorned with beautiful stones and gifts dedicated to God, he said, [6]"As for these things that you see, the days will come when not one stone will be left upon another; all will be thrown down."

On their way back to Bethany they stop on the Mount of Olives and look out over the city. His disciples inquire about his prediction:

Mark 13:3–4	Matt 24:3	Luke 21:7
[3]When he was sitting on the Mount of Olives opposite the temple, Peter, James, John, and Andrew asked him privately, [4]"Tell us, when will this be, and what will be the sign that all these things are about to be accomplished?"	[3]When he was sitting on the Mount of Olives, the disciples came to him privately, saying, "Tell us, when will this be, and what will be the sign of your coming and of the end of the age?"	[7]They asked him, "Teacher, when will this be, and what will be the sign that this is about to take place?"

In response, Jesus goes on to describe, in apocalyptic language, a period of conflict and chaos:

Mark 13:5–8	Matt 24:4–8	Luke 21:8–11
[5]Then Jesus began to say to them, "Beware that no one leads you astray. [6]Many will come in my name and say, 'I am he!' and they will lead many astray. [7]When you hear of wars and rumors of wars, do not be alarmed; this must take place, but the end is still to come. [8]For nation will rise against nation, and kingdom against kingdom; there will be earthquakes in various places; there will be famines. This is but the beginning of the birth pangs."	[4]Jesus answered them, "Beware that no one leads you astray. [5]For many will come in my name, saying, 'I am the Messiah!' and they will lead many astray. [6]And you will hear of wars and rumors of wars; see that you are not alarmed; for this must take place, but the end is not yet. [7]For nation will rise against nation, and kingdom against kingdom, and there will be famines and earthquakes in various places: [8]all this is but the beginning of the birth pangs."	[8]And he said, "Beware that you are not led astray; for many will come in my name and say, 'I am he!' and, 'The time is near!' Do not go after them. [9]"When you hear of wars and insurrections, do not be terrified; for these things must take place first, but the end will not follow immediately." [10]Then he said to them, "Nation will rise against nation, and kingdom against kingdom; [11]there will be great earthquakes, and in various places famines and plagues; and there will be dreadful portents and great signs from heaven."

Many modern Christians, especially dispensationalist Christians, will take this language to be descriptive of present-day realities. But in fact all of this occurred between the inception of the church and the destruction of the temple in 70 CE. This is apocalyptic language and is thus hyper-real. Earthquakes are a common feature of apocalyptic visions of the end—they represent a world in convulsions, or as Mark has it, "the beginning of the birth pangs." This is a description of an old world in labor, ready to birth a new order. Nevertheless, all of the phenomena described herein took place within the approximately forty-year time frame between the inception of the church and the destruction of the Jerusalem temple by the Romans. Palestine was plagued with famines, one of the central factors contributing to what Richard Horsley calls the "spiral of violence"[21] in Roman-occupied Palestine during this period. The famines led to greater desperation on the part of those who were suffering under the exploitative economic system and military occupation of Rome. This led to "wars and rumors of wars." Around this time, many prophets and messianic hopefuls rose up, including "the Samaritan," Theudas, "the Egyptian," Jesus ben Hananiah, Menahem, and Simon bar Giora.[22] Some of these men gathered large militias, often numbering in the hundreds, and purported or promised to perform signs (such as parting the Jordan River, as Moses had the Sea of Reeds, or bringing down the walls of Jerusalem *à la* Joshua). Invariably their attempts to mount a successful revolution were squelched by the Roman police. These are the messiahs about whom Jesus warns his disciples. His disciples are not to be led astray by the promise of liberation. The time is not yet right. Nevertheless, nation did in fact rise against nation, when Jerusalem clashed with the Roman powers. A war beginning in 66 CE seethed for years. This was the beginning of the end. Jesus warns his disciples that throughout this time they will be put to the test:

Mark 13:9–13	*Matt 24:9–14*	*Luke 21:12–19*
[9]"As for yourselves, beware; for they will hand you over to councils; and you will be beaten in synagogues; and you will stand before governors and kings because of me, as a testimony to them. [10]And the good news must first be proclaimed to all nations. [11]When they bring you to trial and hand you over, do not worry beforehand about what you are to say; but say whatever is given you at that time,	[9]"Then they will hand you over to be tortured and will put you to death, and you will be hated by all nations because of my name. [10]Then many will fall away, and they will betray one another and hate one another. [11]And many false prophets will arise and lead many astray. [12]And because of the increase of lawless astray. ness, the love of many will grow cold. [13]But the one who en-	[12]"*But before all this occurs*, they will arrest you and persecute you; they will hand you over to synagogues and prisons, and you will be brought before kings and governors because of my name. [13]This will give you an opportunity to testify. [14]So make up your minds not to prepare your defense in advance; [15]for I will give you words and a wisdom that none of your opponents will be able to

21. Horsley, *Jesus and the Spiral of Violence*.

22. On these and other revolutionary figures from the period, see Horsley, *Bandits, Prophets, and Messiahs*.

Mark 13:9–13	*Matt 24:9–14*	*Luke 21:12–19*
for it is not you who speak, but the Holy Spirit. [12]Brother will betray brother to death, and a father his child, and children will rise against parents and have them put to death; [13]and you will be hated by all because of my name. But the one who endures to the end will be saved."	dures to the end will be saved. [14]And this good news of the kingdom will be proclaimed throughout the world, as a testimony to all the nations; and then the end will come."	withstand or contradict. [16]You will be betrayed even by parents and brothers, by relatives and friends; and they will put some of you to death. [17]You will be hated by all because of my name. [18]But not a hair of your head will perish. [19]By your endurance you will gain your souls."

Luke indicates in verse 12 that all of these things will occur prior to the war in Jerusalem. Christians were put before governors and kings, as the book of Acts recounts. Between 30 and 70 CE, the gospel was proclaimed throughout the world. The known world was of course much smaller then than it is today. But this is the point of the book of Acts, which begins in Jerusalem and culminates with Paul preaching the gospel in Rome—the hub of a world empire and the city to which, according to the proverb, all roads lead. Paul's ministry in Rome is, for Luke (the author of Luke/Acts), the fulfillment of the promise made by the resurrected Jesus at the outset of the book of Acts, that his disciples will be given power after the Holy Spirit had come upon them, and be witnesses "in Jerusalem, throughout Judea and Samaria, and to the ends of the earth" (Acts 1:8; cf. Col 1:23). On account of the gospel, the disciples will be betrayed, lose their families, and suffer persecution, some even to the point of death (Luke 21:16). Yet, as the apocalyptic paradigm dictates, if they are faithful through the period of intense suffering, they will be saved at the end—those who have survived will be delivered from the enemy, and those who have been martyred will be raised in glory. As the next block indicates, all of this takes place prior to the destruction of the temple:

Mark 13:14–23	*Matt 24:15–27*	*Luke 21:20–24*
[14]"But when you see the desolating sacrilege set up where it ought not to be (let the reader understand), *then those in Judea must flee to the mountains;* [15]the one on the housetop must not go down or enter the	[15]"So when you see the desolating sacrilege standing in the holy place, as was spoken of by the prophet Daniel (let the reader understand), [16]then those in *Judea must flee to the mountains;* [17]the one on	[20]"When you see Jerusalem surrounded by armies, then know that its desolation has come near. [21]*Then those in Judea must flee to the mountains,* and those inside the city must leave it, and those out in the

Mark 13:14–23	*Matt 24:15–27*	*Luke 21:20–24*
house to take anything away; [16]the one in the field must not turn back to get a coat. [17]Woe to those who are pregnant and to those who are nursing infants in those days! [18]Pray that it may not be in winter. [19]For in those days there will be suffering, such as has not been from the beginning of the creation that God created until now, no, and never will be. [20]And if the Lord had not cut short those days, no one would be saved; but for the sake of the elect, whom he chose, he has cut short those days. [21]And if anyone says to you at that time, 'Look! Here is the Messiah!' or 'Look! There he is!'—do not believe it. [22]False messiahs and false prophets will appear and produce signs and omens, to lead astray, if possible, the elect. [23]But be alert; I have already told you everything."	the housetop must not go down to take what is in the house; [18]the one in the field must not turn back to get a coat. [19]Woe to those who are pregnant and to those who are nursing infants in those days! [20]Pray that your flight may not be in winter or on a sabbath. [21]For at that time there will be great suffering, such as has not been from the beginning of the world until now, no, and never will be. [22]And if those days had not been cut short, no one would be saved; but for the sake of the elect those days will be cut short. [23]Then if anyone says to you, 'Look! Here is the Messiah!' or 'There he is!'—do not believe it. [24]For false messiahs and false prophets will appear and produce great signs and omens, to lead astray, if possible, even the elect. [25]Take note, I have told you beforehand [26]So, if they say to you, 'Look! He is in the wilderness,' do not go out. If they say, 'Look! He is in the inner rooms,' do not believe it. [27]*For as the lightning comes from the east and flashes as far as the west, so will be the coming of the Son of Man.*"	country must not enter it; [22]for these are days of vengeance, as a fulfillment of all that is written. [23]Woe to those who are pregnant and to those who are nursing infants in those days! For there will be great distress on the earth and wrath against this people; [24]they will fall by the edge of the sword and be taken away as captives among all nations; and *Jerusalem will be trampled on by the Gentiles, until the times of the Gentiles are fulfilled.*"

Jesus refers to the "desolating sacrilege," also sometimes translated as the "abomination that causes desolation." This is an apocalyptic keyword referring to a gentile desecration of the temple. Some background information is in order. The original "desolating sacrilege" was committed in 167 BCE when the Seleucid king Antiochus IV Epiphanes (who had control of Judea at the time) marched into the Jerusalem temple and sacrificed a pig to the Greek god Zeus. This incident, which was utterly devastating to the Jews, instigated the Maccabean revolt. Antiochus outlawed Yahweh worship and ordered the conversion of the temple into a house of worship for foreign gods. A priest from the town of Modin refused to sacrifice to the foreign gods. When a Hellenistic Jew stepped forward to sacrifice, the priest killed him and then killed the Greek official who was there to enforce the policy. This priest's name was Mattathias. He and his sons fled to the mountains, from which they launched a revolt. The sons of Mattathias eventually defeated the Seleucids and enjoyed independence from foreign rule for more than a century, before being brought once again under the hegemony of an imperial power—this time that of Rome, in 37 BCE.

Reexamining the above passage in light of this background, it becomes clear exactly what kind of picture Jesus is painting. He speaks of the "desolating sacrilege," recalling Antiochus's desecration of the temple. Even more significantly, he instructs his disciples, as soon as they see the temple desecrated, to flee to the mountains and wait. The flight to the mountains recalls the flight of David to the mountains, from which he and his mighty men launched their attacks. It recalls the flight of Mattathias and his sons to the mountains, from which they launched their attacks against Yahweh's enemies. Wright correctly identifies this allusion: "Such flight would not betoken cowardice. It would be undertaken with the intention of regrouping as a body, in order subsequently to be vindicated as the true people, indeed the true leaders. Mattathias' flight to the hills ended with his family becoming the new royal house."[23] That is the significance of these mountains. As Wright describes, it is *the* place to regroup until a battle can be waged. The faithful ones will become the rulers and judges of the kingdom, just as Jesus promised: "I tell you the truth, when the renewal of all things comes, when the Son of Man takes his seat on the throne of his glory, you who were faithful to me will likewise take your seats on twelve thrones, judging the twelve tribes of Israel" (Matt 19:28).

Thus, again Jesus warns his disciples that during this period of waiting they are not to follow after those messianic hopefuls who claim to have a divine commission to wage war on Rome. *Yet note that not one of the gospels denies such a war is to be waged.* Luke says that "Jerusalem will be trampled on by the

23. Wright, *Jesus and the Victory of God*, 353.

Gentiles, until the times of the Gentiles are fulfilled." In other words, once they have demolished Jerusalem, Rome's time is up. Matthew says that when the *true* messianic warrior (the "Son of Man"; see Dan 7:13–14) arrives, his identity will be unmistakable. "For as the lightning comes from the east and flashes as far as the west, so will be the coming of the Son of Man." The disciples are charged to regroup in the mountains while Jerusalem is being destroyed. They are to wait until the "times of the Gentiles are fulfilled." Then, as we see next, the Son of Man arrives to judge the nations and deliver God's people:

Mark 13:24–27	Matt 24:29–31	Luke 21:25–28
[24]*"But in those days, after that suffering, the sun will be darkened, and the moon will not give its light,* [25]*and the stars will be falling from heaven, and the powers in the heavens will be shaken.* [26]*Then they will see 'the Son of Man coming in clouds' with great power and glory.* [27]*Then he will send out the angels, and gather his elect from the four winds, from the ends of the earth to the ends of heaven."*	[29]*"Immediately after the suffering of those days the sun will be darkened, and the moon will not give its light; the stars will fall from heaven, and the powers of heaven will be shaken.* [30]*Then the sign of the Son of Man will appear in heaven, and then all the tribes of the earth will mourn, and they will see 'the Son of Man coming on the clouds of heaven' with power and great glory.* [31]*And he will send out his angels with a loud trumpet call, and they will gather his elect from the four winds, from one end of heaven to the other."*	[25]*"There will be signs in the sun, the moon, and the stars, and on the earth distress among nations confused by the roaring of the sea and the waves.* [26]*People will faint from fear and foreboding of what is coming upon the world, for the powers of the heavens will be shaken.* [27]*Then they will see 'the Son of Man coming in a cloud' with power and great glory.* [28]*Now when these things begin to take place, stand up and raise your heads, because your redemption is drawing near."*

Note that both Mark and Matthew make it clear that the coming of the Son of Man follows directly on the heels of the destruction of Jerusalem. They also, however, make it equally clear that the coming of the Son of Man occurs *after* the siege of Jerusalem.[24] In Mark, the coming of the Son of Man takes place "after that suffering," yet still "in those days." Matthew's language is even stronger: "*immediately* after the suffering of those days."

Now the question is what happens at the coming of the Son of Man. The apocalyptic language used may sound strange to us: the sun and moon

---

24. This will become crucial later when we examine Wright's interpretation of this discourse.

go dark, stars fall from the sky, the sea and the waves roar. But this would not have sounded strange to the disciples. They knew exactly what Jesus meant. Jesus was using the traditional language the prophets employed to foretell the fall of Israel's enemies. As Wright acknowledges, the language means no less than that "Babylon will fall—an earth-shattering event!"[25] Jesus is alluding to Isaiah 13:

> Wail! The day of Yahweh is near;
> it is coming, destruction from the Almighty! . . .
> They will be seized with agonizing spasms;
> like a woman in labor, they will be in agony. . . .
> Look, the day of Yahweh comes,
> ruthless, in wrath and ferocious rage,
> to make the earth desolate,
> and to wipe out the wicked from the face of it.
> The stars in the heavens and their constellations
> will no longer give their light;
> when it rises the sun will be dark,
> and the moon will be black.
> I will punish the earth for its evils,
> and the wicked for their wickedness;
> I will crush the pride of the arrogant,
> and humiliate the oppressors in their insolence . . .
> Thus I will put a tremor in the heavens,
> and the earth will be knocked out of place,
> at the wrath of He Who Raises Armies,
> on the day of his ferocious rage. . . .
> And Babylon, the glory of kingdoms,
> the grandeur and treasure of the Chaldeans,
> will be like Sodom and Gomorrah
> when God dethroned them.
> (Isa 13: 6, 8–11, 13, 19)

Again in Isaiah 14:12, Yahweh orders the prophet to taunt the king of Babylon, saying, "How you have fallen from heaven, O Morning Star, son of the Dawn!" The prophet Joel spoke of the day of Yahweh, when Yahweh comes with an army so vast it cannot be counted, to destroy the enemies of Israel. In the wake of the armies of Yahweh, the earth is said to quake and the heavens tremble. "The sun and moon are darkened, and the stars cease to shine" (Joel 2:10). In Joel's vision, it seems as though it is the vast armies of Yahweh themselves that eclipse the sun, moon, and stars. Later, Joel's vision continues:

---

25. Wright, *Jesus and the Victory of God*, 354.

And I will display signs in the heavens and on the earth—blood and fire and billows of smoke. The sun will turn into darkness and the moon to blood, just before the great and terrible day of Yahweh arrives. And whoever calls on the name of Yahweh will be saved. There will be deliverance in Mount Zion and in Jerusalem, the deliverance of the remnant whom Yahweh has called out, just as Yahweh has said. (Joel 2:30–32)

The parallel between Joel's vision and that of Jesus in the Olivet Discourse is clear. Israel is attacked by a foreign power, but Yahweh intervenes and destroys the foreign army, just in time to save the remnant of the faithful. Similarly, Ezekiel speaks of the destruction of Egypt by Yahweh's hand:

I will spread your flesh on the mountains
and fill the valleys with your remains.
I will drench the land with your flowing blood
all the way to the mountains,
and the ravines will be filled with your flesh.
When I snuff you out, I will cover the heavens
and darken their stars;
I will cover the sun with a cloud,
and the moon will not give its light.
All the shining lights in the heavens
I will darken over you;
I will bring darkness over your land,
declares the Sovereign [Yahweh].
(Ezek 32:5–8, NASB)

Here in Ezekiel it is clear that the darkness is an expression of the desolation Yahweh is about to make of the enemy's kingdom. Whether the darkening of the heavenly lights is intended literally or symbolically (or both) is irrelevant. In either case, the least that is meant is that Yahweh is about to heap destruction upon a foreign imperial power.

Thus, when Jesus says that "the sun will be darkened, and the moon will not give its light, and the stars will be falling from heaven, and the powers in the heavens will be shaken," what Jesus means is dreadfully clear: Rome's time is up. The Son of Man is coming with his angels, the heavenly lights are darkened in their wake, and as Matthew says, "all the tribes of the earth will mourn" (24:30). The worldwide mourning of the tribes indicates in no uncertain terms that this is a picture of the final judgment. And while the tribes are mourning, the Son of Man sends out angels in every direction to collect God's people, to gather them out of diaspora and bring them together into the new kingdom about to be established. Thus Jesus can say, "When these things begin to take place, stand up and raise your heads, because your redemption is drawing near" (Luke 21:28). Those who are gathered together in the bandits' mountains, awaiting the arrival of the Son of Man, will know that Rome is about to be brought low, and Yahweh is returning to Israel to establish his kingdom, once and for all.

Recall that Mark and Matthew have both indicated that this will take place immediately after the destruction of Jerusalem. Now this claim is reiterated: "Truly I tell you, this generation will not pass away until all these things have taken place." This claim is repeated verbatim in each synoptic gospel:

Mark 13:28–31	*Matt 24:32–35*	*Luke 21:29–33*
[28]"From the fig tree learn its lesson: as soon as its branch becomes tender and puts forth its leaves, you know that summer is near. [29]So also, when you see these things taking place, you know that he is near, at the very gates. [30]*Truly I tell you, this generation will not pass away until all these things have taken place.* [31]Heaven and earth will pass away, but my words will not pass away."	[32]"From the fig tree learn its lesson: as soon as its branch becomes tender and puts forth its leaves, you know that summer is near. [33]So also, when you see all these things, you know that he is near, at the very gates. [34]*Truly I tell you, this generation will not pass away until all these things have taken place.* [35]Heaven and earth will pass away, but my words will not pass away."	[29]Then he told them a parable: "Look at the fig tree and all the trees; [30]as soon as they sprout leaves you can see for yourselves and know that summer is already near. [31]So also, when you see these things taking place, you know that the kingdom of God is near. [32]*Truly I tell you, this generation will not pass away until all things have taken place.* [33]Heaven and earth will pass away, but my words will not pass away."

What are "all these things"? Jesus has just recounted them: the wars, the famines, the persecutions, the spread of the gospel, the messianic pretenders, the desecration of the temple, the destruction of Jerusalem, the coming of the Son of Man with his angels in judgment, the worldwide mourning of the nations upon the coming of the Son of Man, the gathering of God's chosen out of diaspora, and the redemption of the faithful. "This generation will not pass away until all these things have taken place."

Let's summarize the data so far. With minor variations in phrasing, in each of the synoptic accounts Jesus has said:

1. The temple will be destroyed.

2. Before the temple is destroyed, there will be conflict and a period of testing for his disciples.

3. When the temple is destroyed, Jerusalem will be ransacked and Jesus' disciples are to regroup in the mountains.

4. Immediately or soon after the temple is destroyed, the Son of Man will return to judge the unfaithful and collect the faithful.

5. This will all happen within the lifetimes of Jesus' immediate disciples.

As we can see, the message here is identical to the teaching of Jesus in Mark 8:34—9:1 (with its parallels: Matt 16:24–28; Luke 9:23–27). After a short period of intense suffering, the Son of Man will come to judge the earth and reward the faithful; this will all happen within the lifetime of Jesus' contemporaries.

There seems to be no getting around the fact: if Jesus said what the gospels say he said, then Jesus was wrong. Admittedly, he was right about a lot of it. The good news *did* spread throughout the world. Wars, famines, and plagues *did* occur. His disciples *were* persecuted. Messianic hopefuls *did* attract followings, all of which were squelched. Nation *did* rise against nation. The temple *was* desecrated, and Jerusalem *was* destroyed. He got all of that right! The only part he got wrong was that little detail about the end of the world as we know it. But nine out of ten isn't that bad.

On the other hand, wars, famines, and plagues are always happening. Jewish rebels were perpetually picking fights with the occupying forces. Messianic hopefuls were forever calling down fire from heaven and scorching no one but themselves. Predicting the desecration of the temple and its subsequent destruction wasn't any stupendous feat either. 70 CE would not be the first time the Romans had defiled the Jewish sacred place. Moreover, Jesus wasn't the only prophet in the first century to predict that the Romans would destroy the temple.[26] The signs were very clear to anyone with a savvy eye for politics (which Jesus of Nazareth had in spades): the spiral of violence was getting tighter. Getting all that correct makes Jesus very astute. But the problem is that Jesus interpreted those everyday realities as signs that the world as they knew it was about to end, and that by the power of God a new world order would spring up in its place. This is the apocalyptic script. Jesus had read it. It was a good script, with a thrilling climax. But in this case, life did not imitate art. The real world is always *so* anticlimactic.

---

26. The first century CE oracular prophet Jesus ben Hananiah also pronounced doom upon the temple.

After That Suffering: The Escape Clause

You may think I'm getting a little ahead of myself. You'll have noticed that I stopped quoting Mark 13 at verse 31, precisely where it was convenient for me. If I had kept going, immediately I would have run into a sizeable obstacle. Allow me to allay your concerns:

> But about that day or hour no one knows, neither the angels in
> heaven, nor the Son, but only the Father. (Mark 13:32//Matt 24:36)

I call this the escape clause. Ever since the world as we know it did not end in the late first century CE, Christians have been appealing to this verse as proof that Jesus did not know when the final judgment would occur. After all, how could Jesus predict when the final judgment would occur *and* claim ignorance about it at the same time? In this way, it is thought that Jesus is saved from charges of being a false prophet. He may be ignorant, but he is not wrong.

Unfortunately, this statement cannot legitimately be used in this way, to salvage Jesus' reputation. Let's look at the verse again, and this time we will include the verses that follow:

Mark 13:32–37	*Matt 24:36–44*	*Luke 21:34–36*
[32]"But about that day or hour no one knows, neither the angels in heaven, nor the Son, but only the Father. [33]Beware, keep alert; for you do not know when the time will come. [34]It is like a man going on a journey, when he leaves home and puts his slaves in charge, each with his work, and commands the doorkeeper to be on the watch. [35]Therefore, keep awake—for you do not know when the master of the house will come, in the evening, or at midnight, or at cockcrow, or at dawn, [36]or else he may find you asleep when he comes suddenly. [37]And	[36]"But about that day and hour no one knows, neither the angels of heaven, nor the Son, but only the Father. [37]For as the days of Noah were, so will be the coming of the Son of Man. [38]For as in those days before the flood they were eating and drinking, marrying and giving in marriage, until the day Noah entered the ark, [39]and they knew nothing until the flood came and swept them all away, so too will be the coming of the Son of Man. [40]Then two will be in the field; one will be taken and one will be left. [41]Two women will be grinding meal together; one will be	[34]"Be on guard so that your hearts are not weighed down with dissipation and drunkenness and the worries of this life, and that day does not catch you unexpectedly, [35]like a trap. For it will come upon all who live on the face of the whole earth. [36]Be alert at all times, praying *that you may have the strength to escape all these things that will take place, and to stand before the Son of Man.*"

Mark 13:32–37	Matt 24:36–44	Luke 21:34–36
what I say to you I say to all: Keep awake."	taken and one will be left. [42]Keep awake therefore, for you do not know on what day your Lord is coming. [43]But understand this: if the owner of the house had known in what part of the night the thief was coming, he would have stayed awake and would not have let his house be broken into. [44]Therefore you also must be ready, for the Son of Man is coming at an unexpected hour."	

Note first that in each case, the emphasis remains on the *imminence* of the coming of the Son of Man. The exhortation is to remain alert because the Son of Man could come *at any minute*. Note also that the alleged statement of Jesus' ignorance found in Mark 13:32 and Matt 24:36 is omitted in Luke. In its place is the exhortation to "be on guard so . . . that day does not catch you unexpectedly" (21:34). Moreover, notice the dual reference in Luke 21:36 to the destruction of Jerusalem ("that you may have the strength to escape all these things that will take place") and the coming of the Son of Man. It is clear in Luke that Jesus' exhortation to watchfulness is not based on an ambiguous agnosticism about the time of the final judgment. The exhortation to watchfulness applies to those who will be there when Jerusalem is under siege. The appeal is not to miss the signs that are soon to begin, heralding the imminent end.

In the same way, the declaration that "no one knows the day or hour" is not, in its proper context, a declaration that the end might potentially come at some indefinite time in the distant future. The verse just prior to it makes it clear that all of this will happen within the generation of Jesus' immediate disciples. The focus of "no one knows the day or hour" is to encourage the disciples to stay faithful *precisely because* the end is imminent. In Matthew 25 for instance, the same phrase recurs in the parable of the ten virgins. The point of the parable is not that the master could return anytime within the next several centuries. The point is that his return is imminent, that it is going to happen any minute, that there is not even time enough for the virgins to run to the market to purchase oil. Jesus concludes the parable, saying, "Therefore keep watch, because you do not know the day or hour" (25:13).

Here it is clear that not knowing the day or hour is not an expression of agnosticism or of ignorance, but a statement of immediate urgency. It means "any minute now."

Moreover, Jesus' statement that not even *he* knows the day or hour of the final judgment does *not* erase or contradict the fact that twice (Mark 9:1; 13:31) he promised that the day in question would come within the span of a single generation. Not knowing the day or hour is to be understood *within* that timeframe of one generation. Jesus knows that it will happen soon, has promised that it will happen before the last of his disciples tastes death, but he does not know the precise date or hour that it will occur *within those boundaries*. The point of the statement is not to express his ignorance, but to disparage the disciples from focusing on the precise date when they *should* be busy about the business of preparing the way for the imminent kingdom.

The same logic prevails in Acts 1:6–8. After his resurrection, the disciples want to know if Jesus is now going to restore the kingdom to Israel. Jesus never denies that this is what he intends to do. Overthrowing Rome and restoring the kingdom to Israel is exactly what he said he would do in the Olivet Discourse. Jesus does not deny that is his intention, but rebukes them for their need to know the times and dates. Instead of answering their question, Jesus redirects them to their mission, telling them that although knowledge of the hour is not theirs to have, *power to be witnesses* is. Despite the popular reading of this text, Jesus does not rebuke them for their conception of an earthly kingdom, nor does he correct it. His response assumes it, while refocusing their attention on their immediate task.

It is clear, therefore, that there is no escape clause. Mark 13:32 only came to be seen as such on account of the fact that the final judgment did not eventuate as Jesus had said it would; cognitive dissonance ensued, and an escape clause became necessary. The reason these passages are said to be "obscure" or "difficult to interpret" is not that these passages *are* obscure or difficult to interpret. It is simply that their very plain meaning is difficult for some of us to stomach.

A Pun-Free Section Heading on Wright's Eisegesis[27]

For those who find themselves reeling from the loss of the escape clause, N. T. Wright offers another alternative. I do not think it is a very good alternative,

27. Exegesis is what happens when an interpreter reads a text and comes away with an interpretation that is derived from the text. "*Ex*" means "out of," and so with exegesis one is getting one's ideas straight out of the text—or so the theory goes. Eisegesis is when an interpreter brings his or her own ideas *to* the text, reads the text looking for those ideas, and—surprise of surprises—comes away from the text with those selfsame

and I will show why, but it is an alternative nonetheless. Rightly abandoning the attempt to find some way to push Jesus' language of the final judgment off into the indefinite, distant future, Wright has gone the other direction— denying that Jesus ever made reference to a so-called "second coming" at all. On Wright's reading of Mark 13, everything Jesus predicted was in fact fulfilled by 70 CE, with the destruction of the temple, *including* the coming of the Son of Man. If Wright's reading is correct, then Jesus wasn't wrong. For this reason, Wright's interpretation has become somewhat popular among a new generation of Christians, despite the fact that the vast majority of historical Jesus scholars tend to read Wright's thesis with one eyebrow raised. Here are the primary interpretive claims Wright makes about the Olivet Discourse:

1. No literal "end of the space-time universe" is envisioned here.[28] What comes to an end is the age—namely, "the end of Israel's period of mourning and exile and the beginning of her freedom and vindication."[29]

2. The destruction of the temple in 70 CE and the coming of the Son of Man are not two separate events, but one single event. When the temple is destroyed, that *is* the coming of the Son of Man (metaphorically speaking of course). What this means is that the Son of Man (Jesus) is vindicated *by* the destruction of the temple.[30]

3. The allusions to the destruction of Babylon and Egypt in the Olivet Discourse are *not* (as one would expect) discrete predictions of the destruction of Rome in the wake of its war with Jerusalem. In a radical role reversal, this time, according to Wright, *Jerusalem* is Babylon. The destruction of Jerusalem takes up the space that the destruction of Babylon usually occupied in the prophetic doom oracles.[31] And "when Jerusalem is destroyed, and Jesus' people escape from the ruin just in time, *that will be* YHWH becoming king, bringing about the liberation of his true covenant people, the true return from exile, the beginning of the new world order."[32]

4. When the text says that they will see the Son of Man "coming on the clouds," this is not to be taken literally. Moreover, the words

---

ideas. "*Eis*" means "into," and so with eisegesis, one is projecting one's own ideas *into* the text and fooling oneself into thinking that one found them there.

28. Wright, *Jesus and the Victory of God*, 345.

29. Ibid., 346.

30. Ibid., 342, 360, 362.

31. Ibid., 354–58.

32. Ibid., 364.

here that are regularly translated into English as "coming" do not necessarily mean "coming." One means "presence," and the other could mean either "coming" or "going."[33]

In cogent outline form like this, and abstracted from the actual text of Mark 13, the picture Wright paints here seems to have an air of plausibility. It is an alluring proposal for a number of reasons, and it is one I once accepted myself. Let's take some time to address each of these four points individually, and see how they hold up to a touch of scrutiny.

(1) For some reason Wright is adamant that we acknowledge that the "end of the age" does not mean the "end of the space-time continuum."[34] It is understandable why Wright would need to point this out at least once, since a popular understanding of the day of judgment entails the notion that the world will be destroyed and all souls will go on to live forever in either disembodied bliss or disembodied physical torment. On the other hand, apart from a few fundamentalist Bible commentators, I have never come across a biblical scholar who thinks that the "end of the world" means, literally, the end of the world. When the phrase "end of the world" is used in biblical scholarship, almost invariably it means "end of the world *as we know it.*" It is shorthand for the idea that the world as we now know it will be radically transformed, "recreated," as it were. The "great divorce" between heaven and earth will be mended. The righteous dead will be raised to life and bodies will be sprinkled with angel dust (Matt 22:30). Grass will be greener, and the wolf will lie down with the lamb (Isa 11:6). These are essentially the sorts of things that the standard apocalyptic vision expected would transpire once the "present evil age" had passed away (Gal 1:4) and the nations had been judged.

But Wright does *not* think all this is what is meant by the end of the age. For Wright, the "end of the age" is simply "the end of Israel's period of mourning and exile and the beginning of her freedom and vindication,"[35] and this is what Wright thinks happens in 70 CE. By Wright's idiosyncratic defini-

---

33. Ibid., 341, 361, 364. A fifth claim of Wright's will not be treated in the body but may be treated here. Wright avers that the reference in Mark 12:27 to the angels who "gather his elect" is not, as one would suppose, a typical reference to the eschatological return of God's people to Jerusalem, marking the end of diaspora and exile, but rather (since "angel" can simply mean "messenger") the angels who are sent out to gather the elect are really the disciples, sent out to evangelize the Gentiles (ibid., 361 fn. 152, 363). There are two fatal problems with Wright's interpretation here: (1) angels also accompany the Son of Man in Mark 8:34—9:1, but they are clearly not human evangelists there; (2) Jesus said that the spread of the gospel throughout the whole world would already be accomplished *prior* to the coming of the Son of Man (Mark 13:10).

34. Ibid., 345–46; Wright, *New Testament and the People of God*, 285.

35. Wright, *Jesus and the Victory of God*, 346.

tion of "freedom and vindication," the destruction of the temple somehow puts an end to Israel's exile, puts an end to their mourning, and liberates and vindicates the people of God. How does the destruction of the Jewish temple accomplish all this? Metaphorically, of course. When Jesus identifies the destruction of the temple as the "desolating sacrilege," what he *really* means, according to Wright, is that it is the "liberating vindication" of Israel. But Luke's account flies in the face of Wright's reading. Luke 21:28 describes the liberating vindication of faithful Israel; yet it takes place *after* the desolating sacrilege (21:20). As in Matthew and Mark, in Luke also the destruction of the temple and the coming of the Son of Man are two separate events. Luke characterizes the latter event, and not the former, as Israel's vindication.

(2) Wright argues that the coming of the Son of Man *is* the destruction of the temple, or rather that the "coming" of the Son of Man is a metaphor for the fact that Jesus was vindicated as a prophet when the temple was destroyed. Because Jesus predicted its destruction, Jesus (who was executed as a false prophet) was vindicated when the temple was finally destroyed.[36] There are at least three problems with this claim.

First, Wright's claim that Jesus interprets the destruction of the temple as his own personal vindication is a claim that is not substantiated by anything in the text. Now it is true in a sense that Jesus' prediction of the temple's destruction *was* vindicated when the temple was destroyed, but why should that serve as proof that Jesus was everything else he said he was? It wouldn't. After all, Jesus ben Hananiah had also predicted that the temple would soon be destroyed by the Romans. Did the destruction of the temple mean that Jesus ben Hananiah was a prophet sent from God? Such a claim would be tenuous, at best, which is likely why the claim is *not made in the text*. There is no language in the Olivet Discourse to indicate that the suffering in Jerusalem is to be seen as vindication for Jesus of Nazareth. All of the language describing the destruction of the temple is negative.

Second, and most importantly, the text of Mark and Matthew make it unmistakably clear that the coming of the Son of Man occurs *after* the destruction of Jerusalem. (We will have to reiterate this point again later, because Wright's claims are frequently undermined by this very obvious fact.) Mark places the coming of the Son of Man "in those days, *after that suffering*," and Matthew places it "immediately *after* the suffering of those days." If Jesus had wanted to relay the idea that the destruction of the temple *was identical to* the coming of the Son of Man, why did he say that the Son of Man would come *after* the fact? The answer is simple: Wright's reading is not correct. The actual text seems to indicate that the destruction of the temple

36. Ibid., 362.

was the *very impetus* for the coming of the Son of Man. The destruction of the temple was not the Son of Man's vindication. On the contrary, the coming of the Son of Man was *Jerusalem's* vindication!

That brings us to the third objection to Wright's schema: the Son of Man's coming is global in scope; it is emphatically *not* limited to Jerusalem. Matthew says that "all of the tribes of the earth will mourn" at his coming (24:30),[37] and Luke says that the judgment of the Son of Man will come like a trap "upon all who dwell on the face of the earth" (21:35). This is unequivocally the language of a worldwide judgment. Thus, it is sensible to conclude that Wright's attempt to identify the Son of Man's coming *as* the destruction of the temple has failed.

(3) Wright argues that in the Olivet Discourse, Jerusalem occupies the space within the doom oracle normally reserved for foreign oppressors such as Babylon. Recall our examination earlier of the prophetic oracles in Isa 13:6–19; 14:12; Ezekiel 32:5–8; and Joel 2:10, 30–32. In each of these oracles we found parallels to the language in Mark 13:24: "the sun will be darkened, and the moon will not give its light, and the stars will be falling from heaven." In each of the oracles, this language was an expression of doom to a foreign oppressor (Babylon, Egypt, and other gentile nations). It therefore makes perfect sense to conclude that by quoting this language from the doom oracles, Jesus was predicting the destruction of Rome and a worldwide judgment. After all, the darkening of the heavenly lights coincided with the coming of the Son of Man *after* the destruction of Jerusalem. Moreover, subsequent to these portents of doom, "all the tribes of the earth" would mourn (Matt 24:30).

Despite the data, however, Wright insists that in the Olivet Discourse it is Jerusalem and not Rome who should be seen as Babylon. On what grounds does Wright make this counterintuitive claim? As it turns out, Wright's entire argument here relies on one interpretive move: Wright claims that when Jesus tells his disciples to flee to the mountains, Jesus is echoing oracles from Isaiah, Jeremiah, and Zechariah in which the Judeans are told to flee Babylon.[38] But why should Jesus' instructions to flee from Jerusalem be read as an "echo" of earlier instructions to flee from Babylon? Essentially, the only thing linking the one to the other is the word "flee." Is that enough

---

37. Wright tries to deal with this statement in Matthew by citing Zech 12:10–11, in which *Jerusalem* mourns. See ibid., 360 fn. 151. I am unsure how Wright thinks he can take a text about worldwide mourning and transform it into a text about Jerusalem, simply by declaring by fiat that Zech 12:10–11 is "echoed" in Matt 24:30. The only thing to connect the two texts is the word "mourning." Is Wright trying his hand at *gezerah shawah*?

38. Wright, *Jesus and the Victory of God*, 356–58, quoting Isa 48:20; 52:11–12; Jer 50:6, 8, 28; 51:6–10, 45–46, 50–51, 57; Zech 2:6–8.

on which to build a case? Wright's move is at best tenuous, but here are two reasons why it fails.

First, there is no reason why we should accept Wright's declaration that the *flee Babylon oracles* specifically are echoed in the Olivet Discourse. On what grounds does Wright say that Jeremiah 6, for instance, is not the oracle that is echoed by Jesus from the Mount of Olives?

> Flee for safety, O sons of Benjamin,
> From the midst of Jerusalem!
> Now blow a trumpet in Tekoa
> And raise a signal over Beth-haccerem;
> For evil looks down from the north,
> And a great destruction.
> The comely and dainty one,
> the daughter of Zion,
> I will cut off.
> (Jer 6:1–2, NASB)

This doom oracle appears to be a fine candidate. Here, just as in Mark 13, a foreign army is coming to destroy Jerusalem, and the Judeans are told to flee the city. It seems to me the echo is much stronger here than in an oracle in which Jews are told to flee Babylon before it is destroyed by another imperial power. Or why not Jer 4:5–6? There also the Judeans are told to flee Jerusalem to the fortified cities before it is overrun by armies from the north. Is this not a viable candidate for one of Wright's reverberating background texts?

The interesting thing is that Wright has *already* identified a text to which he believes the warning to "flee to the mountains" alludes. Wright has already told us (as we noted on page 179) that the warning to "flee to the mountains" is a clear allusion to the story of Mattathias and his sons,[39] who fled to the mountains in 167 BCE, from which they launched a successful campaign for liberation from Seleucid hegemony. So which is it? Is "flee to the mountains" an allusion to Mattathias and his militia fleeing Jerusalem after the all-important *desolating sacrilege*, or is it an allusion to Jews being told to flee Babylon (jubilantly) before Babylon's destruction? Can Wright have it both ways?

That brings us to the second problem. Wright selects a variety of oracles to "show" that Jesus is comparing Jerusalem to Babylon by use of the word "flee." Undermining Wright's argument are those very oracles themselves. In Mark 13:14–18 the Jews are fleeing Jerusalem out of fear for their very lives. Yet in Isa 48:20, which Wright quotes as evidence, the Jews are leaving Babylon in jubilation!

---

39. Ibid., 353.

> Depart from Babylon, *flee* from Chaldea,
> announce with a shout of joy, proclaim it,
> dispatch the message to the ends of the earth;
> say, "Yahweh has redeemed his servant Jacob!"

Again, in Mark 13:14–18, there is no time to collect one's possessions, or even to grab a coat. Yet in Isa 52:11–12, which Wright quotes as evidence, the Jews are expressly told to take their time:

> Depart, depart, get out of there!
> Touch nothing that is unclean on your way out;
> get out from their midst and purify yourselves,
> you who carry the very vessels of Yahweh.
> *But you shall not go out in haste,*
> *you shall not go out fleeing;*
> for Yahweh himself will go in front of you,
> and the God of Israel will be your rear guard.

It is difficult to see how anyone familiar with these two passages in Isaiah could have heard them echoed in Jesus' words in Mark 13. The circumstances are precisely the opposite. Wright then quotes Jer 50:6 and 50:28, in which the Jews are told to flee Babylon. Why? Because Yahweh is coming to take vengeance on Babylon *for destroying his temple*—precisely what Rome would do to Jerusalem in 70 CE. If anything in Mark 13 echoes these verses in Jeremiah 50, it would not be the instruction to flee but the proclamation of doom against Rome as repayment for the desecration of the temple. Again, the passage Wright chooses to make his case that Jerusalem is Babylon only supports our earlier intuition that the role of Babylon in Mark 13 is, as would be expected, played by Rome.

The final passage quoted by Wright is from Zechariah 14. Initially, this text seems to make Wright's case for him very well. I will quote here the portions quoted by Wright:

> I will gather all the nations against Jerusalem to battle. . . .
> Then Yahweh will go forth and fight against those nations as when
> he fights on a day of battle. On that day his feet shall stand on the
> Mount of Olives, which lies before Jerusalem on the east; and the
> Mount of Olives shall be split in two from east to west by a very wide
> valley; so that one half of the Mount shall withdraw northwards,
> and the other half southwards. And you shall flee by the valley of
> Yahweh's mountain, for the valley between the mountains shall
> reach to Azal; and you shall flee as you fled from the earthquake in
> the days of King Uzziah of Judah. Then Yahweh my God will come,
> and all the holy ones with him. . . . And Yahweh will become king
> over all the earth; on that day Yahweh will be one and his name one.
> (Zech 14:2a, 3–5, 9, NRSV)

This passage may indeed make a strong case for Wright's position. In it we learn that Yahweh gathers together all of the gentile nations to launch an attack against Jerusalem. Yahweh is said to stand on the Mount of Olives, a point not without significance to those listening to Jesus as he stands on the same mount, again foretelling the destruction of Jerusalem. Portents in the form of earthquakes foretell of impending doom upon Jerusalem, and the inhabitants of the city must flee for their lives as the foreign armies approach. Then, almost as if representative of the foreign armies, Yahweh and his angels come out to war. And on that day, when Jerusalem is attacked by the foreign armies, Yahweh becomes king over all the earth.

Wright's reading of Zechariah 14 is his interpretation of the events of 70 CE in brief. Yahweh calls down the wrath of the Gentiles against Jerusalem; Jerusalem is attacked and destroyed; Yahweh is made king and glorified as Jerusalem is punished for its sins. There is only one difficulty with Wright's use of this passage: the omissions. Let's pick up again from verse 5d, this time filling in Wright's gaps and continuing on where he stopped:

> Then Yahweh my God will come, and all the holy ones with him. On that day there shall not be either cold or frost. *And there shall be continuous day (it is known to Yahweh), not day and not night, for at evening time there shall be light. On that day living waters shall flow out from Jerusalem, half of them to the eastern sea and half of them to the western sea; it shall continue in summer as in winter. And Yahweh will become king over all the earth; on that day Yahweh will be one and his name one.*
>
> The whole land shall be turned into a plain from Geba to Rimmon south of Jerusalem. *But Jerusalem shall remain aloft on its site* from the Gate of Benjamin to the place of the former gate, to the Corner Gate, and from the Tower of Hananel to the king's wine presses. *And it shall be inhabited, for never again shall it be doomed to destruction; Jerusalem shall abide in security. This shall be the plague with which Yahweh will strike all the peoples that wage war against Jerusalem: their flesh shall rot while they are still on their feet; their eyes shall rot in their sockets, and their tongues shall rot in their mouths. On that day a great panic from Yahweh shall fall on them, so that each will seize the hand of a neighbor, and the hand of one will be raised against the hand of the other; even Judah will fight at Jerusalem. And the wealth of all the surrounding nations shall be collected—gold, silver, and garments in great abundance.* And a plague like this plague shall fall on the horses, the mules, the camels, the donkeys, and whatever animals may be in those camps. *Then all who survive of the nations that have come against Jerusalem shall go up year by year to worship the King, He Who Raises Armies, and to keep the festival of booths.* (Zech 14:5d–16, NRSV)

Now this tells a very different story. In *Zechariah's* version of Zechariah 14, Jerusalem is only *half* destroyed by the gentile armies, while the other half is given more glory and honor than ever. The vision is an eschatological one. The battle described on this day is the *final battle*. Nights desist and daylight perseveres forever. Living waters flow year round out from Jerusalem and it becomes the eschatological temple at which all the nations of the earth come to worship Yahweh. More significantly for our purposes, on that same day, Yahweh executes terrible vengeance on all the armies who fought against Jerusalem in that last battle. The wealth of the fallen nations will be collected and brought to Jerusalem as Yahweh's spoil. Those among the nations who survive Yahweh's swift vengeance will travel to Jerusalem to worship him. The passage goes on to say that if any nation does not come to the Jerusalem temple to worship, Yahweh will cause a famine to come upon their land.

Thus, contrary to Wright's shrewdly selective reading of the text, Yahweh does not become king of the whole earth because Jerusalem is destroyed. Rather, Yahweh becomes king of the whole earth because Jerusalem is spared, and all the nations on that day are brought under the yoke of the God of Israel. This passage hardly supports Wright's interpretation of Mark 13, and it hardly reflects the events of 70 CE. It does, however unfortunately, reflect very much what Jesus of Nazareth predicted would take place at that time. In both Zechariah 14 and Mark 13, Yahweh punishes Jerusalem with foreign armies, before immediately turning around and punishing the Gentiles that were used to punish Jerusalem. In both oracles, after the judgment of the nations, a new age of unfathomable glory ensues. In neither case were the oracles fulfilled.

(4) Wright asserts that the coming of the Son of Man on the clouds is not to be taken literally but should be taken as a metaphor for role reversal.[40] Moreover, the Son of Man's *coming* is not a coming at all, but rather a *going*. What are we to make of this first claim? In substantiation of the claim that the "coming on the clouds" is to be taken metaphorically, Wright appeals to little more than our common sense. But *our* common sense isn't necessarily the common sense of apocalyptic Jews in the ancient world. Neither does Wright's common sense appear to be that of Paul, who wrote that "the Lord himself, with a cry of command, with the archangel's call and with the sound of God's trumpet, will descend from heaven, and the dead in Christ will rise first. *Then we who are alive, who are left, will be caught up in the clouds together with them to meet the Lord in the air*" (1 Thess 4:16–17). Paul does not appear to be speaking metaphorically here. Compare this with Jesus' language in the Olivet Discourse: "And they will see 'the Son of Man coming

---

40. Ibid., 341; following Caird, *Jesus and the Jewish Nation*, 20–22.

on the clouds of heaven' with power and great glory. And he will send out his angels with a loud trumpet call, and they will gather his elect from the four winds, from one end of heaven to the other" (Matt 24:30–31). Paul and Matthew seem to rely on a common tradition here, and Paul at least does not seem to take it as a metaphor.[41]

Dale Allison has extensively critiqued Wright's assumption that such language would have been taken to be metaphorical, providing multiple examples of ancient sources (Jewish and otherwise) which took such cosmic signs very literally.[42] As we await Wright's response to Allison's challenges, the jury is still out on what grounds Wright might have to support his claim. Regardless, more important than the question of whether such language is to be taken metaphorically or literally is the question of what such language would be meant to signify even if it *were* metaphorical. And this is where Wright begins to deviate from the parameters established by the Mark 13 discourse itself. Wright insists that the "coming of the Son of Man" is a metaphor for the vindication of Jesus of Nazareth with the destruction of the temple. Yet as we have seen, Mark and Matthew both place the Son of Man's coming temporally *after* the temple has already been destroyed. Moreover, the effects of his coming are said to be global in scope, not local as Wright maintains.

Now what of Wright's claim that the *coming* is in fact not a *coming* but a *going*? The word translated "coming" in Mark 13:26 is in Greek the word *erchomenon*. *Erchomenon* can mean either "coming" or "going," depending on the context. Wright's point is this: the vision of the Son of Man on the clouds in Mark 13 is derived from an earlier vision in Daniel 7:

> And behold, with the clouds of heaven
> One like a Son of Man was coming,
> And He came up to the Ancient of Days
> And was presented before Him.
> And to Him was given dominion,
> Glory and a kingdom,
> That all the peoples, nations and men of every language
> Might serve Him
> His dominion is an everlasting dominion
> Which will not pass away;
> And His kingdom is one
> Which will not be destroyed.
> (Dan 7:13–14, NASB)

41. Dale Allison makes this point in Allison, *Jesus of Nazareth*, 159–60; and again in Allison, "Jesus and the Victory of Apocalyptic," 134–35, 312 n. 36.

42. See ibid., 130–34; and Allison, *Jesus of Nazareth*, 153–67. See further the incisive critiques of Wright's thesis offered in Adams, *Stars Will Fall from Heaven*, 5–16.

Here in the Danielic vision, Wright points out, the Son of Man is not coming from heaven to earth, but is going *from earth to heaven*.[43] Thus, according to Wright, the image in Mark 13 is not of the Son of Man coming down to earth on the clouds, but of the Son of Man ascending up to heaven on the day of his vindication. It is, Wright avers, a metaphor. Wright also points out that the word for "coming" that Matthew uses (four times: 24:3, 27, 37, 39) is the Greek word "*parousia*." *Parousia* does not technically mean "coming" at all, but rather "presence," as opposed to "absence" (*apousia*). Yet this is certainly an equivocation. What else does one call the presence of someone who had been absent? Wright himself concedes this—though the significance of the concession seems to be lost on him—when he writes: "hence it denotes the 'arrival' of someone not at the moment present." Significantly, Wright continues, "and it is especially used in relation to the visit of a royal or official personage."[44]

The significance of this last point must not be overlooked. In the Greco-Roman world, when an emperor had been away from the city in battle or on some other venture, his return to the city was always a celebrated event. Especially after military victories, the crowds would go outside the gates to meet the emperor upon his arrival and to usher him into the city, showering him with gifts and adulation. The emperor's *parousia*, his "presence," was celebrated at the gates. And this is precisely the image painted in the Olivet Discourse. As noted above, in Matthew, "*parousia*" is used four times to refer to the arrival of the Son of Man. His arrival is displayed first by signs in the heavens and then, Matthew says, "when you see all these things, you know that he is near, *at the very gates*" (Matt 24:33; also Mark 13:29). The imagery is crystal clear: the king has returned to Jerusalem; he is already outside the gates. He has returned to deliver his people from the hand of the enemy. Thus, we cannot take seriously Wright's claim that the "coming of the Son of Man" envisioned in the Olivet Discourse is not a literal coming to earth. To make such a claim based on the fact that in Daniel 7 the Son of Man is going

---

43. Ibid., 361. This is already a mistaken claim. Nowhere in Daniel 7 is it said that the "one like a son of man" has come *from* earth. This is because originally the "one like a son of man" was an angelic figure, possibly Michael, who fought on Israel's behalf. Thus, he was *already* in heaven when he was brought before the throne of Yahweh. Wright denies that the Danielic "one like a son of man" is a superhuman figure (ibid.), but offers no justification for his denial; nor does he justify that assumption when he makes it in *New Testament and the People of God*, 291–92. Collins, *Apocalyptic Imagination*, 103–04, has shown convincingly that the "one like a son of man" in Daniel 7 was originally portrayed as an angelic warrior. In later apocalyptic texts the identifier "one like a son of man" would be shortened simply to "son of man," and this would account for the understanding, which we see in some texts, of the figure as a human being.

44. Wright, *Jesus and the Victory of God*, 341.

to the throne room in heaven is to commit a sort of etymological fallacy. Just because the imagery in Mark 13 is derived from Daniel 7 does not require the former to follow the latter's every beat—which it doesn't.

We have already noted that Paul (in 1 Thess 4:16–17) understood the coming of the Son of Man on the clouds to be a literal return of the resurrected Jesus of Nazareth at the time of the end when the dead are raised and the nations are judged. Another corroborating interpretation of the coming of the Son of Man can be found in Acts 1:11. After the disciples watched Jesus ascend into heaven among the clouds, an angel informed them that he "will come in the same way you saw him go." Finally, Wright's conflation of the *parousia* with the destruction of the temple is further vitiated by Rev 1:7, which is based again on the same tradition as the Olivet Discourse:

> Look, he is coming with the clouds,
> and every eye will see him,
> even those who pierced him;
> and all the peoples of the earth
> will mourn because of him.
> So shall it be! Amen.

This was likely written decades after the destruction of the temple, and yet it looks *forward* to the coming of the Son of Man on the clouds ("so shall it be").

With all this in view, and after scrutinizing the four pillars of Wright's argument in light of the text of Mark 13 and its parallel passages, it is reasonable to judge Wright's idiosyncratic reading of the data to be a failure. Wright has not been able to save Jesus from being wrong. In counterdistinction to Wright's strategy, James Dunn finds it "impossible to deny that Jesus had expressed expectation for the *imminent* happening of events which did not happen." Against his own confessional inclinations, Dunn is obliged to admit "that Jesus had entertained hopes which were not fulfilled. There were 'final' elements in his expectation which were not realized. Putting it bluntly, Jesus was proved wrong by the course of events."[45]

After That Suffering: Conclusion

In this section we have examined the Olivet Discourse. Let's summarize our findings again. Each of the synoptic gospels tells us:

1. The temple will be destroyed.

---

45. Dunn, *Jesus Remembered*, 479. My thanks to John Loftus for bringing this page in Dunn's tome to my attention.

2. Before the temple is destroyed, there will be conflict and a period of testing for Jesus' disciples.

3. When the temple is destroyed, Jerusalem will be ransacked and Jesus' disciples are to regroup in the mountains.

4. Immediately or soon after the temple is destroyed, the Son of Man will return to judge the unfaithful and collect the faithful.

5. This will all happen within the lifetime of Jesus' immediate disciples.

Our look at the "escape clause," in which it is said that no one knows the day or hour at which the cataclysmic end will occur, has shown that its import is to stress *imminence*, not *ignorance*. Moreover, the "escape clause" is not sufficient to expunge from the record the clear statements in Mark 9:1 and 13:30 that this "end" will take place within one generation's time. Rather, the statement must be understood to obtain only *within* that timeframe of a single generation. Likewise, our examination of Wright's attempt to conflate the destruction of the temple with the coming of the Son of Man, thereby (conveniently) exonerating Jesus from charges of failed prophecy, has shown that Wright's ideas have been projected *onto* the data (for example, in his selective use of the oracle in Zechariah 14), not derived *from* them.

In the end, as much as we would like to find one, there seems to be no way to maneuver around the fact that—if we take the gospel portrayals of Jesus to be accurate—Jesus predicted the end of the world would occur within his generation. Yet this fact should hardly be surprising to us, since that is precisely what the New Testament tells us his early followers expected.

What Early Christians Expected

The earliest Christian documents we have come from the apostle Paul. One thing that has become increasingly clear to scholars in recent decades is the pervasiveness of the apocalyptic paradigm within Paul's thought.[46] Paul believed that the old world order, which is the world in bondage to hostile heavenly and earthly powers, was dying—in its last gasps. With Jesus of Nazareth a new world order was inaugurated and would be consummated within his lifetime. He characterized the Christian life between the first and second comings of Christ as a foretaste of the world to come. In the illuminating words of Paul Sampley, Paul believed Christians were currently

46. For an overview, see Beker, *Paul the Apostle.*

"walking between the times."[47] Their lives were no longer to be constituted by the characteristics of the old world order, but were to be reflective of the constitution of the age to come. Paul believed this new age, which was foreshadowed in the lives of Christians, would soon overcome the world. Thus, Paul is able to speak of the cosmos as being already "in labor," the birth of the new creation imminent. To extend Paul's analogy, we might say that Paul's proclamation of Christ was like the midwife who encourages the mother, saying, "I can see the head!" Paul writes:

> I consider that the sufferings of this present time are not worth comparing with the glory about to be revealed to us. For the creation waits with eager longing for the revealing of the children of God. . . . We know that the whole creation has been groaning in labor pains until now; and not only the creation, but we ourselves, who have the first fruits of the Spirit, groan inwardly while we wait for adoption, the redemption of our bodies.
> (Rom 8:18–19, 22–23, NRSV)

Paul's moral instructions were informed by his expectation of the imminent end of the old world order. Paul allowed marriage as a concession to those who would otherwise be tempted with sexual desires, but he preferred for believers to be like him, unmarried. Because of his belief that the time was short before the return of the Messiah, he saw marriage as an entanglement, preventing believers from devoting themselves fully to preparing the way for the coming kingdom of God (1 Cor 7:32–35). For Paul, all social norms were topsy-turvy in light of the imminent reconstitution of the cosmos:

> I think that, in view of the impending crisis, it is well for you to remain as you are. . . . I mean, brothers and sisters, the appointed time has grown short; from now on, let even those who have wives be as though they had none, and those who mourn as though they were not mourning, and those who rejoice as though they were not rejoicing, and those who buy as though they had no possessions, and those who deal with the world as though they had no dealings with it. For the present form of this world is passing away.
> (1 Cor 7:26, 29–31, NRSV)

Paul believed that he would live to see the final nail hammered into the coffin of the old world order. This is evident in multiple places. For instance, in 1 Corinthians 15, Paul explains to the church what will happen when the Lord returns and the dead are raised: "Listen, I will tell you a mystery! We will not all die, but we will all be changed, in a moment, in the twinkling of an eye,

47. Sampley, *Walking between the Times.*

at the last trumpet. For the trumpet will sound, and the dead will be raised imperishable, and we will be changed" (1 Cor 15:51–52). In other words, Paul makes a distinction between resurrection and transformation. When the Lord returns, those who are dead will be raised to life in transformed bodies. The bodies of those who are still alive will be transformed instantaneously. When he writes that "*we* will be changed," Paul indicates that he expects to be alive when the change occurs. In another letter, Paul again includes himself among the number of those who are still alive on the last day:

> *We who are alive*, who are left until the coming of the Lord, will by no means precede those who have died. For the Lord himself, with a cry of command, with the archangel's call and with the sound of God's trumpet, will descend from heaven, and the dead in Christ will rise first. *Then we who are alive, who are left,* will be caught up in the clouds together with them to meet the Lord in the air; and so we will be with the Lord forever.
> (1 Thess 4:15–17, NRSV)

Another facet of Paul's apocalypticism was his conviction that the coming of the kingdom of God would spell the end of the Roman order. For instance, Paul describes what will happen to God's enemies when the Lord returns "like a thief in the night": "While people are saying, '*Pax et Securitas,*' destruction will come on them suddenly, as labor pains on a pregnant woman, and they will not escape" (1 Thess 5:3). Paul's language here is an "ironic allusion to the official theology and propaganda of the Pax Romana,"[48] an official slogan popularized under Augustus: *Pax et Securitas*, or "Peace and Security." The ones proclaiming *pax et securitas*, of course, are the imperial propagandists, the rulers, and all those who have given their faith/loyalty to the Pax Romana. They are the ones living "in darkness" (1 Thess. 5:4),[49] upon whom the divinely apportioned destruction will fall. According to Abraham Smith, Paul sees this as the "eschatological battle in which God will bring the imperial order under judgment."[50] By it, "the pretensions of imperial propaganda are torn away."[51] Paul's vision of the kingdom was, according to Richard Horsley, directly "contesting the legitimacy of Rome."[52]

This element can be detected also in Paul's letter to the Romans. Paul encourages the Christians in Rome to avoid conflict by loving their enemies

---

48. Georgi, *Theocracy in Paul*, 28.

49. Wengst, *Pax Romana*, 77–78.

50. Smith, "Unmasking the Powers," 48.

51. Elliott, *Liberating Paul*, 190, quoting Ernst Bammel.

52. Horsley and Silberman, *The Message and the Kingdom*, 156.

and blessing their persecutors (Rom 12:14–21), reminding them that God will take vengeance on their enemies on their behalf (Rom 12:19). Therefore, Paul immediately goes on to counsel subordination to the Roman authorities, warning them that attempts to protest or to resist Roman injustices will be met sternly with the Roman sword (Rom 13:4).[53] Paul is able to recommend a strategy of political quietism because he believes their subjection to Roman authority will not continue much longer. This is evident in the verses immediately following his espousal of subordination to the government. Paul writes: "Besides this, you know what time it is, how it is now the moment for you to wake from sleep. *For salvation is nearer to us now than when we became believers*; the night is far gone, the day is near. Let us then lay aside the works of darkness and put on the armor of light" (Rom 13:11–12, NRSV). Notice that Paul's discussion of the Roman government is sandwiched between two adjoining claims: that God would execute vengeance on the enemies of God's people (12:19), and that God would save them very soon (13:11).

The expectation of an imminent *parousia* can also be seen throughout 1 Peter, where Christians are reminded that they are "being protected by the power of God through faith *for a salvation ready to be revealed in the last time. In this you rejoice, even if now for a little while you have had to suffer various trials*, so that the genuineness of your faith—being more precious than gold that, though perishable, is tested by fire—*may be found to result in praise and glory and honor when Jesus Christ is revealed*" (1 Pet 1:5–7). The same basic imminent apocalyptic paradigm is clear here: (1) their salvation will come in "the last time"; (2) their suffering is "for a little while," indicating that their salvation will come soon. This is implied again later: "Conduct yourselves honorably among the Gentiles, so that, though they malign you as evildoers, they may see your honorable deeds and glorify God when he comes to judge" (1 Pet 2:12). This reflects an expectation of imminent judgment, or else how would those who see the behavior of the churches be alive to glorify God on the day of judgment? This is made explicit in 1 Pet 4:7: "The end of all things is near; therefore be serious and discipline yourselves for the sake of your prayers." As with Paul, the impetus for moral behavior increases as the time of the end draws nearer. Therefore, in view of the imminence of the end, *now* is the time to conduct oneself with the utmost seriousness.

If Acts 2 reflects an accurate portrait of Peter's expectations, then it is clear that as early as 33 CE, Peter believed that they were already living in the "last time" to which 1 Pet 1:5 referred. In the account in Acts 2, after the

---

53. There is certainly a heavy dose of irony intended in Paul's overblown positive evaluation of Roman justice in Rom 13:1–7. See Herzog, "Dissembling, A Weapon of the Weak"; Carter, "Irony of Romans 13"; Elliott, "Strategies of Resistance."

apostles had been empowered by the Holy Spirit, some in the crowd mocked them, supposing they were drunk. Peter responds that they are not drunk, but that their state is evidence that the last days had arrived:

> This is what was spoken through the prophet Joel:
> "In the last days it will be, God declares,
> that I will pour out my Spirit upon all flesh,
> and your sons and your daughters shall prophesy,
> and your young men shall see visions,
> and your old men shall dream dreams.
> Even upon my slaves, both men and women,
> in those days I will pour out my Spirit;
> and they shall prophesy.
> And I will show portents in the heaven above
> and signs on the earth below,
> blood, and fire, and smoky mist.
> The sun shall be turned to darkness
> and the moon to blood,
> before the coming of the Lord's great and glorious day."
> (Acts 2:16–20, NRSV)

The outpouring of the Spirit upon the apostles was evidence that they had now entered the last days immediately prior to the earth-shattering day of Yahweh's vengeance. Peter went on to exhort the crowds, urging them, "Save yourselves from this corrupt generation" (2:40). The "corrupt generation" is clearly the *final* generation before the judgment.

Recall once again the question the disciples put to Jesus at the beginning of the book of Acts. Now that he had been raised from the dead and therefore vindicated by God, the disciples ask if he is now going to restore the kingdom to Israel, meaning, deliver Israel from Rome. Note the response of Jesus (Acts 1:7–8). He does not *deny* that he intends to deliver Israel from Rome. He simply declines to tell them *when*.[54] Since Acts is the sequel to the Gospel of Luke, Luke's readers are already aware that Jesus has promised to establish the earthly kingdom of God within the lifetime of his disciples (Luke 9:27; 21:32). Jesus does not want them fixated on the precise date; instead, he tells them that they will receive special power to testify about him in anticipation of his return. *Pentecost is therefore presented by Luke as the*

---

54. *Contra* Allison, *Jesus of Nazareth*, 165–66, who argues that Luke is here attempting to dissociate Jesus from an imminent expectation of the end. Note that in Luke's version of the Olivet Discourse, the statement found in Mark 13:32 and Matt 24:36 is missing. I contend that Acts 1:7 is simply where Luke opted to insert that saying. The point in both contexts is identical: "Do not focus on the time, but on the task."

empowerment of the disciples to prepare the world for the Messiah's coming to restore the kingdom to Israel.

The remarkable thing is how little the expectations of the early Christians are modified by Luke, given that Acts was written decades after the destruction of the Jerusalem temple. This is true also of other late first century writings, such as 1 John, where the writer encourages Christians to prepare for the coming of the Lord, now that they are in "the final hour" (2:18, 28). Equally so in the Apocalypse to John, where the refrain, "Surely I am coming soon," is repeated throughout (Rev 1:1–3; 3:11; 22:6–7, 10, 12, 20) as an exhortation to those who are desperately anticipating tangible deliverance from Rome.

The above review makes it clear that an expectation of an imminent end is a consistent feature of canonical strands of Christian expectation from the earliest to the latest periods in the first century. Given this fact, it would be surprising if Jesus had *not* predicted an imminent end. If he had not, it would be difficult to explain why such a belief was so pervasive among his followers.[55]

The Death of Apocalyptic

Nevertheless, as the years after the destruction of the temple turned into decades, widespread disillusionment ensued among the faithful. Many began to grow restless. As we have seen, some late writers, such as the John of Revelation, continued to insist on an imminent *parousia*. But cognitive dissonance caused others to distance themselves from such expectations. The pseudonymous letter of 2 Peter, which was very probably composed in the early second century,[56] reflects such a trend. The author cites those who mock and scoff at Christian expectations, saying "Where is the promise of

55. Apologists will often say that his followers simply misunderstood him, but our exegesis rules out such an excuse. Further, Allison, *Jesus of Nazareth*, 166–67, exposes the pretensions behind that particular apologetic strategy.

56. Outside of fundamentalist circles, scholars are virtually unanimous on the pseudonymous and late status of 2 Peter. It certainly could not have been written by the apostle Peter. This is obvious because the Greek in the epistle is very specialized and reflects advanced familiarity with Hellenistic and Hellenized Jewish literature, whereas the historical Peter was an uneducated fisherman from Galilee. It is highly improbable that a fully grown man from rural Judea, who was commissioned to preach the gospel in anticipation of the end of the world, would have sought and acquired an advanced Hellenistic education in the three decades between Jesus' ministry and Peter's death. Therefore, it is clear that the epistle was written in Peter's name, which is evidence of Peter's importance as a figure in the early church. Many other internal and external factors indicate a late date for 2 Peter. It is the latest attested and one of the most disputed documents in the New Testament canon.

his coming? Since our ancestors died, everything continues as it has since the beginning of creation" (3:4). The author responds by adapting and reconfiguring their expectation, providing an apologetic for the "delay" of the return of the messiah:

> But do not ignore this one fact, beloved, that with the Lord one day is like a thousand years, and a thousand years are like one day. The Lord is not slow about his promise, as some think of slowness, but is patient with you, not wanting any to perish, but all to come to repentance. But the day of the Lord will come like a thief, and then the heavens will pass away with a loud noise, and the elements will be dissolved with fire, and the earth and everything that is done on it will be disclosed. (2 Pet 3:8–10, NRSV)

In verse 8 the author quotes Ps 90:4. This reflects an attempt to find answers for their upset expectations within the pages of scripture. Moreover, the author offers a divine motivation for the delay, a "morally sufficient reason for the divine sufferance of evil,"[57] claiming that the delay is explained by God's desire to see all come to repentance. Two things can be said in response to this attempt.

First, note that it represents a different theodicy from the apocalyptic paradigm to which it is indebted. It is abandoning the apocalyptic response to the problem of evil, which says that God will not allow God's people to suffer for long. Instead, the author of 2 Peter suggests that God is allowing God's own people to continue to suffer in order to save *others* from suffering in an afterlife. Second, the theodicy does not work. The longer God waits, the more people perish. Since I do not think any omniscient being "greater than which none other could be conceived" would be without the foresight to figure that out, it is much more likely in my mind that the author is straining desperately to explain an embarrassing and disheartening reality. Notice, however, that in 3:10, the apocalyptic motif of a literal coming of the Son of Man in judgment is unscathed by the unexpected "delay." So in 2 Peter's revision, the apocalyptic nature of the end remains the same; only the expectation of imminence disappears. In other words, the author is stopping the hole in the apocalyptic boat with a non-apocalyptic plug.

---

57. See O'Leary, *Arguing the Apocalypse*, 198. See further, ibid., 199: "Every apocalyptic sect that has survived the failure of its predictions has done so through a process of symbolic negotiation in which its initial epochal formulations are reconstructed into a more durable form of historical self-definition, as the original declaration of the imminent End comes to mark a foundational moment in the institutional narrative of the sect or church."

Another attempt to reconfigure early Christianity's apocalyptic expectations is reflected in the Gospel of John, which is a late document, written a few decades after the expectation of Jesus' return had already been disappointed.[58] The Gospel of John has almost entirely abandoned the apocalyptic framework; or rather, it has spiritualized it. Whereas in the synoptic gospels the expectation is for that of an earthly kingdom (e.g., Matt 6:10), in the Gospel of John that expectation has been left behind and replaced with a spiritual, otherworldly kingdom (e.g., John 18:36). The abandonment of the expectation of an imminent end is also reflected in the second ending to the gospel, John 21:23: "The rumor spread in the community that this disciple would not die. Yet Jesus did not say to him that he would not die, but, 'If it is my will that he remain until I come, what is that to you?'" Allison writes that the second ending "reflects consternation that the Beloved Disciple has died although Jesus has not yet returned."[59] He avers that in the background of this apologetic commentary is Jesus' promise in Mark 9:1 that some of the disciples would not taste death before they witness the arrival of the kingdom of God.

An important factor, also, is Christianity's transformation from a sect within Second Temple Judaism to a predominantly gentile religious institution. This transformation took place over a relatively short period of time. Furthermore, after the destruction of the temple in 70 CE, apocalyptic strands of Judaism found themselves in their death throes. In the early second century CE, the rebel leader Simon ben Kosiba was hailed by so great a rabbi as Akiva as the long awaited messiah and renamed bar Kokhba, meaning "son of the star." But this turned out to be the swan song of Jewish messianic cults. Bar Kokhba's revolution was crushed by Rome in 135 CE, and apocalyptic Judaism with it. The rabbis would again change ben Kosiba's name, this time to ben Kozeba, meaning "son of the lie," a statement which neatly sums up Judaism's sentiment toward apocalypticism for centuries to come.

In the meantime, mainstream Christianity's severance from Judaism was all but complete. Early apocalyptic expectations having been dashed by the failure of Jesus to return as promised, allegorical and metaphorical interpretations of biblical apocalyptic language became the order of the day. By the third century, Origen could authoritatively ridicule Christians who interpreted kingdom of God language literally, characterizing such Christians

---

58. Disambiguation: Most scholars do not believe that the John of the book of Revelation and the John to whom the fourth gospel is attributed are the same John. One reason for this is that the theological and philosophical differences between the two documents are too fundamental. In neither of the two texts is there any claim that the two authors are to be identified with one another.

59. Allison, *Jesus of Nazareth*, 166.

as "those who comprehend the scriptures in a kind of Jewish sense, and taking from the scriptures not a thing worthy of the divine promises" (*Princ.* 2.11.2). Allison points out that, "beginning with Origen, most of the church fathers disparaged chiliasm and literal eschatological expectations as 'judaizing.' They were right," Allison comments, "not to disparage, but to make the association with Judaism. For the literal interpretation corresponds to the original intention of the texts, which were forged within the Jewish tradition."[60]

A Paradoxical Conclusion

The astute reader will have noticed that the case I've made in this chapter has not been against biblical inerrancy. In fact, the case I've made has depended on the assumption of the reliability of the synoptic gospels. I have argued that if the gospels are right, then Jesus was wrong. In the inerrantist universe, this is surely a paradox of cosmic proportions. But what must we conclude from this? What follows from the recognition that Jesus' own utopian expectations and predictions were trampled underfoot by the stubborn persistence of one damned thing after another? Does it follow, in the words of John Loftus, that "at best Jesus was a failed apocalyptic prophet"?[61] Or can Christians legitimately continue to claim that he was more? Should we just chalk it up to the "man" part of the God-Man? Does this mean he was wrong about everything? If he was wrong about this, how can we trust him on other matters? How significant *is* it, anyway? Does it mean he just got the timing wrong? Should Christians continue to expect his coming "like a thief in the night"? Or is a two-thousand-year margin of error indication enough that we ought to abandon the apocalyptic framework wholesale?

Your guesses on these questions are certainly as good as mine, but chapter 10 will be reserved for my own attempts to find a way forward for Christians. For now suffice it to say that I do not believe all is lost. In fact, I think there is much to be gained from the discovery that Jesus was wrong.

60. Ibid., 169.
61. Loftus, "Failed Apocalyptic Prophet."

9 TEXTUAL INTERVENTIONS
ON THE NEED FOR DIRECT CONFRONTATIONS WITH SCRIPTURE

OVER THE COURSE OF THE PAST FIVE CHAPTERS, WE HAVE SEEN that the Bible suffers not only from scientific and historical problems, but also—and much more significantly—from moral, ethical, theological, and ideological problems. We have seen that the Israelites, right up until the time of the Babylonian exile, possessed a polytheistic worldview. We have seen that up until that time, not only was human sacrifice practiced in Israel, it was considered efficacious and commendable, even by the authors of scripture themselves. We have seen that the Yahweh depicted in the conquest narratives was a genocidal dictator—a god, I have argued, created in the image of men. We have seen, moreover, that at least some of the Bible consists of invented traditions, ideological and propagandistic in nature, as in the case of the legend of David and Goliath. Finally, we have seen that not even Jesus himself (or at least Jesus as depicted by the Synoptic gospels) was immune to fallibility. In all of this, the fact is that we have only begun to scratch the surface of the problems that exist within the Judeo-Christian scriptures; these chapters have only been a sampling.

In the face of such overwhelming evidence against the doctrine of inerrancy, what is the next recourse for the committed believer? If *some* of the scriptures cannot be trusted, how do we know we can trust *any* of them? What is to be done with the texts that are morally and theologically deficient? What place, if any, do they have in our canon? In the next chapter, I will offer some potential answers to these very important questions. Before I do that, however, it is necessary to address some alternative reading strategies— strategies which function to relieve the problematic nature of the text, yet which, I argue, ultimately reinforce those selfsame problems.

Enabling the Text

In addition to modern inerrantist strategies, there are at least three additional unsatisfactory strategies for managing problematic texts, employed at both the popular and academic levels. One of these strategies—the allegorical method—we have already seen; additionally there are canonical and subversive readings which function to dispense with problematic texts in various ways. I call these three strategies "enablers." An enabler is someone who despite being cognizant of a person's self-destructive behavior nevertheless permits and even reinforces those tendencies. In various ways, allegorical, canonical, and subversive readings of scripture function as enablers, permitting and reinforcing the destructive power of texts by ignoring their profound problems, either for the sake of convenience or out of fear of the consequences of a direct confrontation.

Allegorical Readings

As I argued at the end of chapter 6, the upside of allegorical readings is that, in some cases, those who choose to employ an allegorical hermeneutic do so because they are fully cognizant of the problematic nature of the text when taken literally. As with Origen and Gregory of Nyssa, such interpreters have come to grips with the texts soberly and have concluded that if they are to continue to be of any use to the church, the literal interpretation must be rejected in favor of a metaphorical reading that produces a message more worthy of God's character and Christian discipleship. Of course, the problem here is that not every practitioner of the allegorical hermeneutic is fully cognizant of the problematic nature of the text. When spiritual readings of scripture become the tradition, within a few generations, the motivation for such readings tends to be lost, and only the practice itself remains. Today, millions of Christians apply spiritual or allegorical interpretations to the conquest narratives, but do not do so for any other reason than that is how they were taught to read the text. Unlike Origen and Gregory, these Christians have not chosen an allegorical reading after having confronted and condemned the literal meaning of the text. This fact leaves open the possibility (too frequently the reality) that literal readings of the morally problematic texts might creep back in through the back door. After all, as the allegorical readings of the Church Fathers gave way to the literal readings of the middle ages, the conquest narratives were reenacted in the Crusades. The allegorization strategy is an evasion of the truth; it is just one more way to doom ourselves to repeating history.

What allows this to happen is the absence of an established tradition of confrontational readings. Allegorical readings do not directly confront the text; they simply discard the text's meaning. Such readings are the functional equivalent of ripping the texts from the canon. They rewrite the text, based on their own immediate inclinations, but there is nothing to guarantee that later generations of Christians or Christians in other contexts will share those same inclinations. Such readings are dishonest with the text, and can blind believers to problematic aspects of their faith heritage, whereas confrontational readings of the scriptures produce humility in religious believers. Knowing that my texts are not perfect prevents me from being quick to execute judgment against those with different readings of my texts, or against those with different texts altogether. Conversely, the assumption that my texts and my readings of them are flawless and spiritually superior leads to self-righteousness and intolerance. Put a picket sign in my hand and I am a fundamentalist bigot. Put a sword in my hand and I am a crusader.

A final reason why Christians cannot in good conscience employ allegorical or spiritual interpretations of the conquest narratives is that such readings are profoundly disrespectful to actual victims of genocide, and to their survivors and descendents. To spiritualize the conquest narratives is to whitewash them. In effect, it makes us the equivalent of Holocaust deniers. To fail to confront the genocidal narratives in our scriptures is to deny the reality that our faith tradition was in a very sober sense founded upon acts of genocide. Any attempt to justify those acts, or to evade their reality, makes us (morally speaking) accessories after the fact. In doing so, we diminish the moral significance of the suffering of every victim of genocide. Although we as individuals are not culpable for the moral crimes of our spiritual ancestors, as participants in a collective faith tradition we have been baptized into moral culpability. This reality need not cripple our faith tradition, but as the people of South Africa have recently reminded us, there can be no reconciliation without truth.

Canonical Readings

In the academic world, Brevard Childs has led the pack of those who espouse a "canonical hermeneutic."[1] Proponents of so-called canonical readings may be but are not necessarily inerrantists. Most acknowledge the composite nature of the biblical texts and are aware of the evidence for multiple and pseudonymous authorship, redactional layers, and the like. Yet for canonical readings, such considerations are rendered irrelevant. What matters is nei-

1. See especially Childs, *Biblical Theology of the Old and New Testaments*.

ther the original layer of the text nor the processes by which the text came to take the shape it presently takes. What matters to proponents of canonical hermeneutics is the final form of the text. After all, they say, the church is not a community of historians but of believers. It was the faith community that originally saw fit to bring these disparate texts together; it was the faith community that canonized these texts in their present form. If the texts are going to continue to be useful, they will be useful not as objects of historical curiosity but as dynamic scriptures which are the rightful property of the community of faith. They were not brought together with the intention of providing historians with fodder for discussion; they were brought together with the intention of providing the community of faith the inspiration it needs to be faithful in a trying world. As a result, readings that challenge the truthfulness of this or that text, or readings that are primarily concerned with discerning multiple layers within a composite text in order to get to the historical core—these readings, according to proponents of canonical herme- neutics, render the texts useless for their intended purpose: encouraging the faith community in its faith. Thus, canonical hermeneutics is not concerned with pitting one set of texts against another, but with discerning the "big pic- ture." Canonical readings seek to discover the macro-narrative that underlies the minutiae. The important thing is the forest, not the trees.

There are at least three problems with this approach to the scriptures. First, the premise of canonical hermeneutics is that the final form of the text is authoritative because that is what the faith community chose. The problem with this is that the final form of the text was *not* chosen by "the faith com- munity," but by the religious and political elites in order to serve their own interests.[2] Moreover, the vast majority of biblical texts were written by elites, not by "the faith community." Proponents of canonical hermeneutics are ei- ther unintentionally or willfully naïve here—in most cases the naïveté is will- ful. Canonical readings simply act as if the evolution of the text is irrelevant to its meaning; usually this is because it is deemed to be more expedient for the purpose of exhorting a faith community if such considerations are put aside.

Second, and consequently, the diverse voices of scripture are lost, and problematic texts are swept under the rug. Individual biblical narratives take on new and foreign significances when they are read in light of the proposed "canonical" narrative. Marginal voices, such as those found in Ecclesiastes, Job, and elsewhere, are made to conform to the voices at the center. Problematic texts are immunized by appeal to some supposed grand narrative that rela- tivizes or recasts their significance. For instance, as we saw in chapter 6 with

2. See Coote and Coote, *Power, Politics, and the Making of the Bible.*

Millard Lind and John Howard Yoder's readings of the conquest narratives, the genocidal narratives are recast in the light of a macro-narrative of nonviolence. In order to do this, however, the reader must foreground certain texts (e.g., the supposed weaponless victory of the Israelites over the Egyptians at the Reed Sea) and background other texts, while ignoring the evidence from comparative ancient war literature that casts the Yahweh wars in a different light altogether from the nonviolent readings.

This leads us to the third problem with canonical readings: who determines what the "canonical reading" is? Is there some sort of consistent, methodologically controlled technique for determining what the underlying narrative is? How do we know what the "central theme" is supposed to be in the light of which all biblical texts are to be read? Walter Brueggemann criticizes Childs on precisely this point, writing that Childs "proceeds as if the 'canonical' is simply there and involves no reader, not even Childs."[3] Although Childs gives lip service to diversity within the texts, "he insists that the text is stable, that it has a persistent, clear meaning." Yet "when one arrives at the stability of the text as quickly as does Childs, much of the power, energy, and, I dare say, truth of the text is lost in a kind of reductionism. The notion of instability is not an enemy of faith but, in fact, an honoring of the detail and nuance of the text that dogmatic closure does not easily entertain or allow. Childs's hermeneutical innocence is not only against our own interpretive context, but more important, against the very character of the text itself, which refuses to be so innocent."[4] The canonical reader paints biblical theology in broad strokes, "flattening and homogenizing" the text, but "such an approach fails to take seriously the detail of the text, which is not so flat or homogeneous."[5] The result of such readings is not a *biblical* theology; it is a theology that is imposed upon the text in a way that is methodologically uncontrollable.

In short, the reader does not seek to be faithful to the individual text; rather, the individual text is remade to be faithful to the reader's own conception of a broader canonical message. Of course, this conception of the broader message is more often than not informed more by ecclesiastical and dogmatic standards than by the scriptures themselves, which resist such reductionism. This may be all very well, and no insult to those who revere ecclesiastical tradition on the same level as they do the scriptures, but it is dishonest when such "readings" are performed under the guise of "biblical" theology. More significantly, canonical readings manage to evade confrontation with problematic texts that do not fit the reader's mold.

3. Brueggemann, "Against the Stream," 282.

4. Ibid., 282–83.

5. Ibid., 283.

Subversive Readings

A similar strategy is to use the text in such a way as to subvert its original meaning. This is a technique employed not just by modern interpreters but by ancient interpreters as well. For instance, the New Testament writers frequently took language from the militant psalms (such as Psalms 2 and 110) and appropriated that language in service of a suffering messiah trope. Texts that originally depicted violent military victories over physical enemies were subverted by incorporating them into the narrative of Christ's victory over the powers in his suffering.[6] Furthermore, the tribalism of Psalm 110 is subverted in Mark 12:35–40 (also Luke 20:41–47) where the Jewish elites, rather than the Gentiles, are implicitly identified as the enemies in the psalm.

Another example of the subversion strategy pertains not to the subversion of biblical texts but to broader cultural scripts. For instance, recent scholarship on Jesus and Paul has reexamined their ostensibly pro-Roman language in light of the anthropological work of James C. Scott,[7] arguing that as representatives of an oppressed minority, Jesus and Paul utilized the official "public transcript," which says that the Roman imperial order is benevolent and just, while at the same time making allusions to an offstage "hidden transcript," discernible by the dominated classes, a hidden transcript which criticizes Rome for failing to live up to the official transcript and also speaks of Rome's impending doom at the imminent arrival of the kingdom of God.

Take Mark 12:13–17 for instance. When asked if it is right to pay taxes to Caesar, Jesus responds by holding up a Roman coin for his audience to see. Jesus says, "Give to Caesar what belongs to Caesar, and give to God what belongs to God." On the surface, this appears to legitimize taxation to Caesar. But the reality is that Jesus and his audience knew full well how crippling the Roman taxes and tributes were on the peasant population.

Moreover, inscribed on the Roman coin held up by Jesus was a claim of divine sonship for the Roman emperor. Every self-respecting Jew would know the meaning and the subtext of Jesus' response. To give to Caesar what is Caesar's is to purify Israel of its idolatrous participation in the Roman economic system. The audience knew how to parse out Jesus' aphorism. What rightfully belongs to Caesar? Nothing. What rightfully belongs to God? Everything. Mark comments that the crowds were "amazed at him." There is hardly anything amazing about Jesus' response if it is simply a regurgitation

---

6. See for example Hebrews chapter 2. See also the extensive discussion in Enz, *The Christian and Warfare*, 69–80. On my broader disagreement with Enz, see my comment on p. 133 fn. 55.

7. Scott, *Domination and the Arts of Resistance.*

of the official Roman ideology. What was amazing is that Jesus was able to evade the Pharisees and Herodians' attempt to expose his anti-imperial message without compromising his commitment to those who suffered under Roman domination.[8]

It is in this light that the language of Jesus' identity and the language used to describe the gospel of the kingdom must be understood. The titles "son of god," "savior," and "lord" were titles that according to the official transcript belonged to Caesar. But these titles were subverted by Christians and applied to Jesus of Nazareth—a man crucified as a political revolutionary by the Romans. In fact, many Christians suffered for refusing to apply these titles to Caesar. Jesus even applied two of Caesar's favorite titles (son of god and peacemaker) to the peasant classes (Matt 5:9). Moreover, the terms used frequently by early Christians to describe the kingdom of God were taken directly from Roman propaganda. Terms such as gospel, salvation, faith, grace, and righteousness figured centrally on billboards throughout the Pax Romana. As Sylvia Keesmaat rightly remarks, "these are all terms weighted with symbolic and mythic import in the empire."[9] She characterizes early Christians' use of this language as a "direct challenge to the empire."[10]

On the one hand, this kind of subversive use of an official transcript (whether it be the unwritten transcript of the Pax Romana or the written transcript of the Jewish scriptures) is perfectly understandable: it is the recourse of those who are disempowered. Absent the means to directly reconfigure dominant society with its conceptual structures and cultural mores, the dominated classes will always use the dominant language in subversive ways. This phenomenon is ubiquitous, seen everywhere from national revolutionary politics to intra-office politics. Those with less power learn to use the official terminology in ways that subvert the official intention. Thus, we can hardly fault Jesus and Paul, as representatives of the dominated classes, for perpetuating the categories of empire through the subversive use of imperial language; doing so was a prudent strategy for survival in an extremely volatile environment.

On the other hand, as Elisabeth Schüssler Fiorenza rightly reminds us, "If one does not deliberately deconstruct the language of imperial domination in which scriptural texts remain caught up, one cannot but valorize and re-inscribe it."[11] Schüssler Fiorenza criticizes scholarship that focuses on the

8. For a reading of Jesus and Paul along these lines, see Herzog, "Dissembling, a Weapon of the Weak."

9. Keesmaat, "If Your Enemy Is Hungry," 143.

10. Ibid., 142.

11. Schüssler Fiorenza, *The Power of the Word*, 6.

way Roman imperial language is subverted by Christian scriptures without paying attention to the way that language and its categories remain intact and to the effects that such categories can have on future generations of readers. If Jesus was alluding to a hidden transcript of opposition to Rome when he said to give to Caesar what Caesar has coming to him, that is not how his words have been read throughout much of church history. If Jesus' language was a subversion of the official transcript, the reality is that his language has only been subject to counter-subversion by the ruling elites ever since. Mark 12:17 has been used by governments to impose the most oppressive of taxes upon populations for centuries.

In the same way, "by claiming that the gospel of Paul is counter-imperial, such a reading is no longer compelled to inquire as to how such inscribed imperial language functioned in the past, and still functions today, and what this type of language does to readers who submit to its world of vision."[12] If Rom 13:1–7 is surrounded by allusions to a hidden transcript in which Rome is about to be dethroned by the soon-to-arrive Messiah (Rom 12:19; 13:11), the moment the text becomes the property of the "Christian emperor," the subverted language of imperial hegemony is recaptured by the establishment and put to work again in service of the official transcript. Thus, "let everyone subordinate themselves to the ruling authorities" ceases to be an ironic statement of temporary subordination to an illegitimate regime in light of the imminent end of the world and instead becomes a prescription for the perpetual subjection of the weak to the strong. It is used by Christian governments to club dissenters over the head. Schüssler Fiorenza argues that more needs to be done than to "reclaim" the subversive meaning of the text:

> Attempts by scholars to rescue early Christian scriptures as anti- or counter-imperial literature tend to overlook that the language of empire and its violence, which are encoded in them, have shaped Christian religious and cultural self-understanding and ethos throughout the centuries and still do so today. Such language of subordination and control is not outdated historical language. Rather, as belonging to sacred scripture, this language is performative language, which continues to determine Christian identity and praxis today. Consequently, such language needs not merely to be understood but also to be made conscious and be critically deconstructed. . . . One cannot simply continue to engage in a purely historical reading. Rather, it becomes necessary to engage in a critical interpretation that seeks to investigate the impact of the discourses of empire on the language, imagery, and message of Christian scripture. Such a reading, which seeks to decolonize the

---

12. Ibid., 4.

religious imagination, has as its goal not to whitewash the Christian
scriptures, nor to absolve Paul from the blame of having inscribed
empire, but rather to make us conscious of such inscriptions. . . .
For Christian scriptures and interpretation could and can be used in
the service of empire, colonialist expansion, racist exploitation, and
heterosexist discrimination, because they have been formulated in
the context of Roman imperial power and therefore are determined
by this rhetorical political imperial context. They advocate and in-
still the ethos of empire: submission, violence, and exclusion; they
speak, as well, about G*d and Christ by analogy to imperial rulers,
who are presumed to be male.[13]

What Schüssler Fiorenza is calling for is a move beyond the mere acknowl-
edgment that violent, imperial, and patriarchal language is subverted in
various ways in certain texts; what is necessary is an analysis of the way that
the perpetuated inscription of the categories of empire and patriarchy have
impeded progress toward human rights, democracy, and authentic human
freedom. Categories such as "lord" and "master" must be critically decon-
structed rather than simply reapplied, uncritically, to God or Christ. If we do
not come up with new language to depict our relationship with the divine,
then the categories of empire will continue to dominate our thinking, even if
their use by Paul and other early Christians was only *ad hoc* and subversive.
Applying the language the emperor used for himself to God only legitimates
the ideology of empire, and ensures that categories of domination and subordination will continue to be second nature to human societies, generation
after generation. This is why the abolitionists had such a difficult time defeating the institution of slavery in the United States—precisely because the
ideology of slavery *is inscribed and legitimated* by the text of scripture. This is
also why subversive readings of the official transcript ultimately function as
enablers to morally and theologically problematic texts.

Textual Interventions

Despite any merits allegorical, canonical, and subversive readings might
have, the reality is that such strategies cannot but enable problematic texts to
continue to wreak havoc upon the church and the world around it. The best
of intentions notwithstanding, these strategies fail to do what is necessary in
order to help future generations of readers to understand what is at stake. In
order for this to take place, Christians must establish habits and traditions of
confrontational readings, what I call "textual interventions."

13. Ibid., 6.

Certain texts in our scriptures are like that alcoholic uncle we all know. It is easy enough to avoid the problem. Like the uncle, many of the texts don't show up on our doorstep very often. But when they do show up (and they inevitably do) they are only going to do damage to the family unless the family is willing to sit down and hold an intervention, to confront the problem directly, and to set the ground rules for interaction within the community. Once these ground rules have been set in place, fruitful interaction between the troublesome text and the faith community becomes possible. The "alcoholic uncle" can continue to be a part of the family, and he can actually learn to participate in unique and fruitful ways, providing he is able to acknowledge that he has, and always will have, the disease. In order to save such texts, they must be confronted, their troublesome nature must be truthfully characterized, and they must be branded for life. Only then will they be able to serve a useful function within the life of the community. As I will argue in the next and final chapter, it is precisely as "condemned texts" that such texts will have value as scripture.

10 Into the Looking Glass
What Scripture Reveals When It Gets God Wrong

In the last chapter I argued that reading strategies which fail to confront morally and theologically problematic texts *directly* ultimately enable those texts to wreak havoc on church and society. In this chapter I will attempt to suggest what such "textual interventions" might look like and how, through them, problematic texts may be retained as scripture, "useful for teaching, for censure, for correction, and for training in the exercise of justice" (2 Tim 3:16). The question looms: what are we to do with those texts we find ourselves wanting to condemn? While the scriptures advocate monotheism, the dissolution of the sacrificial system, and the love of enemy, they also advocate a polytheistic tribalism, human sacrifice, and religiously motivated genocide, among other deplorable things. What should our strategy for dealing with these damnable texts be? Should we simply ignore them? Excise them from our canon?

The only honest answer to the question I have been able to come up with is this: *they must be retained as scripture, precisely as condemned texts. Their status as condemned is exactly their scriptural value. That they are condemned is what they reveal to us about God.* The texts themselves depict God as a genocidal dictator, as a craver of blood. But we must condemn them in our engagement with them—sometimes with guidance from other passages of scripture, sometimes without. That they stand as condemned is what they mean for us as scripture.

Why this? Why not simply excise them from the canon? Why not flatly ignore them? The answer is that to do so is to hide from ourselves a potent reminder of the worst parts of ourselves. Scripture is a mirror. It mirrors humanity, because it is as much the product of human beings as it is the product of the divine. When we peer into the looking glass and see the many faces of God, we see ourselves among them. The mirror reflects our doubt and our mediocrity. It mirrors our best and worst possible selves. It shows us who we can be, both good and evil, and everything in between. *To cut the condemned texts out of the canon would be to shatter that mirror. It would* be to hide from ourselves our very own capacity to become what we most loathe. It would be to lie to ourselves about what we are capable of. It would be to doom ourselves to repeat history.

Gathering Honey from the Weed

There is nothing novel about the observation that good can come from evil, that—as the apostle Paul wrote—God is able to make all things work together for good (Rom 8:28). In Shakespeare's *Henry V*, the wise king reminds us that "there is some soul of goodness in things evil," if only we would "observingly distil it out." These "things evil" are "preachers to us all," admonishing us to prepare ourselves for the challenges that lie ahead. "Thus," insists the king, "may we gather honey from the weed, and make a moral of the devil himself."[1] It is precisely because of the morally dubious, even devilish nature of so many of our scriptures that this principle is so relevant for our purposes. As John Collins elucidates, "there is no reason in principle why a text that is shocking might not be inspired. Such a text can raise our moral consciousness by forcing us to confront the fact that immoral actions are often carried out in the name of religion. . . . Rather than ask whether a text is revealed (and by what criteria could we possibly decide?), it is better to ask whether a text is revelatory, whether we learn something from it about human nature or about the way the world works. A text that is neither historically reliable nor morally edifying . . . may be all too revelatory about human nature."[2]

Though in many cases to take the text at face value would be to obscure, and not to hear, the authentic word of God, this does not prevent us from acknowledging that God may still speak to us *through* the text. God may not have breathed *out* the text, but God still may breathe *into* it, giving it a life and a purpose its human authors did not themselves intend. This does not mean that the text has some hidden meaning, as in an allegorical or metaphorical reading, but that the author's intended meaning, taken very seriously, takes on a new significance for us, guided by the discernment of the Spirit-filled community, as an object lesson of sorts.

What follows are some attempts to "gather honey from the weed" in just this way. These are my own applications of the text, and I do not pretend that they are necessarily the right or the only applications that should be drawn from the text. Of course, what is the appropriate use of the text will vary from context to context. Each confessing community must decide for itself how to make these and other texts useful for its own purposes. In what follows I am merely attempting to show how it is possible to hear God's word, despite it.

1. Act 4, scene 1 of *Henry V*.
2. Collins, *Introduction to the Hebrew Bible*, 601.

From Polytheism to Monotheism and Beyond

Thus, we take the text seriously when it tells us that Yahweh was one god among many national deities in the ancient Near East. We take it seriously when it tells us of Yahweh's origins as a son of the Most High God (El Elyon), and then later of Yahweh's meteoric rise, his own ascendancy to the throne as king of the pantheon. Through these texts, we are able to discern the human faces of the gods. In the ancient cosmology, the plurality of the gods reflected and reinforced the tribalisms and nationalisms of human design. Such structures underwrote the ideologies of slavery, war, genocide, and racism. Though most of us today no longer feel the need to explain the conflicts between tribes and nations as conflicts between the gods, these ancient texts are hardly irrelevant to us. On the contrary, they mirror our own nationalisms and the ideologies by which we justify the othering of those who do not look, speak, or behave as we do. Although ancient justifications for dividing up humanity according to artificial political boundaries are significantly different from ours, these texts reveal to us that we ourselves are little different from our ancient ancestors. They expose the perpetual human need to distinguish the self from "the Other," and to concoct criteria for determining who are the first and who are the second class citizens of the world. Through these texts the voice of God speaks to us today, calling us to reject self-serving ontologies of difference, to abandon any allegiances to tribes or nation-states that take precedence over our allegiance to humanity itself and to the world we all inhabit together.

On the other hand, we must also take seriously the logic behind the eventual rejection of the polytheistic cosmology in the Hebrew Bible. Attributing the move from polytheism to monotheism in the Hebrew scriptures to some conception of "progressive revelation" is too easy and too uncritical a solution. The reality is that the move toward monotheism was in large part a byproduct of the rise of the monarchy in Israel and of the centralization of political power under a militarized government. Just as Marduk's rise to the top of the pantheon in Babylonian literature corresponded to Babylon's rise to supremacy over the nations, the ascendancy of Yahweh in Hebrew literature reflected the aspirations of the Judean kings to political power. This is reflected in numerous texts which express hope for a future in which the nation of Israel enjoys political and religious hegemony over the nations—a future in which every tribe is made subservient to the empire of Israel and all are forced (under threat of famine and plague) to do obeisance before Yahweh and his royal agent, the king (e.g., Zech 14:12–19).

Through these texts the word of God comes to us, exposing our own imperialisms, our own nations' aspirations to political domination through globalized economies underwritten by universalistic meta-narratives that seek to homogenize cultures in the name of the holy trinity of McDonald's, Wal-Mart, and Exxon Mobil. This kind of "monotheism," although it presents itself as the antidote to tribalistic polytheism, is really only tribalism writ large. Its goal is the same; only the means are different. Neither tribalistic polytheism nor imperialistic monotheism is willing to live with the Other. The difference is that tribalism defines the Other ethnically and geographically, whereas monotheism defines the Other in terms of culture, practices, and economic structures. Monotheism says, *if you cannot kill or enslave them, convert them.*

Both tribalistic polytheism and imperialistic monotheism are operative today, and critical and sober readings of our scriptures help us to see that fact. Even in monotheism, we can discern a human face of God staring back at us in the mirror, reinforcing our own self-destructive proclivities. Yet God still speaks through the text, calling on us to break the cycle, to abandon self-reinforcing ontologies of difference. The divine nature is revealed through the inadequacies of our texts. Neither polytheism nor monotheism accurately reflects the divine, for both encourage us to see the Other's otherness as a threat. The inadequacies of the text reveal the need for a conception of divine nature that is difference in harmony, unity in diversity. The divine is not one, but neither—in its plurality—is the divine at odds with itself. Thus, while polytheistic and monotheistic conceptions of God have been exposed as mirror reflections of our worst selves, a conception of the divine as difference in harmony represents an ontology—a divine reality—that calls upon humanity to better itself and to become the mirror image of the sacred reality.

The Human Face of Human Sacrifice

In the same way, rather than deny the fact that the logic of human sacrifice is sustained and promoted in our scriptures, a critical reading of the text makes it possible for this to become revelatory for us. It is exactly our willingness to confront and condemn these texts that enables us to hear the voice of God speaking through them, exposing our own complicity in institutions of human sacrifice. In the ancient world, it was believed that sacrifices made to the gods helped humans to earn divine favor, to secure life's necessities. In times of extreme duress, it was believed that a human sacrifice to the deity would guarantee a good harvest season, or victory against enemies who threatened the homeland. In many cultures, to be the object of sacrifice was considered a great honor; by the spilling of innocent blood the people would be saved. To be the object of sacrifice was to become a national hero. This is in fact the ideology that underwrites the early Christian interpretation of the crucifixion of Jesus. Moreover, parents who sometimes offered their own children as sacrifices were considered to be people of great faith, precisely because of their willingness to make the ultimate sacrifice for the common good, or in order to assuage or to satiate the sovereign deity. The archetypical example of this kind of faith is of course Abraham, who was not condemned but praised for his willingness to slaughter his beloved son on the altar.

Today we denounce such practices as inhuman and reject as irrational the belief that the spilling of innocent blood literally affected the outcome of harvests and military battles. Yet we continue to offer our own children on the altar of homeland security, sending them off to die in ambiguous wars, based on the irrational belief that by being violent we can protect ourselves from violence. We refer to our children's deaths as "sacrifices" which are necessary for the preservation of democracy and free trade. The market is our temple and it must be protected at all costs. Thus, like King Mesha, we make "sacrifices" in order to ensure the victory of capitalism over socialism, the victory of consumerism over terrorism. Our high priests tell us that it is necessary to make sacrifices if we are going to continue to have the freedom to shop. Unlike King Mesha, however, in our day it is rarely the king's own son who is sacrificed; rather, the king sacrifices the sons and daughters of the poor in order to protect an economy whose benefits the poor do not reap. (As *Shrek's* Lord Farquaad so profoundly put it, "Some of you may die, but that is a sacrifice I am willing to make.") Like martyrs, our children are valorized because of their willingness to sacrifice their lives in yet another war waged to rid the world of war. We invest their deaths with meaning by forcing ourselves to believe, despite all evidence to the contrary, that their blood affects the productivity of the market and protects a multitude from the threat of violence.

God speaks to us through these texts, if we are willing to listen critically, and calls on us to recognize ourselves in them. When Yahweh demands the sacrifice of Israel's firstborn children in exchange for freedom from slavery to the Egyptians, when he provides victory in battle in exchange for the pleasant odor of human carnage, we see another of the many human faces of God in scripture. Despite all our pretensions to progress, it seems that there is nothing more human than to hope that our futures can be secured by delivering up our young as lambs to the slaughter.

The Exploitative Face of Theodicy

In the same way, when we hear Yahweh declaring his resolve to punish parents by forcing them to consume the flesh of their own children, by tricking them into believing their children were to be offered as sacrifices (as Ezekiel has it), or by sending soldiers to dash their infants to pieces, we do not hear the voice of God but the voices of humans. We are not looking at the true face of God but at the anguished faces of the mother and father who desperately need an explanation for the suffering of their sons and daughters. Or rather, more accurately, we are looking at the faces of the religious and political elites who are ever exploiting the masses, capitalizing on their desperation in order to seize and to maintain political control or economic prosperity by propagating black and white theologies like that of traditional wisdom—a theology represented by the book of Proverbs, the Deuteronomistic historian, the companions of Job, and today's televangelists, among others. These exploitative elites seek to dominate the masses by convincing them that their suffering is the consequence of a failure to live up to a certain set of rules—the transmission and interpretation of which are of course tightly controlled by those very same elites.

Killing in the Name of . . .

When we look at the face of the Yahweh who ordered the extermination of the inhabitants of Canaan, we see our own capacity to kill in the name of God, or in the name of purity, or some ideology or another. We see our own capacity to other and to exclude, our own capacity for racial profiling. These texts cease to be revelatory and become impediments to revelation if they are read at face value as the very voice of God. Such readings produce incoherent moralities and theologies. Neither can these texts go unread. Our theologies would not be grounded without these reminders that theologies themselves are human constructs and can very quickly go horribly wrong. These texts must continue to be read, and they must continue to be read precisely as condemned texts. Whether we realize it or not, these texts have formed us in ways we do not fully understand. To cut them out of our liturgies would be like sweeping the dirt under the rug.

To wit, while most of us are not criminals of the worst sort, we have been trained to think like them. Just as history's madmen have justified their genocides in utilitarian, ideological, and moralistic fashion, we have been trained to justify the genocides of our spiritual ancestors in the name of Israel's physical preservation, Israel's "right" to land, and in the name of the moral depravity of Israel's enemies. Our scriptures have trained us to reason like war criminals, and whether we like it or not, that capacity abides in us. To ignore these texts is to push that reality out of our sight, where we are powerless to chasten it. We must keep these texts in our liturgies, so that God can speak through them, urging us not to be yet another people willing to kill in the name of some land, some ideology, or some god. We must be as familiar with these texts as we are with the Sermon on the Mount and the epistle to the Romans, so that we are able to recognize the pathology embedded in them, so that God can speak through them, calling upon us to see our pathological selves within them, calling upon us to hold *ourselves* in judgment long before we even begin to approach our enemies.

The Divine Faces of Humans

There is revelatory value too in the royal propaganda produced by loyalists to the Davidic dynasty. The hero-worshiping legends built up around the figure of David remind us of the ways we continue to make giant figures out of our own national heroes. In order to reassure ourselves of the rightness of our cause, we project constructs of divine agency onto charismatic figures of our choosing. We reinforce our sense of identity and direction by project- ing our hopes onto our leaders. Since we do not like to question ourselves or the course of our lives, we convince ourselves that our leaders can do little to no wrong because they are men or women "after God's own heart." Propagandists in the ancient world and in ours parade the pious acts of these "divine agents" in order to reassure the people that the powerful are inter- ested only in doing the will of God. Over the course of time, legends about the honesty, integrity, and bravery of the nation's founding heroes are built up and function to defend the legitimacy of the institutions of government.

These legends about past heroes are useful as comparisons are made to present-day political figures vying for popular support, even or especially when the policies of these politicians are extreme by earlier standards. Thus, Josiah's expansion of governmental powers is legitimated by comparisons made between Josiah and fictionalized versions of earlier national heroes such as David and Joshua. In the same way, modern-day politicians such as George W. Bush or Barack Obama appeal to the common traditions about the unassailable integrity of beloved bygone U.S. presidents and present themselves as heirs to Washington or to Lincoln. Popular expectations and official propaganda combine to create fictionalized versions of past and pres- ent political figures so that the disconnect between the collective national identity and the true character of collective action may be disguised; this keeps the populace blissfully unaware and frees behind-the-scenes policy- makers to continue to push their unpublicized agendas.

If Christians could read their scriptures with a critical spirit, the pres- ence of propaganda within the text might become revelatory and might help to prevent Christians from falling prey to the perennial temptation to valorize and to divinize putative national heroes. In the best tradition of the

Hebrew prophets, Christians would be better equipped to distinguish the official narratives from the realities on the ground. But the construct of inerrancy forces Christians to take the political propaganda within the scriptures at face value and thus dooms them to repeat history. Yet the voice of God, as we have seen, does not always speak out of the official narratives. Sometimes the voice of God can only be heard if we are willing to read between the lines. Reading biblical propaganda such as the legend of David and Goliath at face value may have its rewards; it is certainly an inspirational story. But such a reading can also foster delusion. Moreover, such a reading is not as interesting or as relevant as a critical reading. It is the critical reading that prepares us to face the real world where the true giants are the centralized powers that mask themselves with the ruddy faces of shepherd boys and good ol' boys.

Jesus Was Wrong and Right

A critical appraisal of Jesus' apocalyptic worldview and expectations yields both negative and positive insights, all of which may be appropriated by believing communities as revelatory. On the one hand, honest appraisals of the text force us to acknowledge that because of the apocalyptic worldview that Jesus inherited, he necessarily got a few things wrong. In addition to his failed prediction of the imminent end, Jesus' commitment to apocalyptic categories entails a number of intractable problems.

First, there is the problem of apocalyptic dualism. The apocalyptic worldview divides up the entire cosmos into two categories: good and evil, or light and dark. Those on the side of light have given their allegiance wholly to God; everyone else, wittingly or not, has given their allegiance to Satan. Because of Jesus' conviction that he was the last prophet before the imminent end of the world, Jesus was able to equate allegiance to himself with allegiance to God. As with other apocalyptic sects of his day (such as the Qumran community), Jesus believed that *his brand* of Judaism was the only brand that could save the people of Yahweh from the coming destruction and judgment.[3] Of course, this black and white perspective is understandable given the character of the times. Apocalyptic Jews considered themselves to be soldiers (some violent, others nonviolent) in a time of war.

It was a war between the celestial forces of Yahweh and Belial, mirrored on earth as a battle between Israel and the gentile nations. "The dualism of God's agents versus Satan reflected the political-economic situation in which the people's lives were out of their own control and under hostile and/or alien

3. This is not to say that the Jesus movement was not inclusivistic in important ways, but to deny that it was not also exclusivistic in equally important ways.

control."[4] In wartime it is often necessary to draw up sharp dividing lines between sides in the conflict, and this would have been the logic that underwrote apocalyptic sects' extreme claims that failure to join their particular cause was tantamount to treason. Only the narrow road leads to life, but broad is the road that leads to destruction. This conviction led to extreme demands upon the joiners, a set of tests to separate "the men from the boys." Thus, Jesus called his followers to celibacy (Matt 19:12), and expected them to leave their families behind (Matt 19:29). Those who were unwilling to abandon the concerns of everyday existence were unfit for engagement in the final battle before the end. In the mindset that predominates in wartime, those unwilling to make such severe sacrifices are cowards at best, collaborators at worst. Moreover, the consequences for cowards and collaborators are the same. To be "ashamed" of Jesus and his demand to carry the cross—the demand to participate in the revolution even if it meant a revolutionary's death—is to stand condemned when the Son of Man comes (Mark 8:34–38).

The problem, of course, with this black and white dualism is that real human beings cannot be made to fit so neatly into one or the other of the two sharply defined categories. Morality is not always black and white; in fact, only rarely is a moral decision so clear. Furthermore, although in times of war it is usually considered courageous to abandon one's family, when it is not wartime it is considered cowardly and immoral to do so. Perhaps those who refused to follow Jesus to Golgotha did so not out of cowardice but out of moral courage. Tempting as it would have been to believe Jesus' message that the Roman order was about to end, most Jews had heard it all before, and it had never come to fruition yet. Jaded as they had become, perhaps they saw joining yet another radical revolution as the coward's way out of the harder task of commitment to one's family and everyday responsibilities in the midst of a crippling economy and violent world. Yet according to the perspective of Jesus and other apocalyptic Jews of his day, those committed to their families in such volatile times would be tried and condemned when the war was over. From the perspective of the apocalypticists, it was an expression of hope to abandon the affairs of the present world. From the perspective of other Jews, such policies were a counsel of despair.

Related to this is a second problem inherent in the apocalyptic perspective. The sharp dualism between good and evil comes with a corresponding dualism between the believing community and the outside world. The outside world is equated with all things evil, and the demand upon believers not to associate with it is supported by the assumption that the world is "passing away" (1 John 2:15–17). The problem is that within this mindset there is no

4. Horsley, *Sociology and the Jesus Movement*, 98.

room for any form of engagement with the world or for any conception of broader political responsibility. As John Collins explains, "the apocalypses often lack a program for effective action. . . . Their strong sense that human affairs are controlled by higher powers usually limited the scope of human initiative. The apocalyptic revolution is a revolution in the imagination."[5] At most, political responsibility is narrated in sectarian terms. *To be politically responsible is to be sectarian.* This makes sense because the sect believes that what it is doing is directly connected to the fate of the entire world.[6] The trouble is that the world is still waiting for the church to make good on that promise, two thousand years delayed.

If the apocalyptic version of theodicy is that God's justice will not allow God's people to suffer for very long, then as a theodicy the apocalyptic worldview has failed. Time and again, the Christian commitment to justice has been undermined by the expectation of an imminent end. Generation after generation, those who suffer are told to wait it out; authentic justice is impossible this side of the eschaton, but there is hope to be had in the conviction that the end is nigh. Yet the end has never been nigh, and there is no reason to believe that it is nigh today. Meanwhile, human beings continue to suffer and many Christian institutions can do little more than to bandage wounds and send victims back into the very political and economic environments that wounded them in the first place. Comprehensive visions of just societies are rejected by most Christians as utopian fantasies, excepting of course that vision in which God finally and miraculously intervenes in the world to make everything instantly come out right. Until justice magically materializes, sporadic charity will have to suffice. Thus, Jesus' ministry of compassion was depicted as a sign of an impending new world order. Such charity was not a solution to the problem, but a glimpse at what the kingdom of God will look like when it comes. That may be all very well when the consummation of the kingdom of God is expected to take place within a few decades, but with a two-thousand-year margin of error, such charity itself becomes an injustice.[7]

In light of this, the apocalypticism in the Christian scriptures becomes revelatory for us, not in the sense that the scriptures reveal how the present

---

5. Collins, *Apocalyptic Imagination*, 283.

6. For an example of this perspective, see Yoder, *Discipleship as Political Responsibility*. The above criticisms of early apocalyptic Christianity should not be mistaken for criticisms of any or all varieties of Anabaptism, however.

7. Archbishop Dom Hélder Câmara sharply articulated the difference between charity and justice: "When I give food to the poor, they call me a saint. When I ask why the poor have no food, they call me a communist."

world is really going to be transformed into an everlasting utopia, but in the sense that they reveal the very human desire for a quick fix. The quick fix of an all powerful savior (whether it be a messiah or an elected president) is preferable to the hard work of widespread human cooperation over the long haul. The problem with the all powerful savior is that it makes for bad drama. The expectation of the ultimate divine intervention that solves all of our problems for us in one fell swoop is quite literally a *deus ex machina*.

In ancient theater, the conflict of the drama was sometimes resolved not by the protagonists, but by the intervention of some god, lowered onto the stage by a machine. Aristotle was critical of this device, arguing that it was contrived and that the dramatic conflict should be resolved internally, not externally. In modern theater too, this convention is widely considered to be a *faux pas*, and rightly so. What it does is to change the locus of dramatic action from the human protagonists to an outside salvific entity for whom nothing is at stake. The protagonists, therefore, ultimately fail to achieve what they set out to achieve; it is simply handed to them.

The Christian expectation of a miraculous divine intervention at the end of time often has the same effect—it sets up the protagonist for failure. A fundamental axiom of Christian religions is that human beings *cannot* save themselves; a *deus ex machina* is essential to the resolution of the drama. But since this *deus ex machina* is conceived of as an omnipotent deity, there is nothing at stake. No character in the drama can succeed, save one, who cannot fail. Such a resolution to the drama renders world history a cosmic joke. In this narrative, the only thing that human beings can succeed in doing is waiting for the miracle. Because of this, the Christian religion ceases to be about justice—a consideration that is only within the purview of the intervening God at the end of history—and becomes consumed with the ethics of waiting. The interim wartime ethic preached by Jesus becomes the entirety of the religion. Of course, such an interim ethic cannot be sustained over a very long period of time, nor was it meant to. Consequently, post-Constantinian Christian religion is often marked by a frightfully incoherent combination of quasi-revolutionary visions of the end of society with conservative politics and social mores.

This is not to say that Jesus was a thoroughgoing apocalyptic thinker. There are certainly aspects of his teaching that are informed by sources other than Jewish apocalyptic. As with any Jewish apocalyptic movement, the roots of Jesus' teaching go back well before the birth of the apocalyptic worldview. For instance, as Richard Horsley argues, significant strands of Jesus' teaching are rooted in the economic principles of the Mosaic covenant (principles such as mutuality and debt forgiveness, which militate against our modern sensibilities as good capitalists), and are therefore functional outside of an apocalyptic framework. The apocalyptic framework is one that thrives where there is domination and desperation, but it is not a solution to a long-term problem. Yet the elements of Jesus' teaching that are derived from older covenantal sources, if we can tease them apart from other apocalyptic components, may continue to prove useful both among voiceless communities searching for strategies of resistance to domination and for those communities who have voices in democratic societies.[8]

On the other hand, despite some of the problems with the apocalyptic perspective, it is precisely the apocalypticism of Jesus that can be revelatory for us in positive ways. Jesus' belief in an imminent eschatological consummation, even if it was wrong, nevertheless speaks to some kind of pertinent sociopolitical/economic critique. To believe that eschatological consummation (or revolution) is imminent is to speak a curse against the present condition. It is to insist that something has got to give. Although the apocalyptic revolution is one that takes place primarily in the imagination of the apocalyptic community, Collins reminds us that

> the revolutionary potential of such imagination should not be underestimated, as it can foster dissatisfaction with the present and generate visions of what might be. The legacy of the apocalypses includes a powerful rhetoric for denouncing the deficiencies of this world. It also includes the conviction that the world as now constituted is not the end. Most of all, it entails an appreciation of the great resource that lies in the imagination to construct a symbolic world where the integrity of values can be maintained in the face of social and political powerlessness and even of the threat of death.[9]

Thus the realization that Jesus was wrong about the imminent end of the existing world order has opened us up to analyze without encumbrance the sociological factors that contributed to the worldview to which Jesus subscribed, and really for the first time to see its significance. Its significance is that it is a complex, beautiful, and incisively *accurate* expression of outrage at the existing world order, and a clarion call for fidelity to a new social system based upon justice rather than exploitation. The belief that the existing system is so corrupt that it is presently in the very throws of death, and the belief that the new system is so ripe that the world is already in labor with it (Rom 8:22)—this is the cry of the revolutionary spirit. This is not the voice of

8. See Horsley, *Covenant Economics.*

9. Collins, *Apocalyptic Imagination*, 283. See also the similar analysis in Shaull, "End of the World," 30–31.

despair at the world, but the voice of hope, and this, I submit, is the voice of God speaking to us through our scriptures.

Here is what the fact that Jesus was wrong, so far two thousand years wrong, should tell us. The revolutionary impulse was right. The curse upon the existing world order was valid. The expression of hope in a new beginning was vital. The creation of counter-cultural communities which function as signs of this new beginning was not only noble but necessary in order for the revolution to be successful. But the waiting for a miracle to make it all happen—that was wrong. Now when I say it was wrong, I do not mean to condemn the early Christians. After all, Jesus and Paul were prudent to encourage their followers not to do anything that would bring the wrath of Rome down upon their heads. They did not live in a world where the democratic spirit could breathe. Their apocalyptic framework was most likely the best they could do given the limitations of their time, place, and political climate. But we live in a different world. We do not have to wait for the miracle.

There is hope. It is not a hope in some miraculous intervention that will solve all of our problems for us in a single day. Our hope is in the kind of God who lives and breathes and struggles with us, and our hope is in the possibility of justice—the kind of sustained justice our God represents. I thank God Jesus was wrong, because if he was right, the possibility of revolutionary change in our lifetime would not exist, and neither would we. So, in the words of John Caputo, "The next time we look up to heaven and piously pray 'Come, Lord Jesus,' we may find that he is already here, trying to get warm over an urban steam grate or trying to cross our borders."[10] After all, we're not the only ones waiting for an intervention.

* * *

These have been my own attempts to make some of our problematic texts useful as scripture. It should be clear that even as "condemned texts," they are still quite "useful for teaching, for censure, for correction, and for training in the exercise of justice" (2 Tim 3:16). The church has long used flawed biblical characters in just this way. How many times has David been put to work as an object lesson in sermons on lust and adultery? How many Sunday school lessons on lying and telling the truth have found value in Abraham's not infrequent falsehoods? This is not a new way to make problematic texts useful as scripture. It is simply that honest and critical readings of the text compel us to add more passages to this category of "negative revelation" than would otherwise make us comfortable. Nevertheless, these have been my own at-

10. Caputo, *What Would Jesus Deconstruct?*, 30.

tempts, and I do not pretend that my musings should take the place of the discernment of the community. Each community must decide for itself how to make these and other texts useful for its own purposes; I have only made a few suggestions in the hope that my readings may prove useful to some. I have wanted to show how it is possible to hear God's word, despite it. *Beyond my own proposed readings, however, my argument has been that we must be honest with our scriptures, and that in many cases confrontational readings must be adopted, if we are to be honest with ourselves.*

The Specter of Marcionism

Inevitably, positions like mine will be construed by orthodox watchdogs as yet another incarnation of Marcion's heresy. Indeed, where I have expounded my position in the past, the charge of Marcionism has invariably been brought against me. There is a certain logic to it, I suppose. Marcion and I both insist upon historical-grammatical readings of problematic texts, and we both find it necessary, after critical scrutiny, to conclude that the god presented frequently throughout the Hebrew Bible is not worthy to be called a god of love. But about here is where my convergences with Marcion end and our numerous differences begin to emerge. First of all, Marcion made a distinction between the Hebrew god, and the god of Paul. The one was a god of violence, the other a god of love. Conversely, I am inclined to subject every conception of the divine to the same critical scrutiny. Paul's god is as much a god of vengeance as that of Moses, and the god of Moses was sometimes merciful too.[11] In fact, when I speak of "condemned texts," I do not mean to suggest that certain texts must be isolated from the pack as condemned, while the remainder may be read uncritically. On the contrary, all scripture should be read with a critical eye. In many cases, we will need to condemn certain aspects of a text, while extolling other aspects. In rarer cases should entire narratives be condemned (the conquest narratives, I think, come the closest).

Of course, the sharpest distinction between my position and that of Marcion pertains to canonicity. When Marcion rejected a text, he cut it out of the canon (much like Luther wished to do with Esther, Hebrews, James, Jude, and Revelation). Marcion simply abolished the Hebrew Bible and most of the Christian scriptures from his community's curriculum. My position is precisely the opposite. We have to learn to read them not as records of God's

---

11. Of course, slave owners could be merciful to their slaves in one moment and violent and vengeful in the next. Thus, to identify the god as "merciful" in some cases is not necessarily to redeem such a god.

actions, but as failed attempts to act on behalf of God. We have to be able to condemn them completely. But that does *not* mean we are free simply to discard them. They have to stand as failed attempts to speak for God. Discarding them, or trying to take them out of the canon, is tantamount to shattering the mirror. Once properly framed, we need these texts to remind us of the kind of monstrous people we always have the potential to become in the name of some land, some ideology, or some god. To cut them out of the canon would be to hide the worst parts of ourselves from ourselves. It would be to doom ourselves to repeat history.

The reality is that they are a part of our tradition whether we like it or not. Thus to extricate them from the canon would be a massive dishonesty. *In condemning them, we must own them.* As participants in the Judeo-Christian tradition, we are responsible for these texts, just as the good family takes responsibility for the alcoholic uncle. In order to mitigate the damage these texts can do—the extent of which history has borne out—we must keep these texts close to us. Casual dismissals of the Crusades and of missionary colonialism as aberrations of the faith fail to take responsibility for the complicity of our scriptures in such moral atrocities. The true modern-day Marcions are those who refuse to take responsibility for the Bible's role in the violent expansion of Western civilization.

A Problem with Authority

Even if inerrantists are able to concede that the position I have outlined in these pages cannot be identified with Marcionism, they will still have a difficult time accepting this as a viable account of scripture. For inerrantists, after all, any single, miniscule error in the Bible undermines the authority of the whole. So say the Chicago inerrantists: "The authority of Scripture is inescapably impaired if this total divine inerrancy is in any way limited or disregarded."[12] So also B. B. Warfield before them: if a single error or discrepancy is admitted, "we would no doubt need to give up the biblical doctrine of inspiration; but with it we must also give up our confidence in the biblical writers as teachers of doctrine."[13] This is taken to be common sense within fundamentalist Christianity. If one part is in error, the whole is useless. James Barr illustrates this vividly: "For modern fundamentalists . . . St. John's gospel has a more important function than the Book of Numbers, and they do not in fact build a great deal of their living faith upon the talking powers of Balaam's ass, of which they probably do not think more than once in ten

12. Henry, *God Who Speaks*, 212.
13. Warfield, *Inspiration and Authority*, 220.

years. But the moment someone questions the story of Balaam's ass everything is different. Any doubt about this, and the entire edifice of Christianity may tumble to the ground. In this negative sense anything and everything that could somehow suggest some sort of error or imperfection in the Bible, however small, can be fatal to all Christian faith and life."[14]

This "all or nothing" account of biblical authority begs for a psychological evaluation. Inerrantists who espouse this account of authority seem to be stuck in the mindset of adolescent disillusionment. When adolescents first discover that their parents are not infallible, often they become paralyzed and begin to doubt everything their parents have taught them. Many adolescents go through a stage in which *anything and everything* their parents say cannot be trusted; or rather, something is wrong *precisely because* it was uttered by their parents. This seems to be the mindset of the modern-day inerrantists: if the Bible is wrong on one issue, then there is no reason to listen to anything it says. More precisely, inerrantists are like the precocious and obsequious kid brother or sister who insists, despite the evidence, that the parents are still infallible; they must insist on this because they have bought into the faulty "all or nothing" logic of the petulant older sibling.

Yet this is the mark of a profound immaturity. Some adolescents never grow out of this mindset; but a healthy adult is one who has learned that an authority can be trustworthy without being inerrant. A mature individual is one who learns that discernment must be exercised when appropriating the teaching of an authority figure, but also that disagreement with the authority figure does not entail that the figure has ceased to be an authority. I myself have countless disagreements with my parents, but as I have matured and have come to know myself better, I have discovered that my identity is irrevocably shaped by them, whether I like it or not. In the same way, to have disagreements with scripture is not to deny that scripture has been and remains a central authority in our lives. The ability to engage scripture in argument without rejecting its rightful place in the community is a mark of spiritual maturity, a testament to the scriptures' power to fashion authentic, self-determining moral agents. Those who espouse this "all or nothing" account of authority seem to be stuck in spiritual adolescence. It is the inerrantists, and not the critical believers, who have the problem with authority.

Moreover, as everybody already acknowledges, the Bible does not answer every possible moral question for us. We all have to learn how to think morally in situations the writers of the Bible did not envision. Thus the notion that we are bereft of any resources to come to a moral conclusion if the Bible does not give us one is ludicrous. We reason morally beyond the limitations of the

14. Barr, *Fundamentalism*, 69.

Bible every day. So the approach to scripture I am advocating does not change anything, except to undermine a construct some of us *thought* was holding everything in place, even though it was not (like Dumbo's magic feather). The truth is, in reality we do not depend upon the Bible for our knowledge of what is moral. If we did, we would be paralyzed in a world vastly different from the biblical worlds. Moreover, if we did depend upon the Bible for our morality, we would not be able to mount moral arguments against the institution of slavery, or against patriarchal polygamy, among other things. Everything the Bible tells us about these institutions is that they are morally permissible, but most Christians today have found ways to articulate the immorality of these institutions, without the Bible's help. In reality we Christians do not need the Bible in order to become authentic moral agents, but the Bible is a tremendous resource for Christians to utilize as we struggle toward that goal.

Finally, and not insignificantly, the Bible is *our* resource. Christian moral reasoning *begins* with the Bible, even if it that's not always necessarily where it ends. Our scriptures are like our parents. As much as we disagree with them, we cannot escape the ways they have irrevocably shaped us; nor, in many cases, should we want to. In my case, I did not choose the Bible. I was born into a household in which the Bible was the authority figure, just as I was born to my parents. As an adolescent, I discovered my parents' flaws and chose to reject their authority wholesale; I wanted nothing to do with them. But as I matured, I discovered that to deny them was to deny myself. So I took them again as my parents, this time by choice. I committed myself to them, despite their flaws. I have been able to learn as much from their vices as I have from their virtues. In the same way, the Holy Bible is my book because I continue to choose it. For everything I loathe about it, there is at least one thing I love about it: it is a book full of passion and humanity, a book of despair as well as of hope. Both are true. Both are valid. Both inspire me.

Everybody Chooses

> We are conscious too that great and grave confusion results from ceasing to maintain the total truth of the Bible whose authority one professes to acknowledge. The result of taking this step is that the Bible which God gave loses its authority, and what has authority instead is a Bible reduced in content according to the demands of one's critical reasonings and in principle reducible still further once one has started. This means that at bottom independent reason now has authority, as opposed to Scriptural teaching. If this is not seen and if for the time being basic evan-

gelical doctrines are still held, persons denying the full truth of Scripture may claim an evangelical identity while methodologically they have moved away from the evangelical principle of knowledge to an unstable subjectivism, and will find it hard not to move further.[15]

In other words, the Chicago inerrantists claim that by rejecting their (supposedly) evangelical "all or nothing" account of authority, non-inerrantist Christians are either unwittingly or deceptively replacing biblical authority with the authority of the individual's reason. It is not, they claim, the Bible that is authoritative for such Christians; the Christians have become their own authorities. We have already seen why this is a deficient, immature account of authority. The inerrantists' Bible is not *authoritative*, it is *authoritarian*. It is the dictator who declares what is true by fiat. But true authorities are those who command respect by their willingness to subject themselves to critique, and to admit when they are wrong.

There are three further problems with the statement made above. First, the Chicago inerrantists claim that the only alternative to an authoritarian account of the Bible is "independent reason." But this is simply not so. I have argued that the proper place for critical appropriations of scripture is within the believing community. This does not deny the propriety of critical scholarship, but it stipulates that the believing community, not the individual biblical scholar, is responsible for critically appropriating the ancient text *as scripture*. Thus, it is not to "independent reason" that the scriptures are subjected, but to the discernment of the believing community, guided by the Spirit. Second, the Chicago inerrantists claim that critical readings of scripture result in an "unstable subjectivism." Yet as we have seen throughout the course of this book, it is the inerrantist readings of the text that result in unstable subjectivism. Conversely, critical readings of scripture are more methodologically controllable and are *self-consciously critical*. Subjectivism is not the only alternative to authoritarianism; this is a false dichotomy. There are all sorts of more or less objective criteria that are regularly used to govern the processes of critical interpretation and application of scripture.

This leads to the third point of contention. The criticism that the inerrantists make of critical readings of scripture is that they are arbitrary. They accuse readers of arbitrarily picking and choosing which are the "condemned" texts and which are the "inspired" ones. Or rather, they accuse readers of dismissing the texts they do not like, and retaining only those the so-called "liberal worldview" can stomach. Again, however, as we have seen, the inerrantists are no less guilty of picking and choosing which texts they

15. Henry, *God Who Speaks*, 219.

believe and which they deny; it is only that inerrantists hide their disagreement with certain texts by reinterpreting them to conform to the texts they prefer. Inerrantists pick and choose; they simply do not or cannot admit to it. What I am calling for is honesty in this process. We all emphasize certain scriptural perspectives to the neglect of others. *I am suggesting that being conscious and open about that fact will actually help to prevent us from being selective arbitrarily and will force us to struggle to find good reasons to make the choices that we make.* Everybody makes the choices. If they do not realize they are making the choices, then they are more susceptible to having made those choices arbitrarily or for poor reasons. The process of determining which texts to condemn and which to affirm, or which texts to read with caution and caveats, is a process that must not end. It is a struggle that each generation must take up anew, as they seek to be relevant actors in their societies with the Judeo-Christian scriptures as a resource.

Finally, even if we were to concede the claim of inerrantists that the only alternative to an authoritarian Bible is the authoritarian individual, that would not constitute a sufficient defense of inerrancy. This is an example of reasoning from the conclusion to the premise. The logic is that, because we do not like the consequences of the collapse of inerrancy, we must continue to believe in it. But wanting things to be other than what they are does not change what they are. We cannot base our beliefs on what we *want* to be true. Just because we want an infallible authority, just because we crave an unshakable foundation, that does not mean we are going to get one. Obviously this fact makes us uncomfortable, just as we became profoundly uncomfortable when we first discovered that our parents were fallible. We all wish the Bible gave us a consistent morality so that we could use it as an infallible moral textbook. That would make us a good deal more comfortable.

Yet the reality is that no matter how dire we may think the consequences of the collapse of inerrancy are, inerrancy cannot be sustained. We do not reject it because we hate the idea of having access to unassailable truth; in rejecting inerrancy, we lose something that we all long to have. But as I argued in chapter 3, the truth is that despite ourselves we should not want to have that kind of comfort. It is precisely the struggle through moral uncertainty that makes us moral beings. Without that uncertainty, without that struggle, no text, no word from God, is powerful enough to make us virtuous people. So while the Bible can and does help us to learn to think and act morally, it cannot be our only source of moral insight.

Authoritative from the Ground Up

It may be helpful to extend the "parental authority" metaphor for scripture in the following way. Although parents begin as top-down authority figures, as their children mature, the role of parents evolves, and parents become "authoritative from the ground up."[16] In other words, in the beginning, what parents teach is all their children know; it is literally everything. But as children develop into mature adults, the significance of those first teachings is transformed. Those first teachings are no longer authoritative in a top-down sense, but become authoritative in a new way; namely, they provide a basic structure through which the world is seen. In the same way, the scriptures are our basic grammar. They are authoritative from the ground up. That means they provide a basic framework for seeing the world and offer basic metaphors and claims that direct us and help us to make sense of our experiences.

As our grammar from the ground up, however, our scriptures are subject to criticism or challenge from an infinite number of other voices. We need to be able to hear those voices not as threats to us, but as challenges and potential "words from the Lord," even if they are spoken to us in a threatening manner. And we need to have a faith that is mature enough to be able to discern God's voice in the tension between this scripture here, that scripture there, this atheist, that Muslim, and this or that impoverished community. God is not confined to the pages of a book. God has the power to speak to us, and always chooses to speak to us, only to the extent that we are really willing to listen. Listening to God means being willing to listen to the wholly Other—to the alien, to the stranger, to the enemy, to the heretic, to the fundamentalist. If God can speak to Balaam through an ass, God can speak to a Baptist through an atheist. The key is knowing how to listen for God's voice, and that takes practice, and that takes community.

Unfounded Truths

So where does this leave us? The scriptures are not infallible. Jesus was not infallible—or, if he was, we have no access to his infallibility. So where is our foundation? Upon what do we build our worldview, our ethics, our politics and our morality? The answer is that there is no foundation. There is no sure ground upon which to build our institutions. And that is a good thing. That is what I call grace. An infallible Jesus, just like a set of infallible scriptures, is ultimately just a shortcut through our moral and spiritual development. To have a book or a messenger dropped from heaven, the likes of which is

16. I owe this way of characterizing biblical authority to Alex Giltner.

beyond the reach of all human criticism, is a dangerous shortcut. It is no wonder humans have always attempted to create these kinds of foundations. And it is a revelation of God's character, from my perspective, that cracks have been found in each and every one of those foundations.

Yet while we are without a foundation, we are not left without resources. The truth is that God has given us many resources to use together to struggle toward lives that reflect justice and peace. Our scriptures are some of those resources. The unique witness of Jesus of Nazareth within those scriptures is a resource in its own right. But we have other resources. We have our faculties of reason, our experiences, and the experiences of others. We have the voices of the past, the voices of the present, the voices of our elders, our peers, our children, and our enemies. We have the voices of other religions and the voices of atheists. We have the voices of those who suffer. We also have scientific methods of inquiry. We have critical theory, and philosophy, that help us to subject our own basic assumptions and frameworks of thought to critique. We have the Spirit of God. We have our individual minds, and the organic machinations of our communities. We have resources we know not of.

None of these resources is more basic than any other. Each one possesses the right to critique and the obligation to be critiqued by each of the others. Those who ask whether or how we can trust that these resources will lead us in the right direction are motivated by fear—fear of the unknown, fear of uncertainty, fear of the struggle. But the struggle, the pressing on in the face of uncertainties, the commitment to taking the journey together, as Christians, but more basically and more broadly, as human beings—these are the things that make us the kind of virtuous people our scriptures call us to be. The scriptures do not have to be right about everything in order to be useful. They do not have to be the antithesis of darkness in order to give us light. They are clear and cogent and often times conflicting examples of other communities' attempts to find God in this world, sometimes by means we should reject, sometimes by means we should embrace, and always by means to which we should pay close attention. They are God's voice speaking to us, but these are not the only place God speaks. God, whatever God is, is bigger than the stories in our book and the stories of our historical traditions.

Nonetheless, these stories are still a voice from God; they are free to help us along in our struggle only to the degree that we are free to subject them to criticism. Our scriptures can be wrong where other voices are right. The way through this process is not to look for some foundation to cling to that would make the process of discernment easier for us. There is no permanent foundation to cling to. What serves as a foundation in one context may not be foundational in another context. There may always be a consideration that is "more basic" than another. The quest for a "single foundation" of all our knowledge of God and of morality is a particularly modern quest, I think, and is problematic on a number of levels, one being that no such single foundation exists. The process is to reason together, to struggle together, to listen to each other, to learn from each other, to challenge one another, and to change our minds as often as we ask others to change theirs. One voice cannot be privileged in a foundational way against another. Rather, it is up to the believing community to moderate a conversation between the different voices and to leave the outcome up to the collective discernment. This process is guided by the wisdom of the Holy Spirit who is interested in creating a *faithful* community in particular contexts. It is also necessary to recognize that the Spirit's work moves beyond the confines of the church, which is precisely why the process is not properly Spirit-guided if the church is not listening to outside voices when the situation calls for it.

It all comes down to context. What context are we in when we are asking this question? What context are we in when we are asking that question? For the purposes of one situation, one passage may be more foundational than another, and that may be as far down as everybody agrees we need to go. For the purposes of another situation, that foundational passage may be subject to critique from someplace else, some other scriptural text, or some voice outside scripture altogether. We can never answer these questions once and for all in the abstract. To do so is to stack the deck. We never know where a more foundational consideration is going to come from, or even if one will arise. And there may be one, but we may not be aware of it for whatever reason (contingent factors, stubbornness, etc.). What I am describing is not relativism. I am merely saying there is no absolute foundation that is always and forever fixed in place. But relativism is just the flipside to the absolutist coin. What I am talking about is a realism, or contextualism, that accepts neither an idealist absolutism nor a nihilist relativism.

It may be helpful to think of moral reasoning like procedure in a court room. The court room is basically the same. But in each different case, different voices are heard. In one trial, one person may be the key witness, and his or her testimony may be true. In another trial, that same witness may be the accused, and the voices testifying against him or her may be true also. No two trials are alike. Different procedures and different voices are required according to the demands of each specific case. But there is a basic, flexible process that is called "trying a case," just as with moral reasoning and theological reflection. Each context will bring a different set of relevant voices with it. Now Christians, as followers of Jesus, need to be tuned in to look for the voice from the margins that may not be within earshot of the mainstream conversation. But, apart from that, generally speaking, who the relevant voices are will be obvious from context to context.

Of course, not every voice is going to present a significant challenge to our most basic voices as Christians. For instance, it would be disingenuous to say that the Christian needs to hold Stalin and Jesus on equal footing. We are Christians. Some voices are always going to be immediately more basic than others at the outset. Christian moral reasoning *begins* with scripture. What I am saying is that the process of the conversation, if it is a really good conversation, will reveal whether or not one voice that was originally foundational needs to be displaced by an outside voice within the context of that conversation. Which voices become "more basic" for the purposes of a given question is something that is determined throughout the course of that conversation, not at the outset. It is difficult to imagine a conversation, given our vantage point, in which Stalin's *The Road to Power* would ever come to be seen by any Christian community as more basic than the Sermon on the Mount.

Yet when it comes to Jesus' eschatology and, say, a Buddhist activist, the conversation is going to need to be a lot more lively, with room for critique (as contrasted with Stalin) being much more of a live option. Of course, all this depends on the question(s), the context(s), and the voice(s) involved. I am not making a blanket statement that Christianity and Buddhism are equally valid. I would not know how to make sense of a statement like that. I am just suggesting a methodology for moral reasoning in contexts. Nor am I suggesting that a conversation without permanent foundations is one that is completely open-ended. *Contra* Derrida, not much is really completely open-ended. Most questions can reasonably terminate somewhere, at least for the immediate purposes of a given context. Moreover, there is always going to be a basic framework from which Christian reasoning begins. What is important is that that framework is able to be challenged, critiqued, and if necessary expanded or reconfigured in order to make room for strange voices that the community comes through discernment to recognize as the voice of God in context.

The fear that drives us to look to the Bible as an infallible authority is ultimately the fear of being adrift at sea without an anchor. If there are no foundations, what mechanism for self-correction still exists? What can guarantee the faithfulness of the community throughout history? What can guarantee that we have got things right? The answer, of course, is that nothing can offer such a guarantee, and neither can an inerrant Bible. The quest for that kind of an unassailable foundation is, as I have argued, an attempt to find a shortcut. It is motivated by fear, a very reasonable fear: the fear of not being in control. The construct of an inerrant text gives a false sense of certainty; it provides people the illusion that they have some semblance of control over their lives. Even still, it is important to reiterate that the foundationless view of scripture I am articulating here does *not* undercut scripture's ability to facilitate moral self-correction. It merely makes that process more complex—not a case of "the Bible says it, I believe it, that settles it." *In fact, it is the very complexity of the process that makes the process effective in making us moral people, rather than just offering us moral answers.* Scripture still plays a role in correcting the church; it is just not an easy one-to-one application. We have to use discernment, which is a gift of the Spirit.

I have no doubt that not everyone is going to like the approach to scripture I am proposing. I am not proposing it because I think it is easy, or because it frees me up to play fast and loose with the text, to make irresponsible and spiritually immature use of the text. I am proposing it because to me it represents the most honest struggle—it is the only honest way that I know how to navigate our moral universe. Some will be afraid to live in a world without foundations. To them I commend the foundationless nature of agape. The search for a foundation is at base the search for control. But Christians are not called to live in control; they are called to live out of control. *Faith can only begin once we are willing to stop trying to defend whatever it is we think we know.* This letting go is what makes agape possible; agape is the virtue of those without foundations. Others will see a world without foundations and take license from it. To them I commend the words of the apostle Paul: "For you, brothers and sisters, were called to freedom, with a single caveat: do not use your freedom as license for self-indulgence; rather, serve one another in love. For the entire law is summed up in a single maxim: 'You shall love your neighbor as yourself.' But if you bite and devour one another, take heed not to be consumed by one another" (Gal 5:13–15).

Conclusion

Being a Christian means that Jesus of Nazareth takes pride of place at the center of our ethical and theological reflection. Christians believe that he revealed something about God, about the world, and about human beings—something that is very real, to which we are obligated to respond. That response is a whole way of life—or at least an ongoing attempt at one. If Christians are those who seek to emulate Jesus of Nazareth, then Christianity is about speaking truth to power, and more importantly, speaking truth to and in solidarity with the powerless. It is about proclaiming a vision of a new creation in which the old world order has died, and a whole new web of human relationships is about to begin. That is what the writers of the New Testament spoke of as a "new creation." What that will look like, none of us can pretend to articulate in the abstract. It looks like people caring for people just because we are all people.

Being a Christian means rejecting allegiances to nation states and to any artificial lines that have been concocted by powerful men and women in order to divide human beings from one another. It means denying fatalism and nihilism the power to dictate what we do. It means loving the alien among us. It means proclaiming a vision of a society that is actually good news to those who are captive to debt. It means coming together to live as an alternative to inhuman structures (political, economic, and otherwise) that seek to conquer us by dividing us. In Christ, we are all united. That is the vision of what it means to be an ecclesia, and that is the vision the church has to offer up as a gift to the world.

I am a Christian. Not an orthodox one, because no such thing exists, but one who strives to be an honest one. I am a Christian because my parents were Christians, as were theirs, and so on. I am a Christian because I chose to be a Christian. I am a Christian because I am a white male living in the West. I am a Christian because I happen to like Jesus, warts and all. For all of these reasons, I am a Christian. Because I am a Christian, this book we call the "Holy Bible" is uniquely my own book. Whether I want it or not, I am stuck with it. Even if I were never to pick it up again, I could never put it down. It has shaped me in irrevocable ways. I am formed by the Hebrew and Christians scriptures. And although I will always be changing, transforming, regressing, and progressing (toward something or other), I will always be formed by these scriptures in ways that I will never be able to fully understand. Attempting to renounce them would be like attempting to sneak a moment without me. So this Holy Bible is my book. It is the book of my people.

This Holy Bible is also my book because I continue to choose it. For everything I loathe about it, there is at least one thing I love about it: it has the power to show me who I am. When we look into the looking glass we see the aspirations, desires, insecurities, and utter obliviousness of humanity. We see ourselves, thank God, and that is a beautiful and a terrifying thing.

BIBLIOGRAPHY

Adams, Edward. *The Stars Will Fall From Heaven: Cosmic Catastrophe in the New Testament and Its World.* London: T&T Clark, 2007.

Alexander, T. Desmond. "Jonah and Genre." *Tyndale Bulletin* 36 (1985) 35–59.

Allison, Dale C. "Jesus and the Victory of Apocalyptic." In *Jesus and Restoration of Israel: A Critical Assessment of N. T. Wright's* Jesus and the Victory of God, 126–41, edited by Carey C. Newman. Downers Grove: InterVarsity, 1999.

———. *Jesus of Nazareth: Millenarian Prophet.* Minneapolis: Fortress, 1998.

Allison, Dale C., et al. *The Apocalyptic Jesus: A Debate,* edited by Robert J. Miller. Santa Rosa: Polebridge, 2001.

Aly, Götz, et al. *Cleansing the Fatherland: Nazi Medicine and Racial Hygiene.* Baltimore: Johns Hopkins University Press, 1994.

Archer, Gleason L. *Encyclopedia of Bible Difficulties.* Grand Rapids: Zondervan, 1982.

———. *A Survey of Old Testament Introduction.* Rev. ed. Chicago: Moody, 1994.

Avalos, Hector. "Creationists for Genocide." Talk Reason. Online: http://www.talkreason.org/articles/Genocide.cfm.

———. *Fighting Words: The Origins of Religious Violence.* Amherst: Prometheus, 2005.

Barr, James. *Fundamentalism.* Philadelphia: Westminster, 1978.

Beker, J. Christiaan. *Paul the Apostle: The Triumph of God in Life and Thought.* Philadelphia: Fortress, 1980.

Bembry, Jason A. *YHWH's Coming of Age.* Winona Lake: Eisenbrauns, forthcoming.

Binion, Rudolf. "Hitler's Concept of Lebensraum: The Psychological Basis." *History of Childhood Quarterly* 1/2 (1973) 187–215.

Bonfante, G. "Who Were the Philistines?" *American Journal of Archaeology* 50/2 (1946) 251–62.

Boyd, Greg. "Did Calvin Kill Servetus?" Random Reflections. Online: http://gregboyd.blogspot.com/2007/11/did-calvin-kill-servetus.html.

Bratcher, Dennis. "Isaiah 7:14: Translation Issues." The Voice: CRI/Voice, Institute. Online: http://www.crivoice.org/isa7-14.html.

Bruce, F. F. "Pesher." Jewish Virtual Library. Online: http://www.jewishvirtuallibrary.org/jsource/judaica/ejud_0002_0016_0_15650.html.

Brueggemann, Walter. "Against the Stream: Brevard Childs's Biblical Theology." *Theology Today* 50/2 (1993) 279–84.

Caird, George B. *Jesus and the Jewish Nation.* London: Athlone, 1965.

Callaway, Joseph A. "A New Perspective on the Hill Country Settlement of Canaan in Iron Age I." In *Palestine in the Bronze and Iron Ages: Papers in Honour of Olga Tufnell,* 31–49, edited by J. N. Tubb. London: Institute of Archaeology, 1985.

———. "The Settlement in Canaan: The Period of the Judges." In *Ancient Israel: From Abraham to the Roman Destruction of the Temple,* 55–90, edited by Hershel Shanks. Rev. ed. Washington, D.C.: Biblical Archaeological Society, 1999.

Caputo, John D. *What Would Jesus Deconstruct?: The Good News of Postmodernity for the Church*. Grand Rapids: Baker Academic, 2007.

Carter, T. L. "The Irony of Romans 13." *Novum Testamentum* 46/3 (2004) 209–28.

Charlesworth, James H. *Jesus within Judaism: New Light from Exciting Archaeological Discoveries*. Anchor Bible Reference Library. New York: Doubleday, 1988.

"Chicago Statement on Biblical Application." Alliance of Confessing Evangelicals. Online: http://www.alliancenet.org/partner/Article_Display_Page/0,,PTID307086_CHID750054_CIID2094578,00.html.

Childs, Brevard S. *Biblical Theology of the Old and New Testaments: Theological Reflection on the Christian Bible*. Minneapolis: Fortress, 1993.

Christian, Carol and Lisa Teachey. "Yates Believed Children Doomed / Psychiatrist Says Mom Delusional, Fixated on Satan." Houston Chronicle Archives. Online: http://www.chron.com/CDA/archives/archive.mpl?id=2002_3520463.

Cohen, Shaye J. D. *From the Maccabees to the Mishnah*. Library of Early Christianity 7, edited by Wayne A. Meeks. Philadelphia: Westminster, 1987.

Collins, John J. *The Apocalyptic Imagination: An Introduction to Jewish Apocalyptic Literature*. 2nd ed. Grand Rapids: Eerdmans, 1998.

———. *Does the Bible Justify Violence?* Facets. Minneapolis: Fortress, 2004.

———. *Introduction to the Hebrew Bible*. Minneapolis: Fortress, 2004.

———. "Prophecy and Fulfillment in the Dead Sea Scrolls." *Journal of the Evangelical Theological Society* 30/3 (September 1987) 267–78.

Coote, Robert B., and Mary P. Coote. *Power, Politics, and the Making of the Bible: An Introduction*. Minneapolis: Fortress, 1990.

Copan, Paul, "Are Old Testament Laws Evil?" In *God Is Great, God Is Good: Why Believing in God Is Reasonable and Responsible*, 134–54, edited by W. L. Craig and Chad Meister. Downers Grove: InterVarsity, 2009.

———. "Yahweh Wars and the Canaanites: Divinely-Mandated Genocide or Corporate Capital Punishment?" Evangelical Philosophical Society. Online: http://www.epsociety.org/library/articles.asp?pid=63

Cowles, C. S. "A Response to Daniel L. Gard." In *Show Them No Mercy: 4 Views on God and Canaanite Genocide*, 145–49, edited by Stanley N. Gundry. Grand Rapids: Zondervan, 2003.

———. "A Response to Eugene H. Merrill." In *Show Them No Mercy: 4 Views on God and Canaanite Genocide*, 97–101, edited by Stanley N. Gundry. Grand Rapids: Zondervan, 2003.

Craig, William Lane. "Divine Command Morality and Voluntarism." Reasonable Faith. Online: http://www.reasonablefaith.org/site/News2?page=NewsArticle&id=7911.

———. "The Indispensability of Theological Meta-Ethical Foundations for Morality." *Foundations* 5 (1997) 9–12.

———. "Slaughter of the Canaanites." Reasonable Faith. Online: http://www.reasonablefaith.org/site/News2?page=NewsArticle&id=5767.

Cross, Frank Moore. *Canaanite Myth and Hebrew Epic: Essays in the History of the Religion of Israel*. 1973. Reprint, Cambridge: Harvard University Press, 1997.

Dawson, David. *Allegorical Readers and Cultural Revision in Ancient Alexandria*. Berkeley: University of California Press, 1992.

De Wette, W. M. L. *A Critical and Historical Introduction to the Canonical Scriptures of the Old Testament*. Translated by Theodore Parker. 2 vols. 3rd ed. Boston: Rufus Leighton, 1859.

Dever, William G. *Who Were the Early Israelites and Where Did They Come From?* Grand Rapids: Eerdmans, 2003.

Dictionary of New Testament Background, edited by Craig A. Evans and Stanley E. Porter. Downers Grove: InterVarsity, 2000.

Driscoll, Mark. *On Church Leadership*. A Book You'll Actually Read. Wheaton: Crossway, 2008.

Dunn, James D. G. *Jesus Remembered*. Christianity in the Making 1. Grand Rapids: Eerdmans, 2003.

Eerdmans Dictionary of the Bible, edited by David Noel Freedman. Grand Rapids: Eerdmans, 2000.

Edwards, Jonathan. "Concerning the Divine Decrees." In *The Works of Jonathan Edwards*. Edinburgh: Banner of Truth, 1974.

Ehrman, Bart D. *God's Problem: How the Bible Fails To Answer Our Most Important Question—Why We Suffer*. San Francisco: HarperOne, 2008.

———. *Jesus: Apocalyptic Prophet of the New Millennium*. New York: Oxford University Press, 2001.

———. *The New Testament: A Historical Introduction to the Early Christian Writings*. 4th ed. New York: Oxford University Press, 2008.

Elliott, Neil. *Liberating Paul: The Justice of God and the Politics of the Apostle*. Minneapolis: Fortress, 2006.

———. "Strategies of Resistance and Hidden Transcripts in the Pauline Communities." In *Hidden Transcripts and the Arts of Resistance: Applying the Work of James C. Scott to Jesus and Paul*, 97–122, edited by Richard A. Horsley. Atlanta: Society of Biblical Literature, 2004.

Enz, Jacob J. *The Christian and Warfare: The Roots of Pacifism in the Old Testament*. Scottdale: Herald, 1972.

Ferguson, Everett. *Backgrounds of Early Christianity*. 3rd ed. Grand Rapids: Eerdmans, 2003.

Finkelstein, Israel and Neil Asher Silberman. *The Bible Unearthed: Archaeology's New Vision of Ancient Israel and the Origin of Its Sacred Texts*. New York: Touchstone, 2002.

Gard, Daniel L. "Response to C. S. Cowles." In *Show Them No Mercy: 4 Views on God and Canaanite Genocide*, 53–56, edited by Stanley N. Gundry. Grand Rapids: Zondervan, 2003.

Georgi, Dieter. *Theocracy in Paul's Praxis and Theology*. Minneapolis: Fortress, 1991.

Greenwald, Glenn. "When Presidential Sermons Collide." Salon.com. Online: http://www.salon.com/news/opinion/glenn_greenwald/2010/03/25/obama.

Gregg, Brian Han. *The Historical Jesus and the Final Judgment Sayings in Q*. Tübingen: Mohr Siebeck, 2006.

Halpern, Baruch. "Why Manasseh Is Blamed for the Babylonian Exile: the Evolution of a Biblical Tradition." *Vetus Testamentum* 48/4 (October, 1998) 473–514.

Hays, Richard B. *Echoes of Scripture in the Letters of Paul*. New Haven: Yale University Press, 1993.

Heiser, Michael S. "Deuteronomy 32:8 and the Sons of God." *Bibliotheca Sacra* 158 (2001) 52–74.

Henry, Carl F. H. *God Who Speaks and Shows: Fifteen Theses, Part Three*. God, Revelation and Authority 4. Waco: Word, 1976–83.

Herzog, William R. "Dissembling, A Weapon of the Weak: The Case of Christ and Caesar in Mark 12:13–17 and Romans 13:1–7." *Journal of the NABPR* 21 (1994) 339–60.

Hess, Richard S. *Joshua: An Introduction and Commentary*. Tyndale Old Testament Commentaries. Downers Grove: IVP Academic, 2008.

Hitler, Adolf. *Mein Kampf*. New York: Reynal & Hitchcock, 1939.

Hobbs, T. R. *A Time for War: A Study of Warfare in the Old Testament*. Old Testament Studies 3. Wilmington: Michael Glazier, 1989.

Hobsbawm, Eric. "Introduction: Inventing Traditions." In *The Invention of Tradition*, 1–14, edited by Eric Hobsbawm and Terence Ranger. 2nd ed. Cambridge, N.Y.: Cambridge University Press, 1996.

Hoerth, Alfred J. *Archaeology and the Old Testament*. Grand Rapids: Baker, 1998.

Hooker, Morna D. "The Authority of the Bible: A New Testament Perspective." *Ex Auditu* 19 (2003) 45–64.

Horsley, Richard A. *Covenant Economics: A Biblical Vision of Justice for All*. Louisville: Westminster John Knox, 2009.

———. *Jesus and the Spiral of Violence: Popular Jewish Resistance in Roman Palestine*. Minneapolis: Fortress, 1993.

———. *Sociology and the Jesus Movement*. New York: Crossword, 1989.

Horsley, Richard A., with John S. Hanson. *Bandits, Prophets, and Messiahs: Popular Movements in the Time of Jesus*. Harrisburg: Trinity, 1999.

Horsley, Richard A., and Neil Asher Silberman. *The Message and the Kingdom: How Jesus and Paul Ignited a Revolution and Transformed the Ancient World*. Minneapolis: Fortress, 1997.

Hulbert, W. G. "Good King and Bad King: Traditions about Manasseh in the Bible and Late Second Temple Judaism." *Stone-Campbell Journal* 11 (Spring 2008) 71–81.

Hurtado, Larry W. *One God, One Lord: Early Christian Devotion and Ancient Jewish Monotheism*. 2nd ed. Edinburgh: T&T Clark, 1998.

Huxtable, John. *The Bible Says*. London: SCM, 1962.

Kaiser, Walter C., et al. *Hard Sayings of the Bible*. Downers Grove: InterVarsity, 1996.

Kang, Sa-Moon. *Divine War in the Old Testament and in the Ancient Near East*, edited by Otto Kaiser. Berlin: Walter de Gruyter, 1989.

Keesmaat, Sylvia C. "If Your Enemy Is Hungry: Love and Subversive Politics in Romans 12–13." In *Character Ethics and the New Testament: Moral Dimensions of Scripture*, 141–58, edited by Robert L. Brawley. Louisville: Westminster/John Knox, 2007.

Kenyon, Kathleen M. *Digging Up Jericho*. London: Ernest Benn Limited, 1957.

Kitchen, Kenneth A. *On the Reliability of the Old Testament*. Grand Rapids: Eerdmans, 2003.

Koch, Klaus. *The Rediscovery of Apocalyptic: A Polemical Work on a Neglected Area of Biblical Studies and Its Damaging Effects on Theology and Philosophy*. Translated by M. Kohl. London: SCM, 1972.

Koenigsberg, Richard. "Genocide as Immunology: The Psychosomatic Source of Culture." Richard Koenigsberg. Online: http://home.earthlink.net/~libraryofsocialscience/gi.htm.

Kugel, James L. *The Bible As It Was*. Cambridge: Belknap, 1997.

Kugel, James L., and Rowan A. Greer. *Early Biblical Interpretation*. Library of Early Christianity 3, edited by Wayne A. Meeks. Philadelphia: Westminster, 1986.

Kvasnica, Brian. "Shifts in Israelite War Ethics and Early Jewish Historiography of Plundering." In *Writing and Reading War: Rhetoric, Gender, and Ethics in Biblical and Modern Contexts*, 175–96, edited by Brad E. Kelle and Frank Ritchel Ames. Symposium Series 42. Atlanta: Society of Biblical Literature, 2008.

Levenson, Jon D. "Abusing Abraham: Traditions, Religious Histories, and Modern Misinterpretations," *Judaism* 47 (1998) 259–77.

———. *The Death and Resurrection of the Beloved Son: The Transformation of Child Sacrifice in Judaism and Christianity*. New Haven: Yale University Press, 1993.

Lim, Timothy H. "The Qumran Scrolls, Multilingualism, and Biblical Interpretation." In *Religion in the Dead Sea Scrolls*, 57–73, edited by John J. Collins and Robert A. Kugler. Grand Rapids: Eerdmans, 2000.

Lind, Millard C. *Yahweh Is a Warrior: The Theology of Warfare in Ancient Israel*. Scottdale: Herald, 1980.

Loftus, John W. "At Best Jesus Was a Failed Apocalyptic Prophet." In *The Christian Delusion: Why Faith Fails*, 316–43, edited by John W. Loftus. Amherst: Prometheus, 2010.

Lohfink, Gerhard. *Does God Need the Church?: Toward a Theology of the People of God.* Translated by Linda M. Maloney. Collegeville: Liturgical, 1999.

Malherbe, Abraham, and Everett Ferguson (trans.). *Gregory of Nyssa: The Life of Moses.* Mahwah: Paulist, 1978.

Mazar, Amihai. *Archaeology of the Land of the Bible: 10,000–586 B.C.E.* The Anchor Yale Bible Reference Library. New Haven: Yale University Press, 1992.

McCarter, P. Kyle, Jr. "The Apology of David." *Journal of Biblical Literature* 99/4 (1980) 489–504.

———. *I Samuel: A New Translation with Introduction, Notes, and Commentary.* The Anchor Bible 8. New York: Doubleday, 1980.

———. *II Samuel: A New Translation with Introduction, Notes, and Commentary.* The Anchor Bible 9. New York: Doubleday, 1984.

Merrill, Eugene H. "The Case for Moderate Discontinuity." In *Show Them No Mercy: 4 Views on God and Canaanite Genocide,* 61–96, edited by Stanley N. Gundry. Grand Rapids: Zondervan, 2003.

Niditch, Susan. *War in the Hebrew Bible: A Study in the Ethics of Violence.* New York: Oxford University Press, 1993.

Noth, Martin. *The Deuteronomistic History.* Journal for the Study of the Old Testament Supplement Series 15. 2nd ed. Sheffield: Sheffield Academic, 1991.

O'Leary, Stephen D. *Arguing the Apocalypse: A Theory of Millennial Rhetoric.* New York: Oxford University Press, 1994.

O'Sullivan, John L. "The Great Nation of Futurity." *The United States Democratic Review* 6/23 (1839) 426–30.

Piper, John. *Desiring God: Meditations of a Christian Hedonist.* Sisters: Multnomah, 2003.

———. "How Can Evil Have a Good Purpose?" Desiring God. Online: http://www.desiringgod.org/ResourceLibrary/AskPastorJohn/ByTopic/43/3415_How_can_evil_have_a_good_purpose/.

Pritchard, James Bennett, ed. *Ancient Near Eastern Tets Relating to the Old Testament.* 3rd ed. Princeton: Princeton University Press, 1969.

Proctor, Robert N. *The Nazi War on Cancer.* Princeton: Princeton University Press, 1999.

Radmacher, Earl D., and Robert D. Preus, eds. *Hermeneutics, Inerrancy and the Bible: Papers from the ICBI Summit II.* Grand Rapids: Zondervan, 1984.

Rollston, Christopher A. "The Rise of Monotheism in Ancient Israel: Biblical and Epigraphic Evidence." *Stone-Campbell Journal* 6 (2003) 95–115.

Rollston, Christopher A., and Heather Dana Davis Parker. "2 Kings." In *The Transforming Word: A One Volume Commentary on the Bible,* 329–52, edited by Mark Hamilton. Abilene: Abilene Christian University Press, 2009.

Rowlett, Lori L. *Joshua and the Rhetoric of Violence: A New Historicist Analysis.* Journal for the Study of the Old Testament Supplement Series 226, edited by David J. A. Clines and Philip R. Davies. Sheffield: Sheffield Academic, 1996.

Sampley, J. Paul. *Walking between the Times: Paul's Moral Reasoning.* Minneapolis: Fortress, 1991.

Sanders, E. P. *Paul and Palestinian Judaism: A Comparison of Patterns of Religion.* Minneapolis: Fortress, 1977.

Schaff, Philip. *History of the Reformation.* Vol. 2. New York: Scribner's, 1892.

Scott, James C. *Domination and the Arts of Resistance: Hidden Transcripts.* New Haven: Yale University Press, 1990.

Schüssler Fiorenza, Elisabeth. *The Power of the Word: Scripture and the Rhetoric of Empire.* Minneapolis: Fortress, 2007.

Schweitzer, Albert. *The Quest of the Historical Jesus: A Critical Study of Its Progress from Reimarus to Wrede.* 1910. Reprint, Mineola: Dover, 2005.

Seibert, Eric A. *Disturbing Divine Behavior: Troubling Old Testament Images of God.* Minneapolis: Fortress, 2009.

Shaull, Richard. "The End of the World and a New Beginning." In *Marxism and Radical Religion: Essays Toward a Revolutionary Humanism,* 27–48, edited by John C. Raines and Thomas Dean. Philadelphia: Temple University Press, 1970.

Siddiqui, Abdul Hamid, trans. "The Book of Jihad and Expedition." University of Southern California Center for Muslim-Jewish Engagement. Online: http://www.usc.edu/schools/college/crcc/engagement/resources/texts/muslim/hadith/muslim/019.smt.html.

Smith, Abraham. "Unmasking the Powers: Toward a Postcolonial Analysis of 1 Thessalonians." In *Paul and the Roman Imperial Order,* 47–66, edited by Richard A. Horsley. New York: Trinity, 2004.

Smith, Mark S. *The Early History of God: Yahweh and the Other Deities in Ancient Israel.* 2nd ed. Grand Rapids: Eerdmans, 2002.

———. *The Origins of Biblical Monotheism: Israel's Polytheistic Background and the Ugaritic Texts.* New York: Oxford University Press, 2001.

Stager, Lawrence E., and Samuel R. Wolff. "Child Sacrifice at Carthage—Religious Rite or Population Control?" *Biblical Archaeology Review* 10/1 (January 1984) 31–51.

Stern, Philip D. *The Biblical Herem: A Window on Israel's Religious Experience.* Brown Judaic Studies 211, edited by Ernest S. Frerichs et al. Atlanta: Scholars, 1991.

Stout, Jeffrey. *Ethics after Babel: The Languages of Morals and Their Discontents.* 1988. Princeton: Princeton University Press, 2001.

Swift, Louis J. "Early Christian Views on Violence, War, and Peace." In *War and Peace in the Ancient World,* 279–296, edited by Kurt A. Raaflaub. Malden: Blackwell, 2007.

———. *The Early Fathers on War and Military Service.* Message of the Fathers of the Church 19. Wilmington: Michael Glazier, 1983.

Torrey, R. A. *Difficulties in the Bible.* Chicago: Moody, n.d.

Van de Beek, A. *Why? On Suffering, Guilt, and God.* Translated by John Vriend. Grand Rapids: Eerdmans, 1990.

Vermes, Geza. *The Complete Dead Sea Scrolls in English.* Translated by Geza Vermes. Rev. ed. London: Penguin, 2004.

Von Rad, Gerhard. *Holy War in Ancient Israel.* Translated and edited by Marva J. Dawn. Grand Rapids: Eerdmans, 1991.

Warfield, Benjamin B. *The Inspiration and Authority of the Bible.* Phillipsburg: P&R, 1948.

Wengst, Klaus. *Pax Romana and the Peace of Jesus Christ.* Philadelphia: Fortress, 1986.

Williams, Thomas. "Biblical Interpretation." In *The Cambridge Companion to Augustine,* 59–70, edited by Eleonore Stump and Norman Kretzmann. Cambridge: Cambridge University Press, 2001.

Wright, Christopher J. H. *The God I Don't Understand: Reflections on Tough Questions of Faith.* Grand Rapids: Zondervan, 2008.

Wright, N. T. *Jesus and the Victory of God.* Christian Origins and the Question of God 2. Minneapolis: Fortress, 1996.

———. *The New Testament and the People of God.* Christian Origins and the Question of God 1. Minneapolis: Fortress, 1992.

———. *The Resurrection of the Son of God.* Christian Origins and the Question of God 3. Minneapolis: Fortress, 2003.

Yoder, John Howard. *Discipleship as Political Responsibility.* Herald, 2003.

———. *The Original Revolution: Essays on Christian Pacifism.* Eugene: Wipf & Stock, 1971.

Younger, K. Lawson. *Ancient Conquest Accounts: A Study in Ancient Near Eastern and Biblical History Writing.* Journal for the Study of the Old Testament Supplement Series 98. Sheffield: Sheffield Academic, 1990.